BLUE YARN

A Memoir About Loss,
Letting Go,
& What Happens Next

CARRIE CLASSON

Black Rose Writing | Texas

First printing

The author has tried to recreate events, locales and conversations from his/her memories.

ISBN: 978-1-68433-226-7
PUBLISHED BY BLACK ROSE WRITING
www.blackrosewriting.com

Printed in the United States of America
Suggested Retail Price (SRP) $19.95

Blue Yarn is printed in Book Antiqua

I'd like to send out a great big thank you to my agent, Jane von Mehren, at Aevitas Creative Management for her tenacity and faith in this book. I would like to thank Andrew Jensen for encouraging me to start writing, Nora Lichtenecker for giving me the time and place to write, and my former husband for giving me something to write about. Thank you to Michael Noltemeyer for his sharp eyes, Cat Hubka for being my writing pal, Jerry Shea for giving me confidence when I needed it most, and Peter — for everything.

—Carrie Classon

BLUE YARN

yarn *noun*
A long or rambling story, especially one that is implausible.
—Oxford English Dictionary

PART ONE

WHAT HAPPENED

I'm sitting in front of an antiquated PC in a hot Internet café in Lagos, Nigeria, reading my e-mail. I am in this café because I no longer have a computer. I can't use my phone, because I no longer have that either.

The computers in this café do not run well and I assume they are infected with a variety of viruses and other malware. Several keys on the yellowed keyboard stick and some do not work at all, so I have devised a variety of workarounds in order to employ the full alphabet. Sitting on either side of me are young Nigerians, busily doing things on the rented computers. While Nigeria is notorious for its scammers, I am not assuming the worst of the young people on either side of me. Actually, I am not assuming anything anymore.

The loss of my computer and phone was recent, as was the loss of my husband, my job, and my home. This loss upon loss has left me shell-shocked and numb and questioning all my assumptions. With each loss, I was certain I had nothing left to lose; but today I see that I was—once again—mistaken.

In today's mail is a note from my lawyer in the U.S. She is writing to tell me that a warrant has been issued for my arrest in Nigeria. It appears my freedom might also be lost, and this seems less unimaginable than it would have even a week ago. The fact that I am fairly certain I have committed no crime seems strangely irrelevant.

I sit in the very hot Internet café, staring at the screen before me, reading this message from my lawyer several times. For a moment, I do not feel the rising panic and fear which would certainly have been appropriate and will surely soon hit. For a long moment, before the fear has time to settle in, I simply marvel at how I managed—in such a remarkably short time — to go from a happily married businesswoman in Wisconsin to a homeless, unemployed, single woman in Lagos, wanted by the Nigerian police.

What happened?

•   •   •   •   •

It's always hard to know where a story begins, just as it is almost impossible to say exactly when it ends, but this one began before cell phones, before the Internet, when I was a twenty-year-old acting student living in New York with three roommates in two rooms. Two of my roommates were depressed. They spent much of their time bingeing on snack food and late-night television and the rest of their time talking about all the things they hated. The third roommate was a dancer with a broken ankle hobbling around on crutches. She was the cheerful one.

The rooms were tiny and the atmosphere was claustrophobic but I was not depressed — even though my living situation was dismal and my acting classes were not what I had hoped for when I moved from Chicago, even though it was winter in New York and I didn't have money to go to shows or eat out. I couldn't stay sad for long because every day I would go down to the lobby of our apartment complex, to the wall of mailboxes with brass doors, open our mailbox, and get the mail.

Sometimes my roommates would get a care package from home or a tuition bill or an opportunity to subscribe to magazines they could not afford. But most days, I was the only one who got mail because — every day — there was a letter from the boy who loved me.

I opened the mailbox with the little brass key. The letter was there. This one was in an envelope made from a brown grocery sack. I smiled; he had run out of envelopes again. I tucked the letter in my pocket before I headed back up to my room because I was a smart girl and I knew how this looked, how my two cynical roommates would smirk. I knew the love affairs of twenty-year-olds were unlikely to survive. I suspected this one was less likely to survive than most. We met when

I had just turned nineteen. We spent a part of one summer together in Alaska. No one expected it to last. I would go back to school. He would get a job somewhere. We would have some sweet memories.

But — just as I was leaving — I wrote him a letter. And — on his way out of town, checking the mail one last time — he got it.

He wrote back. And I replied. He moved to Chicago to be with me. I moved to New York to study. And we kept writing. The distance brought us closer as we shared the most intimate moment of every day with one another — with a pen on paper. And that is how it went for hundreds of letters over the course of twenty months: love letters, promises, the growing realization that this love was the story that defined us, the awareness that our love story was who we were.

In the quiet of my room, I could hear my two grumpy roommates bickering and the sound of the television. I carefully cut the envelope open with a knife and started to read.

You were falling asleep, drifting away peacefully and your dream made a left turn into oncoming traffic, some ludicrous tangent brought you back to me laughing. I shared your laughter and held you close, you slipped away again, I lay there treasuring you and all that I had come to know, the scent of your hair scattered on the pillow, the sensuous warm curve of your derriere against my thigh. Racing through a museum or a zoo, leaving the former on the wrong bus and making you late for rehearsal. I wonder sometimes if I have ever taken the "wrong" bus.

I think not.

As I recall I held your hand, I held your hand on the el and I held your hand the night we walked out of Dr. Zhivago for a walk on the shore of Lake Michigan. Nothing could compare with the simplicity of our own love story. Drinking too much wine on a cold afternoon in Grant Park, did I tell you then that I love you? I had mangled the bread, in my rush to meet you, going through the turnstiles, you laughed when I told you. I was late, again. There were deadlines to meet, you had a class you couldn't miss so I spent the afternoon in the art institute wishing I could cry.

Deadlines to meet, priorities to decide, it was all so very temporary, the winter was coming fast what would hold my sanity? The mornings we stayed in bed having intended to get up "bright and early" but how could I share you with the rest of the world? I knew then, or thought I did anyway, just how long the winter lasts.

No more. This is the last winter I will spend alone. I do not know how I survive, without you I am nothing, I have nothing, this must never be repeated. I look forward to seeing you the way a condemned man must look for a reprieve. My supply of goodbyes is exhausted. Fair warning: one day soon I will foreswear all goodbyes.

A thought suddenly occurs; I would like to put in all the letters you've written and I, you, bundled together with a heavy blue yarn. I want that thought, that warm sensation in the back of my mind. Ah yes, somewhere up in the attic...

So finally (because there really was no choice in the matter) we married. And even though we were young and had no money and were both still growing up into the people we would become, this love—built and recorded and made sublime over the course of hundreds of letters—this love survived. It surprised everyone who doubted it. It survived against the odds. It survived for one decade and then it survived for two. I left acting and went into business. He became an expert in computers. But through all the changes, this love we created remained. We loved one another just as they had planned and pledged to love in those letters—letters that were eventually tied together with heavy blue yarn.

Then one evening in August, shortly after our twenty-second anniversary, I was in Lagos, Nigeria, on business. I had only recently completed an MBA and started traveling on foreign business trips and I was still rather awed and amazed by all I was seeing. I was staying at a hotel frequented by American and European businessmen who had read about the latest kidnappings in the Niger Delta and had been sent by their nervous companies to this overpriced hotel surrounded by concrete walls topped with razor wire. The carpet smelled of mildew from the constant humidity and black mold climbed inexorably up the white cement walls. The hotel took credit cards, which was still a rarity, and the bar was filled with well-dressed prostitutes. All prices were given in dollars.

It was after dark and I was standing by the pool when my husband, who was also traveling on business, called from Brussels. The pool in Lagos was reflecting a larger-than-life moon overhead. There was distant music coming from a boom box outside the hotel compound and the sound of palm fronds rattling in the breeze.

"Hey, how are you?" he asked. He was always eager to hear where I was and what I was up to in my new, globe-trotting incarnation.

I smiled, hearing his voice. "I'm good, good. Still staying in lovely Lagos. What's up?"

"I dunno, I was just wondering…" He paused for a moment and I realized he had called for a special reason. "How would you like to live abroad for a while?"

I was relieved to hear him sound eager and excited instead of depressed or distant as he had more and more often lately. For the first time in our marriage, we were both making a significant salary, saving and investing most of what we made in pursuit of an early retirement. We were both traveling to places we had never been, then reconvening to swap stories in our Wisconsin farmhouse under the maple trees. While he traveled for extended periods to Brazil to work on large computer projects, I willfully ignored the growing emotional and geographic distance between us.

Yes, I knew he had withdrawn from me in recent months and, no, I did not know why. Questioning him had yielded only repeated promises that things would be better soon.

"But what's wrong?" I'd persist, and he would look at me with the same sad eyes and sideways grin.

"Not a lack of love," he'd say.

I observed his melancholy and occasional indifference as I would a storm that had unexpectedly settled in. It would pass, I assured myself. While he had battled depression intermittently throughout our marriage, I knew our love was a constant; it was a setpoint which did not fluctuate with his sometimes-tumultuous emotional weather.

Between my trips abroad, I would sit on our sunny porch and tally up our little pile of savings. The story I told myself was, once we had enough money, once we hit our "magic number," we would leave behind these fancy jobs and ridiculous business clothes and again be the people we had known we were all along. After more than twenty years of marriage, we would put on our backpacks and raggedy jeans and start all over. My story did not include the fact that he did not want to touch me, that he had not made love to me in a very long time. My story insisted it was only jobs and continents that kept us apart.

Now, it seemed, he was suggesting something that would bring us together, an adventure, a new chapter in our marriage. After months of simply assuring me that things would be better "soon," he was now making a suggestion that offered romance and novelty and new experiences together.

I would work in Lagos, but (in my story) I didn't imagine it as the place I would really live. My husband would work in Belgium for a couple of years while we continued to save for retirement, and I would hop over the beautiful Mediterranean to be with him whenever I was free. Instead of flying over the Atlantic to reconvene under the maple trees, we would enjoy the long vacations given to expats and have more time together than we'd had in years. I imagined seeing Italy and Greece and Spain together. I imagined how it would feel to leave behind our quiet life under the maple trees and discover the world, how it would feel to discover one another all over again. I imagined hotels on the coast overlooking the sea and white curtains flapping in the breeze and nothing to do on a long weekend but explore old streets, drink coffee out of tiny cups, make love on crisp hotel sheets, and swim in the deep blue Mediterranean. I thought that would be nice. Very nice indeed. I would gladly move to Nigeria to hear that eager and excited voice more often. I would bridge the distance between us by moving across an ocean.

Perhaps I was not afraid of putting this distance between us because it was at a distance our love had grown. We had fallen in love at a distance and perhaps, I thought, this is what we needed to bring us back together again.

How would I like to live abroad for a while?

The palm trees rattled as I listened to him waiting on the other end of the line.

"Yes," I said. "Yes, I think I would like that."

Snow would soon be falling on our farmhouse under the maple trees. While there was much about Lagos that was unpleasant, the weather was almost always fine.

•   •   •   •   •

My company was surprised and delighted I was willing to move to Lagos once I presented the idea. We were dabbling in Nigerian business, but without someone there full-time it was difficult to get a foothold. I had only been with the company for a short time but had a string of small successes and a proven willingness to jump into projects where others were more wary. Almost immediately I was busy preparing budgets and marketing materials for the new venture I would be heading up. I was lining up possible house sitters for our farmhouse. I was wondering what my life would be like. Would I enjoy spending time in Belgium? What would it be like to work full-time in Lagos? While I had spent much of the past two years traveling, I had never lived abroad before.

Perhaps that is why I was unprepared, why I was completely unprepared, when my husband came home from Brussels on October 20th, less than three months before we were to leave, with something important he needed to tell me. He said he had some news he needed to share. We went upstairs and sat on our bed that fall afternoon. Late afternoon light filtered through the maple trees.

"I figured out why I've been so depressed lately," he told me. His voice was soft and I leaned closer to him. "I realized what it was on the flight over and I spent the whole time I was in Brussels trying to persuade myself I was wrong."

He looked at me earnestly. I looked at his handsome face I knew as well as my own, the fine lines that had only recently appeared at the corners of his eyes and the touches of gray at his temples. I knew he had been under a lot of stress and I was anxious to hear his news. I had waited a long time to find out what was wrong—what had gone missing—so we could make things better again.

"I finally realized," he told me, "I don't love you anymore."

SCATTERED

Running through the woods is what I remember next.

He has just told me he does not love me, and I cannot sit still with this knowledge. So now I am running, running through the woods on this cloudy, cold day in late October. I am running and crying until I am exhausted and finally stop and lie down next to an outcropping of rocks beneath a tree. I curl up under the low branches of the tree in the damp leaves and stay there for some time. I don't know how long I lie there. All the things that happen before something and after something else have become irrelevant. I heave great, aching sobs that do not sound like human crying but sound as if a wounded animal has crawled beneath the tree. I sob until I am hollow and there is nothing left inside. It is cold, but I am not cold. There is nothing left in me to be cold. I look up through the branches of the tree and stare at the very white sky for a long time.

"What happens next?" I ask whoever might be listening.

I am not a religious person in any ordinary sense of the word and so, while I know what happens next is true, I also know it makes no sense at all.

"Get ready," She says, this voice I have never heard before, "Get ready for the next big thing."

I am thoroughly unimpressed with this divine advice.

I'm thinking it's just my luck that when I finally hear the voice of the divine She ends up sounding like a cheap self-help book. I am certainly not interested in any "next big thing" when everything that has been essential for more than half my life is disappearing before my eyes. I am absolutely not going to "get ready" for anything. I am going to dig in deep under this tree and do everything in my power to ignore this awful new truth that makes my twenty-two years of marriage seem like a sad and pointless joke.

Then, in one moment, I do not believe any of it has happened.

I know he loves me. He will be waiting for me just outside the woods, his eyes will be sad, and he will be so worried about me. He will take me home and this will be over.

"I'm so sorry," he'll say. "What I was thinking?" And he'll take me in his arms and tell me again he loves me and he will never stop loving me.

I walk out of the woods. He is not waiting for me. I go home. I walk into the house and I see him watching football. I don't know what I expected, but I somehow did not expect he would be watching the Packers.

Before I can say anything, he says, "I know we need to talk about this—but not all the time." He glances up at me briefly, then looks back at the television screen. "I can't talk about this all the time."

While there is a lot I can't remember, this part I remember explicitly.

I am standing in our living room watching him watch television. Green and yellow uniforms swim across the screen and I am thinking he is probably right, we probably can't talk about this all the time. But I cannot think of one other thing to talk about.

Not one thing.

•　　　•　　　•　　　•　　　•

I was carried to Lagos on the power of inertia.

It was actually an airplane, but I remember very little of the time after my husband told me he no longer loved me and before I arrived in Lagos. I insisted on an intense weekend of marriage counseling and he went without protest. I asked the counselor how successful he had been in the past.

"Not very," the counselor admitted. "Couples usually come too late."

I do not remember what we said in that terrible, cheery room for two long days. I was, as always, hopeful. We had always stood united as a couple. In all my years with him, I cannot remember him saying a word against me. In all the times he had been depressed and pushed me away, I had never confessed my loneliness to another soul. Whatever troubles there might have been behind closed doors, we always emerged with smiling faces and a united front. This loyalty had lasted more than half our lives, and it persisted in counseling.

Even as I knew this was likely my only opportunity to save our marriage, I could not speak ill of this man I had married. I did not tell the counselor my husband would not touch me. My husband did not tell the counselor he no longer loved me. Perhaps we believed if our naturally agreeable natures could succeed in persuading the counselor all was well, it would be. Perhaps the inexplicably lost love had simply been mislaid. The counselor seemed persuaded by our performance; we remained the amicable couple we had always been in public. We left the counseling session together on that sunny fall day in late autumn and I realized, after twelve hours of counseling, I was still the only one who knew he didn't love me anymore.

But something within me rebelled. I did not understand how twenty-two years of love could be lost. Love did not just fall out of your pocket and end up lying behind the dresser or stuck between the sofa cushions. Through all the changes: changing jobs, changing locations, changing identities, I was tethered to the surety of our love. I knew he was not happy. Being happy was as difficult for him as it was easy for me. But I could not believe I had suddenly been identified as the cause of his depression over the course of twenty years. Always in the past, when I asked him what was wrong, his answer was the same.

"Not a lack of love," he'd say.

Not a lack of love, until there was no more.

We concluded our counseling on an optimistic note. Then he moved out.

Still lacking any kind of explanation for his removal from the marriage, still hoping this was just a particularly severe squall which we would inevitably weather, I never told my family or friends I no longer had a functioning marriage. I wouldn't have known what to say and I didn't want them to blame him for something I could not explain. I knew my husband was depressed. He had been before and had always returned. With less than two months before I was scheduled to move to Lagos, I packed up our house so it could be occupied by house sitters. My husband and I showed the house-sitting couple our home and he talked about our move as if we were still together.

"We're looking forward to seeing a little more of the world before we retire," he told them.

"What a wonderful opportunity!" the prospective house sitters exclaimed approvingly.

I wanted to keep talking to these strangers all afternoon. I was so comforted by the easy lies my husband told them in front of me, the way he explained to strangers the thing he would never say to me: how everything was going to work out, how everything was going to be fine.

We decided our small deaf cat, Lucy, would come to Nigeria with me. In preparation for the house sitters, I packed my husband's clothes and mine. I remember wondering if I should put our clothes in the same box or in separate boxes. I stopped and stared at a favorite T-shirt of his, unable to imagine a future when that shirt would be unpacked, utterly stymied by the enormity of this decision I was about to make, incapable of putting the shirt in either box.

I do not know how long I held the shirt in my hand, motionless, before I continued to pack. I might have held that shirt for a very long time. (I suspect I did.) At some point, I must have decided where to put it, because I followed the checklist I had written that told me what to do next and, as each item was finished, I checked it off.

"Lucy to veterinarian." Check.

"Dinner with Mom and Dad." Check.

Is it possible I never confided to anyone that my marriage was over? Is it possible I never reconsidered my move to Nigeria, never tried to stop the chain of events already set in motion? Maybe I did confide my doubts to a friend or two. Maybe there was a tear-stained confidence shared over a drink. Or perhaps I did not tell anyone anything had changed because I believed, if I told the story aloud, I might make it real; I might give it a life it did not previously possess.

I must have known, somewhere deep within, that continuing with plans as if nothing had happened was madness. But the whole thing seemed mad to me. His loss of love was so sudden and inexplicable I was simply unable to accept it. It was easier to deny what I had heard, deny what I now knew, than to deal with the unimaginable consequences. If I went along as if everything was fine then, perhaps somehow, it would be. This brand of magical thinking was encouraged by a particularly persistent brand of optimism, but also by a Midwestern upbringing that deeply valued damage control.

People throughout the Midwest remembered the North Dakota boy who had both arms ripped off by a tractor while he was working alone. He made it back to the house, dialed "911" with a pencil between his teeth, and then (and this is the important part) he waited in the bathtub for the paramedics to arrive so he wouldn't get blood on his mother's carpet. We read about this boy and admired him. We admired him for the last part in particular. Because, when things have suddenly gotten more terrible than we ever imagined possible, we figure we might as well do whatever we can to keep them from getting worse—even if it isn't much, even if it's just keeping blood off the carpet. This made a great deal of sense to me at the time.

I do not remember doing most of the things on my list, but I have check marks assuring me I did them. I don't remember the dinners with family or friends or what I said to them. I don't remember my company's goodbye lunch or buying supplies to take with me to Nigeria or visiting the travel clinic for the shots I would need to live abroad. (Although I know I received eight shots: I had four marks on each arm.) I know I did these things. I imagine I did other things that were not on the list, but I have no recollection.

My brother-in-law called me. He was the only one who knew what had happened because my husband had moved in with him.

"What's going on?" he demanded. "He's crazy and won't talk about it."

"I don't know," I told him. I didn't know.

A few days later, my husband came back to the house under the maple trees and I was filled with hope again. Optimism had won out. Persistence had been rewarded. But nothing changed. He had nothing to say. I followed him around like a ghost. An unbreakable silence lay between us.

Another month passed. I have only the vaguest memory of the most miserable (the only miserable) Christmas of my life. We attended all the family festivities together and I thought perhaps being with my family, who loved him as a son, would make obvious how foolish this idea of not loving me really was. I remember very little except what I got my husband for a present: it was a traditional Nigerian stool. The stool was made for sitting and relaxing in the yard. I imagined a time when people didn't fly around the globe to make a living or to be with one another, when instead they sat under a shady tree on a comfortable stool and talked things over with their friends. Counseling and crying had not worked. The stool did not work either.

I have a few fragmented memories of a really dreadful New Year's Eve. I have a clear recollection of spending the night naked and weeping in the dark with my head pressed against the cold wooden farmhouse floor. (Was I in the closet? It seems to me I was in the closet, but that can't be right.) But there was no breakdown. A breakdown was not on the list.

My husband suggested we go to Mexico after New Year's and I was again filled with optimism. My supply of hope appeared to be inexhaustible. We decided to go to a little fishing village we had visited several times before. I remembered those midwinter trips, traveling with only a small daypack each, wearing zip off trousers and sandals with heavy wool socks. When we heard the announcement that we were about to land, we'd give one another a secret smile, zip off the legs of our trousers in unison, and stuff the unneeded trouser legs and wool socks into our daypacks. We'd emerge into the sweet-smelling tropical heat in shorts, sandals, and sunglasses, hop on a rickety bus, and in a few hours' time we'd land on a gentle curve of the Pacific where we would scout up a simple room and spend a blissful week. I remembered those trips, when we were two carefree travelers, as we took the familiar long bus ride over the lush forested mountains. I was sure he remembered them too.

This is why we came to Mexico, I thought, as I waited for him to talk to me. But any resemblance to those early trips remained a memory. I tried to talk to him, but my talking irritated him, so I remained quiet and watched him instead. I watched him as we rode the small bus with the worn-out seats over the mountains to the sea. We did not talk the entire bumpy ride over the mountains, and when we reached the ocean he still had nothing to say. I watched him while he slept in the hotel room with the brightly colored walls. I watched him on the warm, coral beach.

Only in the ocean was there peace. Floating far from shore I lay in the tranquil sea, protected from the large waves and undertow. I swam for hours far out in the bay and around the two small islands. I lay on my back a long way from shore and slowly spun round and round like a compass dial to see the church in the distance, the hills rising above the shore, the wide blue sky. I felt a surprised fish brush against me and occasionally a cold finger of water stealing in from the open sea. A wave lifted me and I saw my husband under a straw hat on the shore; the wave lowered and I saw only the hills and the sky. I wanted to stay there, suspended in time, in that peaceful limbo where he was always on the shore, always waiting for me.

Just as the sun was setting, we walked in silence along the beach. He traced a long, curving line in the sand with his toe as he walked several yards ahead of me. He looked so impossibly sad. He was still that wistful boy—a little older now, but in his raggedy shorts, still the boy I loved. My heart ached for this boy, lost in thoughts he could not share, gone to some place where I could not join him. I stopped walking and stood still, watching him make a curving line with his toe in the sand. I wanted to run and catch him. I wanted to hold him and bring him back. But there was nothing I could do. If I approached I knew he would pull away, become annoyed. I would break the spell. I had no words to reach him, wherever he had gone. Caught in the setting sun's light, this lonely boy I loved kept walking slowly, farther and farther away from me, drawing loops of curving lines in the sand. He never looked back.

As we prepared to leave Mexico, we sat with bare feet in the cold airport before dawn drinking bad coffee. He finally had a few words for me. His eyes were red. My feet were cold.

"I'd like six months to think things over," he said quietly. He wanted six months to decide if he still wanted to be married.

"Okay," I said.

Why? Why did I agree?

I agreed because I could not say no. To reject this suggestion, the only one he had made in the two and a half months since announcing he no longer loved me, would be to close the door on hope. I would not be the one who gave up on love, even after it had moved out without a forwarding address, even after it made no logical sense whatsoever to keep the porch light on.

I had lived my entire life without giving up on anything that was important to me and now, clearly defeated, I simply did not know how it was done. As I saw my life going into a tailspin, I would not be at the wheel. I kept my hands gripped tightly onto thin air.

We returned from Mexico and I continued to mark my list with neat check marks indicating what I had accomplished. I did not know then, and I did not know for a very long time, there was another story I did not know.

I did not know my husband had been engaged in a yearlong affair while traveling to Brazil. I did not know they shared a home. I did not know they shared a bed. I did not know the story of this beautiful dark-haired girl with a young son in a poor country whom my husband met while getting his hair cut. I did not know this story as I packed my boxes and prepared to leave for Nigeria. As I packed to leave for Lagos the affair was over, but the story was untold.

And so, my husband created a new story for himself, a story he did not share with me — perhaps out of fear, perhaps out of pride, perhaps out of kindness. In my husband's new story, it is easier just to let me go. He is deeply pained and ashamed of what he has done and, eventually, his guilt persuades him to believe this new story, this story of why it is necessary to slip away without explanation. It would be better this way, he believes, it would be better for me if he says nothing. It would be better for us both. He believes it would be better to simply disappear, with no story at all.

•　　　•　　　•　　　•　　　•

On a snowy day in early January, dressed entirely in black, I loaded my cat, Lucy, in her pet carrier and my two carefully packed boxes onto a luggage cart in a lonely corner of the airport parking lot. I was hanging on, but barely, to a story that explained my life, a story that bore little relation to the truth. I did not know, that day in January, how fragile my grasp was on this illusory world. I was too terrified to speculate how little of my world would be left when my belief in the impossible was no longer possible.

Suddenly, I slipped. The cart toppled. The boxes fell. I found myself lying in the snow, dressed in black, everything scattered under the white winter sky.

FLYING IN THE DARK

I was flying in the dark — flying to Lagos, flying over an ocean at night. The cabin lights low, I took Lucy out of her carrier beneath my feet and put her on my lap.

"Where are we going, Lucy?" I asked.

Lucy lay in my lap purring, her head bobbing and twisting in the odd way she had in order to capture with her eyes what her ears could not.

"Where are we going, Lucy?" I asked again, as we flew in limbo between the earth and sky, my entire life quite literally up in the air. Lucy looked up at me and purred, barely five pounds of fur-covered devotion. I did not allow myself to think of where we were going or what we had left behind. I was as alone as I could be — except for Lucy. I held tight to this fierce purring ball of fur as we flew over an ocean and into the unimaginable.

I had adopted Lucy the year before. My intent had not been to find a companion for world travel, but a bit more pedestrian. Living in a farmhouse in the woods, I needed to keep the sizable mouse population in check. I wanted a mature female cat to take charge of my mouse eradication program before the cupboards were overrun. The Humane Society's website advertised a number of mature felines looking for gainful employment (some sporting flattering photos), and I thought the chances of finding my next farmhouse mouser looked good.

All the cats were in cages labeled with index cards stating the occupant's name, gender, age, a brief biography, and any medical conditions of interest. Most of the information was fairly routine except for one cage that required an additional index card to list all the medical abnormalities of its occupant. I quickly passed by this cage and proceeded to acquaint myself with the other inmates, but none had that something special I was looking for. (But then, how could I ever have known what I was looking for?) I was thinking I would drive to another shelter when I decided, in the interest of fairness, I should at least say hello to the unfortunate cat with all the medical conditions.

The tiny mottled gray cat was sleeping when I opened her cage. The door made a loud noise but she didn't stir. I worried she might be dead. Given the amount of medical information on her index cards, this didn't seem impossible. I gently poked her with my finger to see if rigor mortis had set in. She let out an enormous squeal and leapt out of the cage. I assumed she was attempting to escape and I was going to be reprimanded for letting loose this mad, half-dead animal.

But she didn't dash. She dove straight into my arms and instantly began to purr loudly, making no effort to do anything but hang onto me. Stone-deaf and starved for attention and stimulus, she hung on tight as we walked around the shelter, her head bobbing and spinning as she looked at everything with incredulous wonder. The longer I held her, the more I doubted anything on those index cards could possibly be important.

Lucy was found in a state park on September 17th, which was, whether by coincidence or fate, the exact day of my 20th wedding anniversary. She was very near death; her body was covered in scabs, she had lost her lower teeth, and she was hosting the worst case of ear mites the veterinarian had ever seen. The mites had eaten through her eardrums, leaving her totally deaf. They had so thoroughly invaded her nasal passages that she was left with a perpetual sinus infection. The shelter had an "open admissions" policy, meaning they did their best to find a home for every poor creature that landed on their doorstep, regardless of the odds against it. Without this policy, it is unlikely Lucy would ever have become a frequent flier with KLM.

Flying in the dark, this little cat in my lap, I didn't appreciate at the time the beautiful absurdity that my sole comfort and consolation came from a tiny deaf cat with a perpetual nasal drip. Because I had agreed to give my husband six months to decide what he wanted to do, I had no one else to confide in. Because I had been given no reason for our separation, I had no righteous rage or rational narrative to comfort me. All I knew was he had lost his love for me in an utterly mysterious fashion and the only explanation I had was that the depression which had dogged him all his adult life had succeeded in siphoning from him his joy in life, his interest in sex, his sense of humor, and, finally, even his ability to love. I had spent the last two years reading articles and books about the loss of libido related to depression. I had tried lingerie and sex toys and seductive chat, trying to lure him into intimacy. I had cried silently into my pillow, so as not to upset him when he rejected me, again and again. It was not his fault, I told myself, he was trying, he said. It was not a lack of love. I had never once — not once — imagined he would be unfaithful. Because I had known him for a quarter century and never once seen him lie about anything important, it never occurred to me he would lie or could lie to me about this. Anger would have been such a comfort.

Instead, I was locked in a grief I could not give voice to, could not even fully respect, because I sincerely believed his loss was greater than mine. Yes, I had lost the only man I ever loved. He was lost to me as if he were dead. But I still had my love for him. After years of fighting, he had lost his battle with the demons that had plagued him all his adult life. I felt ashamed of my own grief. I knew I was still capable of happiness. Even in moments of overwhelming sadness, I could recognize the humor or pathos of the situation. I could step outside myself and see the many reasons I had to be grateful and happy, the many ways in which I was blessed. I realized he could not, and this knowledge broke my heart.

Except it was all a lie.

I was mourning and grieving all the wrong things. I did not have the comfort of justifiable fury, or a plausible explanation, or the knowledge he had betrayed my love and faith in him in the most profound way. I was flying in the dark — flying to an unknown future, flying to a place where no one knew me — with only a sniffling little cat for company.

•   •   •   •   •

Lucy and I landed in Lagos, a city of seventeen to twenty-one million people (no one knew for sure), in the late morning. The airport's air conditioning wasn't working, as was usually the case. Bare light bulbs dangled from disassembled fluorescent panels above the threadbare carpeting of the jetway as we entered the stifling hot terminal. The airport was always in disrepair, as if to prepare arriving passengers for the reality that Lagos, the largest city in Africa, did not function in any meaningful way. Because I had been to Lagos several times by now, I knew more or less what to expect, although Lagos never lost its capacity to surprise and shock.

I made the decision to move to Lagos thinking I would be escaping to Europe at every opportunity, never imagining Lagos would really be "home," but more of a temporary work assignment. Thoughts of life in Lagos—actually living in Lagos—had been pushed entirely out of mind. When people asked me, "What is Lagos like?" I never told them. It was easier that way. It was easier to rationalize this move, which was more a perverse accident than a conscious choice. I didn't tell anyone about the blunt shock I experienced driving through Lagos the first few times. I didn't tell them about the panic I would feel if I allowed myself to imagine making Lagos my home. I didn't tell them for the same reason I didn't tell them my marriage was over and I was completely and utterly lost.

Instead, I told a story—to myself, to anyone who asked—and the story was true, but the story was not what Lagos was like. I told people who asked, and I reminded myself, about the funny and quirky and unexpectedly beautiful things I saw in Lagos. The story I told was like a beam of sunshine that made its way through the razor wire fence, past the crumbling buildings, the piles of refuse, the pervasive human suffering, and landed on a flower inexplicably growing in the cracks of the shattered asphalt.

"I saw a beautiful flower today," I told anyone who asked. "I took a picture."

Lagos is a terrible hard place. People survive by different means.

Some mark their calendars. They were made an offer they could not refuse, a deal with the devil, a short stint in purgatory in exchange for riches—if not enough for a lifetime, enough for early retirement and a handsome nest egg. They watch their calendars, go to their jobs, spend too much at overpriced restaurants, drink too much, and hunker down. They know it will end and they've made their bargain.

Some refuse to see. They see the banks and the billboards but not the corpse in the street or the man with no eyes at the car window. They see the promise of dollars and opportunities and focus on that promise hard enough so as not to see the beggar children running through lanes of traffic. They live in a gated compound and have people fetch things for them and if they spend too much it's okay. They have preserved the illusion they live in just another neighborhood in just another city.

Most have no choice. They ask, "When will you take me to America?" They work in jobs that pay barely enough to survive in this very expensive city, and they live crowded in flats piled on top of each other, if they're lucky. If they're unlucky, they live under the bridge, in houses built on stilts over water filled with sewage and industrial waste, surrounded by a veil of toxic smog.

But Lagos is, first and foremost, a commercial city. Rampant commercialism and brilliant mass marketing pervade every street corner. Between every lane of stalled cars creeping forward in interminable "go-slows" is an endless stream of entrepreneurs. They sell fruit and toiletries and thousands of sausage rolls (filled with meat of a mysterious origin) and soda pop and plantain chips and electrical appliances (guaranteed to work or your money back) and garbage cans and bathroom scales and watches (genuine Rolex) and books (I actually bought the complete works of Shakespeare, right out of my car window) and cologne and sometimes puppies (I was tempted) and reflective stickers to put on your car to comply with some obscure regulation someone says will eventually be enforced (by whom and for what reason?) and newspapers and rat poison (sold on a stick decorated with dead rats so you get the point) and, always and everywhere, phone charge cards.

And because it is a commercial city, at every intersection where traffic may slow, and there are too many to count, there is also at least one entrepreneur in the industry of human suffering. This one has no arms; this one has no legs and propels himself on a skateboard with sandals on his hands. He attaches himself to my car door handle as I try to accelerate; he refuses to let go, a game of Russian roulette where I am dared to drive faster without throwing money out the window. On the next corner is a burn victim, his face melted away, stripped to the waist, demanding his due. I lock the doors and try to look away. But when he sees me look away he begins to berate me, to yell, to cajole, to implore, louder and louder, closer and closer as I pray for the traffic to move. Please let it move.

And tumors so large and in such unlikely places: faces, groins, backs, tumors the size of cantaloupes, tumors the size of watermelons, tumors I cannot comprehend because it does not seem possible they could be covered with human skin.

But worse is the victim with an entourage. A color photo appears in my car window, expertly framed under glass. It is a before-and-after shot, a pretty young girl on the left, something terrible in the photo on the right involving, what? An exploded stove, perhaps? Too awful to tell—her middle is missing, she has her blouse lifted to reveal what has happened, what is no longer there, the terrible wreckage that has replaced it. When I turn my head away, I see in the next lane of traffic, the car next to mine has an identical picture being thrust in its window. I look forward and see the whole phalanx of young men, organized, in formation, moving through the crowded street, pictures in hand, so no car is missed.

And then I see the genius of the organization.

Straight ahead and, since she cannot see, an escort at either side, is the girl herself being led through the crowd, the final act in a perfectly choreographed appeal designed to affect the most hardened skeptic. Money comes out the car windows, crumpled twenty and fifty *naira* notes, slipped through windows by people who cannot help but look and stare.

And the dying are left at the side of the road and in the harbor to wash up against the pier, little left but remnants of clothing and leg bones and torsos that look strangely large and white.

And yes, there are nice restaurants, and yes, I can see a recent motion picture in a real movie theater—the only city in Nigeria where this is possible—but when I leave, I will walk through the crowd of supplicants on skateboards and handmade crutches with signs around their necks explaining the nature and cause of their particular misfortune, and I must decide what to do.

I can pretend I do not see, but they will still come. I can hand out money till my wallet is empty, but they will still come. I can get angry at the country for having no safety net, angry at the beggars for harassing me, angry at God for making life so hideously unfair and inequitable. Or I can just navigate like most of us do, the undeservedly healthy, the absurdly privileged, the inexplicably blessed. I can hand out a few notes to the people who do not frighten me too much and try to escape the horror of the rest.

Stepping into the sticky, near-equatorial heat, I was suddenly confronted with the reality of this Lagos I had refused to acknowledge as my future home. Lucy and I were met by a sea of yelling faces offering cabs and demanding attention as they pushed and fought their way to the barrier erected just outside the airport. In the thick of the crowd I saw Klaus, the foul-tempered Austrian, permanently browned by the African sun, who worked for my company as a project manager on the other side of the country.

Weathered from years of outdoor projects and decades of scowling, Klaus handed my two boxes to his driver and told me curtly, "I fly back tonight. Before nightfall."

We piled into Klaus' SUV and headed to the guesthouse my company had rented. The streets were clogged with beggars and the police, as always, were collecting bribes at every intersection where traffic stalled on the pothole-riddled roads. Lagos had electricity less than half the day in the best parts of town (in poorer neighborhoods the power was out for days at a time) and the air of this island city was blue with exhaust from the tens of thousands of private generators producing light for a city that would otherwise lie in darkness.

We arrived at the guesthouse—an enormous six-bedroom, four-story house with no trees, a concrete yard, and a "boys' quarters" for the staff to live in, all enclosed within a white cement wall topped with razor wire — where we immediately discovered the house was not, in fact, actually rented yet. No lease had been signed and no renovations had begun. This responsibility had been left to our Nigerian "partner," Felix. Felix had little interest in the new Lagos office, telling the CFO he was certain I would fail in Nigeria, and he had skedaddled off to Canada having made no preparations whatsoever. This was significant because properties in Lagos were rented out with a minimum advance payment of two years, and landlords had few obligations. There were no appliances, no fixtures, and no generator — meaning there would be no electricity for much of the day. The electrical wiring might or might not be intact, but the plumbing almost certainly would not work. Every wall would need painting and every floor would require polishing. Many of the windows and doors would need to be replaced. This guesthouse had been vacant a long time.

Klaus squinted at the dirty, uninhabitable hulk of a building. He grunted, "I guess we take you to the hotel then."

I look at this place that was supposed to be my home. It is uninhabitable but I don't see that. I won't let myself see that. Because, if I saw that, I'd have to see a lot of other things too.

I look back on myself, looking at that home that was not a home, and I am filled with an overwhelming sadness for this woman: imagining she was going to find a home or anything resembling one, still dressed all in black, holding tightly onto a small, deaf cat. Yes, I had a briefcase full of papers and a job to do, but none of it — none of it — mattered. I was there preserving a fiction, desperately hanging onto an illusion that was becoming increasingly preposterous, terrified of what would become obvious if I allowed myself to see.

IMPROBABLE ACHIEVEMENT

Lucy and I were deposited at a hotel—the same hotel where I received the call in the moonlight five months earlier, the same hotel where the whole idea started. But first, Klaus introduced me to Ismail.

Ismail arrived at the guesthouse within minutes. A no-nonsense man with thoughtful eyes and prematurely silver hair, Ismail took one look at the dirty, run-down guesthouse, then looked at me. His chivalric instincts took over. "I'll get some guys to start working," he said.

In the next few days, with Ismail's help, I negotiated and signed a lease and Ismail assembled a crew of contractors who, while certainly not efficient, were theoretically capable of doing the required work. My company had provided Felix with a car and, since he was in Canada, Felix's driver drove me in the company car every day from the hotel through the labyrinth of Lagos traffic to the guesthouse where I worked to make it habitable.

It seemed everything that could possibly go wrong did. The well was dry, so I had a new one dug. The first pump for the new well burned out—then the second. The third pump worked, but water from the new well smelled like sulfur. The electricians were arrested on suspicion of possessing stolen property (not stolen—it was actually mine, as it turned out). They spent a night in jail. The floor refinishers got the job half done and someone's uncle died. (If someone related to anyone died, the entire crew took the day off.) The electricians walked over the half-finished floor and ruined it. The days dragged on.

At the end of every day, Lucy and I would return to the hotel, walking past the moneychangers. The banks gave a terrible exchange rate so, while it was technically illegal, I would go to the moneychangers to get more U.S. dollars exchanged to pay for the seemingly never-ending guesthouse renovations. The moneychangers were Muslim, Hausa from the north of Nigeria, dressed in traditional robes and hats. I don't imagine they looked a whole lot different from the money lenders Jesus threw out of the synagogue. The hotel was more tolerant.

With their prayer rugs rolled up next to large locked boxes full of dollars, euros, British pounds, and Nigerian naira, they operated right outside the hotel, on hotel property, in an area ostensibly set up to sell souvenirs. They may have sold a few trinkets from time to time, but their main business was money-changing.

Coming and going, no one at the hotel ever noticed Lucy in her little carrier with the black screen sides. But the moneychangers saw her immediately. They made a living by watching people closely. If a customer was desperate to change money, they would get a terrible rate. If someone could take it or leave it, wait another day, they would get as good a rate as could be found on the mainland.

"Ologbo," the moneychangers said when they saw Lucy. I realize now this is not Hausa, but Yoruba, the language of southern Nigeria. I didn't know that at the time, but I knew what they meant.

"Yes," I replied, "I have a cat. Her name is Lucy."

Cats were generally feared in the southern, Christian part of Nigeria, including Lagos, but the Muslim moneychangers were from the north, where cats were more accepted. Muhammad himself was said to have been very fond of his cat.

"Lucy! Lucy!" the moneychangers yelled every time I came back from another frustrating day at the guesthouse. If she was not with me they asked, "Where is Miss Lucy?" Lucy, "the traveling cat from America!", quickly became a celebrity among the moneychangers.

Sometimes, at night, the hotel room would become too claustrophobic. It was easy to distract myself all day with contractors, but at night the disconnect between myself and an explanation for my current life—an explanation that made any sort of sense—would sometimes become too intense to bear. When this happened, Lucy and

I would go outside the hotel, so I could stop thinking, and sit and chat with the moneychangers instead. They would pour me a cup of hot, sweet tea and I would give them some of Lucy's cat food to feed to the wild cats outside the hotel. Lucy would sit on my lap, transfixed, as the wild cats cautiously came to try the American cat food. They ate the crunchy kibble, glancing nervously up at Lucy, the moneychangers, and me. Soon the moneychangers began feeding the cats scraps from their dinner.

"They will keep the rats away!" the moneychangers told me, happy with their newfound companions. After a couple weeks, I was pleased to see some of the cats had become quite tame. I sipped my tea and watched the feral cats darting around the large metal money boxes, roaming the hotel grounds at night, gingerly enjoying their unlikely haven.

After a month in the hotel, when my threats and entreaties to the contractors no longer seemed to be having any effect, I decided to move into the guesthouse so I could apply more direct pressure. We had installed a generator, so I had electricity in at least a portion of the house. My room had no door, but one was hastily installed when the carpenters realized with alarm I really did plan to spend the night. Security was not in place—so I hired a security firm to start that evening. Lucy and I moved into the huge guesthouse with my two cardboard boxes. There was no one else in the house—except Precious.

Precious came with the house. He had been the security guard for six years and, after the previous tenants left, the landlord kept him on to mind the property. He slept on the cement floor in the unfurnished "boys' quarters" and had lived alone on the vacant property for the better part of two years before Lucy and I arrived.

The realtor advised against hiring Precious. "We don't know that man," he told me in a low voice, gesturing to the muscular young man in a ragged T-shirt with a neatly shaved head. Precious had no references. He was completely illiterate. But Precious seemed determined to make the most of this opportunity. I told Precious, if I kept him on, he would have to be willing to do anything—and that is what he did. Precious helped every contractor who needed help. He swept the giant building after the daily construction. He hauled buckets of cement, chopped up yards of pavement, ran for water, answered the door. He told me when contractors left doors unlocked. He let me know if anyone was looking in a box he didn't think they should be looking in.

Precious also looked after Lucy. When he was working outside, she would watch through the window — covered in iron bars — for Precious to walk by. A parade of young, bald-headed Nigerian contractors passed the window, but Lucy only cried out when she saw Precious. She learned one loud, sustained squall would summon him. Precious would fetch the tiny cat and carry her around like a baby so she could observe the activity, which she seemed to enjoy enormously.

Eventually, I trained Precious to collate papers and operate a hole punch to assist me with the oil and gas contracts I was applying for while construction continued all around us. Precious helped collate the voluminous qualification documents and, since he could not read, he learned to recognize the pages by sight.

Precious had never seen a toaster, but he learned to make toast. Precious had never seen a coffeemaker before he made coffee. When Ismail came to monitor the progress in the afternoon, Precious would serve him with the line he had carefully rehearsed: "Is there anything I can offer you?" He would then slowly list all the beverages we had in the refrigerator. Precious learned about litterboxes and fitted sheets and toilet paper dispensers and how to operate the washing machine (not a total success). Precious also turned on the generator half a dozen times a day when the power went off, and then turned it off again when the electricity returned. I told Precious he would have quite an impressive resume when he was through working with me. He called me "Mum" and occasionally "Mummy," which sounded odd, but was intended as a sign of respect.

I finally prevailed upon the painters to paint the boys' quarters. I had a new iron bunk bed delivered, complete with mattress and pillow, and gave Precious linens for his bed. He stood awkwardly, linens in hand, completely taken aback.

"Thank you, Mum. Thank you," he mumbled, embarrassed. He

said he had told his mother and his pastor about his new employer from America.

"I will work hard for you, Mum. You will not be disappointed."

Did I believe him? Maybe I knew it was wrong to hire someone with no references. Maybe I suspected I would ultimately regret it. But I was happy to have Precious living with us. We made an unusual little family: Precious, Lucy, and me.

Shortly after Lucy and I moved into the guesthouse, Felix returned from Canada. Felix seldom visited the guesthouse but, now that he was back in Lagos, the company car was rarely available for me to use. Every day I supervised the growing army of contractors while preparing qualification documents, creating marketing materials, and introducing my company to the oil and gas companies in Lagos. If the company car was unavailable, I took a cab. If the cab failed to arrive (as frequently happened) I took an *okada*, one of the legions of motorcycles for hire which dodged between the lanes of stalled traffic. Dressed in a black suit and heels, a fat qualifications packet tucked under my arm, I arrived at these surprisingly clean and well-maintained offices, gave a presentation, and hoped no one would notice when I jumped on the back of a battered motorcycle to get home. I usually worked until the Minneapolis office closed at five, midnight my time, then started my day when the first workers arrived in the morning.

After the contractors left, I had a dinner of the greens and rice I bought at the local market. Just before sunset, I went for a run through the darkening streets. While Lagos was a city of constant *wahala* (Yoruba for "troubles") there was little actual danger. As I ran through my neighborhood, little kids stopped and stared. They saw few white women—never a white woman running. I smiled and pantomimed they should run with me. They blushed and laughed. I waved to the line of people walking home: large metal bowls balanced on their heads filled with the things they sold on the roadside, a kerosene lantern in the center of each bowl to light the way, a bobbing row of dusty lanterns in the dark. The palm and banana trees picked up the night breeze; the moon came out. It grows dark quickly, so close to the equator. In the Midwest, sunset is a three-act play. In Lagos, the sun drops and darkness falls in minutes.

At night I sprayed my room to keep the mosquitoes at bay, as Lagos has an alarmingly high rate of malaria. As soon as work stopped for the day, a fine dust would begin to settle. With no furniture or carpets, my steps echoed up and down the four flights of stairs. The walls were white, the floors were white. There was no color anywhere except the batik cloth I bought at the market and threw over my bed to keep the dust and insect spray off my sheets.

Lucy occupied herself killing cockroaches. Lucy was useless as a mouser I learned, immediately after adopting her. It seemed that mousing required hearing. Somehow, I imagined cats smelled mice or saw mice. (Okay, to be honest, I hadn't actually given it a lot of thought.) But, for the record, mousing is a skill that requires hearing, and the mice in my farmhouse under the maple trees quickly learned Lucy posed no credible threat and ran through the house in greater numbers than ever. But the auditory skills required for mousing are apparently not a prerequisite for killing cockroaches. Or perhaps the cockroaches' tiny brains were not adept at sensing the imminent threat of this feline foe. Whatever the reason, Lucy was stacking up a pile of vanquished prey and looking inordinately proud of herself.

Certainly, I was aware this was not what an expat assignment should be. I had no transportation, little furniture, no office assistance. I was living alone in a barely habitable prison of a building with only an illiterate security guard for company. My entreaties for more money and help went unanswered. The year was not off to a good start in Minneapolis. My company was overextended; projects around the world were underfunded, understaffed, and had been poorly managed. I knew, realistically, there was not enough money to properly support this new office in Lagos. It was an impossible situation, I realized even then.

But how can I explain now how difficult it was for me to address one impossible situation when another was already upon me? I had promised to give my husband six months, with little understanding of what that would entail. I had promised to open an office for my company, similarly ignorant. Now, rather than try to imagine what I would do without either of them, I opted to stay the course. It was easier — in fact, it was all I could do — to continue to fill out the necessary paperwork by day and battle the cockroaches by night. It was the best I could do, and it felt like a small but improbable achievement.

When the power went out at night, which it did every night for several hours, the compound went dark. The air conditioners fell silent. Lucy and I rattled around in the large vacant house. I navigated by flashlight. (Lucy loved flashlights.) At night, I sometimes allowed myself a moment to think and to wonder. I wondered how my husband was doing in Brussels. I wondered what his home looked like. I wondered if he would want me to visit him soon. Alone with my small, deaf cat in this big, empty house, it seemed my little piece of the Dark Continent was very dark indeed. I opened the door to the balcony in my bedroom and smelled the fetid breeze coming off the lagoon and green wood burning in the rain.

BARREN SPACE

It was slowly becoming apparent that somehow, without meaning to, I had committed to an indefinitely extended business trip in Lagos, Nigeria. My plan to see the capitals of Europe and the Mediterranean was looking less and less likely, and it slowly sank in that I now *lived* in Lagos and was not going anywhere anytime soon.

How did this happen?

The company I worked for seemed more and more remote and less and less concerned about me. On weekend evenings, when my husband did not call from Brussels and everyone in the Minneapolis office was off doing whatever it was they did on the weekend (what did they do on the weekend? I was having a hard time remembering) I watched the same two old DVDs over and over on my laptop and wondered: *How did this happen? What do I do now? Something. I must do something now.*

Trying to imagine a future life, when this one was so clearly unsustainable (both personally and professionally) was not yet possible. Changing course would have required action, and I was immobilized. The course was set. The iceberg was dead ahead. All I could do at that moment in time was to rearrange the deck chairs.

Ismail was frequently the only person I would see all day besides Precious and an ever-changing cast of contractors. He stopped in on his way home and soon started inviting me to his house to share an occasional meal.

Ismail was born in Lebanon and had moved to Nigeria alone when he was fourteen. One day, he was walking down the beach where Shirene, the beautiful half-Persian daughter of a wealthy man, and her mother were sunbathing. Until that day on the beach, Shirene had intended to marry another wealthy man who had avidly courted her for years. Ismail and Shirene fell in love at first sight. Ismail had no money and no prospects. Shirene's father was skeptical. Shirene's American mother was unperturbed.

"All the women in my family fall in love at the beach," she said.

Shirene's life with Ismail was sometimes hard, but I never heard her indicate she would have made any other choice. Ismail moved with Shirene to Florida, where he completed both his undergraduate and graduate degrees in engineering and they started a family. After fourteen years in the U.S., they decided to try their luck back in Lagos.

Shirene was still a beautiful woman, barely five-foot-tall, with perfectly applied make-up and long, manicured nails. She was understandably concerned I was living alone in an enormous, semihabitable house with only my cat for company. One evening when they had me to dinner, she gave me a copy of *Lagos Easy Access*, a guidebook put out by the American Women's Club—energetic "trailing wives" of oil executives and diplomats—in the hope I would find some excuse to occasionally leave the guesthouse. I dutifully looked through the guidebook, but nothing seemed of any interest until I saw... the Yacht Club.

I'd never sailed before, but I paid my quarterly dues, went through a brief orientation that involved a lot of complimentary cocktails, and three days later I was crewing on a small sailboat for the race held every Saturday afternoon in the Lagos harbor. I didn't care who won the race. I just wanted to be out on the water, away from the guesthouse, far from the smog and the go-slows and the traffic. I sailed on old boats with even older sailors who were cheerful because the glass was always more than half full, as far as they were concerned, any day they could be sailing.

The racecourse was complicated. In addition to the huge barges and container ships, there were masses of floating debris that would catch in the rudder, and fairly frequently there would be a corpse, bleached strangely white from days or weeks in saltwater, floating just below the surface. I learned the accepted protocol was to skirt the corpse and resume the course. No one would retrieve the body because whoever did was responsible for its burial. So, the bodies remained where they were and the race continued: brightly colored sailboats deftly skirting the corpse, ghostly white and ragged, floating just below the surface of the water for a few hours or a day before it slowly disappeared into the harbor.

These cheerful sailors were undeterred because, they told me, it used to be so much worse. They slammed pints of beer on the well-worn bar, polished to a luster and overlooking the harbor in two directions, glistening in the late afternoon light. The club dated back to the time when Nigeria was a British colony and was largely unchanged since then. A silent Nigerian bartender dressed in white refilled the glasses. Drinks were put on a tab; there was no cash and no tipping. Phones were silenced; a ringing phone in the bar incurred the penalty of a round of drinks for the house: a penalty sufficiently stiff to ensure every phone was switched off.

"See a corpse in the harbor today? Why that's nothing," they told me. "Was a time you couldn't drive across Falomo Bridge without seeing four or five bodies floating down below. And the roads, Jesus! They used to just leave bodies on the road and nobody would move them till they were run over flat, just a hand sticking up. Ha! You haven't seen anything!"

They were like survivors of a war, these old sailors. Nothing I had seen or experienced was anything compared to how it used to be. Lagos was a paradise now—you should have seen it back in the day. Those were the days. And how could you not be cheerful when everything was obviously so much improved?

And they stayed ten years, fifteen years, twenty years. They'd been here for decades some of them. They each had a story of why they left wherever they came from—dead-end marriages, a longing for something different, a need to escape a preordained path—and somehow, almost always by accident, Lagos became home. Without really meaning to, they stayed another year, and then another. And by Friday afternoon, over a few bottles of beer, they wondered why they did it. "There's too much frustration!" they complained. "Too much *wahala* in this damned city!"

But Saturday afternoon they were on the water again, shaving a few minutes off a course they knew like the back of their hand, playing in the currents like a bird plays in the air, avoiding the monstrous barges and tugs and container ships that loomed over the tiny sailboat, making it look and feel like a child's toy. And they forgot all about the gloom of Friday afternoon. They had another draft at the bar and congratulated the winner—who (they insisted) had only won due to some totally undeserved piece of good luck that could have happened to anyone in a similar circumstance.

I felt comfortable amidst these expats who had negotiated an uneasy truce with both Lagos and whatever tumultuous past had brought them here. Real intimacy was not encouraged; in its place was a rough-and-ready camaraderie, a stiff upper lip, the cynical humor that comes from living in a place where something is always going wrong, where calamity is a daily occurrence. It was easy to fit in with this doggedly cheerful crowd with no explanation and no expectations.

On Friday nights, I started to receive phone calls from one of several cheery members of the Yacht Club. "Would you like to go out to a movie? We're going to see…"

"Yes."

It didn't matter what the movie was; they were usually bad. It didn't matter where we ate; it was always overpriced. There were six or eight of us, all expats, with nothing much in common except that we were alone—for whatever reason—on a Friday or Saturday night. And I wanted to be anywhere but in that empty white house, anywhere at all. We would go to the only movie theater in Lagos, a brand-new complex with plush seats and giant screens. We'd order sweet and salty popcorn and watch an American blockbuster, a movie I would never have bothered with in the U.S., then leave the frigidly cold air-conditioned theater and step into the hot, moist night of Lagos, surrounded by legless beggars on skateboards congregated in the parking lot. We'd drop a few *naira* into outstretched hands, say our good nights, roll up the car windows, and go home.

I learned to sail from Don. He was Scottish and approaching

seventy. He had a pink face, a pinker nose, and masses of unruly white curls. He had a nameless wife whom he rarely spoke of somewhere in Scotland and a fourteen-foot sailboat with ragged sails that took on water at a furious rate. Yet he won the race more often than not because he knew the currents of the Lagos harbor better than anyone else.

"Throw those double D's over the side, girl!" he'd holler in a thick Scottish brogue, and I'd hang out over the water (with considerably less than double D's to work with), desperately trying to counterbalance the tilting sailboat.

On the water, time seemed to pause, and the limbo I lived in seemed far away. In the bright African sunshine, the city's details in the distance, Lagos looked like any other city. With my life's details in the distance, I could spend a few hours pretending to be just another person sailing in the bright sunshine. I blistered my fingers and learned to fly the spinnaker and had a few hours' reprieve from the awful reality of real life.

I took my wedding ring off during this time. There was no significant moment. I was walking one night, alone in the dark, when I rubbed my thumb against my ring as I always did—but instead of simply reassuring myself it was there, I slipped it off and put it in my pocket. About this time, I also started to tell people I was divorced. It seemed less awkward than the truth, which sounded peculiar even to me.

"I came here to be closer to my husband... who is on another continent... and to wait for him to decide if he loves me anymore."

Silence.

"He's still deciding."

Silence.

"He's very thorough."

•　　•　　•　　•　　•

I'd been in Lagos for more than two months when my husband suggested we meet in Europe, but our first European get-together took some time to get together. First, he was busy, traveling, working. Then he suggested we go to Greece (frantic research on Greece). Two days later, he told me he couldn't make it to Greece. Then it was Turkey (I got as far as hotel listings). Not Turkey. Then it was Madrid. He had clients there. One quick check-in with the clients and we would spend a long weekend — his birthday weekend — in Madrid. No ocean breezes in Madrid, but that was okay. Jackson Browne was playing at a small venue in the old part of town. He liked Jackson Browne. Can we get tickets? We can. I researched hotels, looking for one that was convenient to walk from place to place and, of course, romantic. I found a sweet little hotel with a balcony in an old part of town. I tried to temper my optimism as there were no hopeful developments to hang onto — we had hardly spoken since I arrived in Lagos. But when he called he said, "I've missed you," and I hung tightly onto those words.

Tired of quarreling with Felix over use of the company car, with Ismail's help I bought a used Toyota and leased it to my company at a below-market rate. I hired a skinny and resourceful driver named Emeka, recommended by one of my fellow sailors at the Yacht Club. Because I didn't yet know Emeka well, I left the keys with Precious.

"Don't let anyone drive the car while I'm gone, Precious."

"No, Mum."

"You can give the keys to Emeka to pick me up at the airport, but not before, okay?"

"Yes, Mum."

"The car stays where it is until then, okay?"

"Yes, Mum."

"And take good care of Lucy while I'm away."

"Yes, Mum."

"I'm trusting you, Precious, to take care of things."

"Yes, Mum. Thank you, Mummy."

•　　　•　　　•　　　•　　　•

I arrived in Madrid early and walked around town. Madrid is a delightful city, so unbelievably clean compared to Lagos, full of street musicians and pigeons and funny, skinny buildings crowded together, with peculiar tiny balconies overlooking outdoor tables situated around the sunny courtyards. I bought a necklace I thought I would wear to the concert. Do I look okay? Did I bring the right clothes? It was a little cold. I bought socks and warm tights to wear under my African clothes. March in Madrid is cool, especially in the evening. I waited for him to arrive.

"Hey, how are you?" he said with a tired smile as he hugged me in the hotel lobby.

"I'm good. I'm fine." It felt so good to touch him again.

He'd been working too hard. He was tired. He wanted to take a nap. So, I walked around the city on my own, waiting for him to rest. I got my hair cut and lightened, an adventure with my level of Spanish. (*Papeles de platos*, as it turns out, for anyone looking to get a foil in Spain.) The people were friendly and indulged my poor Spanish patiently.

I felt fine. I had pretty things to wear and I was fit and a little tan, full of interesting stories I had saved up to amuse him. But I was also… anxious. I was anxious in all the word implies—anxious to find out what happened next in my life, anxious things might not go well, anxious for him take me in his arms and make love to me for the first time in… how long had it been? (I knew exactly.) Anxious to know if there was any reason to keep living this surreal double life where everything was wonderful and exciting, according to what I'd told everyone back in the U.S., when the truth was so different and frightening.

Madrid is not an anxious city. It is relaxed and easygoing and has its priorities in order: good coffee, good wine, good food. Sitting in the warm, early-spring sun after he rose from his nap, it seemed our problems may have been imagined. We were so easy together. He heard about Nigeria and I heard about Belgium and… what did we talk about? It is funny how little I remember. I just knew I was with him again and I felt the clock ticking, anxious the time would pass too soon.

It would have been a good time for him to tell me.

It would have been the perfect time to get some sort of explanation for what had happened. He could have told me it was over. He could have told me why. He could have offered my anxious mind and breaking heart something to land on, a reason why our marriage of twenty-two years was now dead after so many years of robust life. Instead, we had a nice dinner. We listened to Jackson Brown. We talked to one another as if we were still lovers, still partners, still friends. Honesty would have been such a kindness. Instead, he allowed me to hope.

Then evening comes and he literally recoils from my touch. It is as if my touch hurts him, as if I am there to do him harm, as if I am not merely undesirable, but physically harmful.

"I just want to sleep," he tells me in the hotel room, his back to me, the dim light of streetlights reflected through the balcony windows. "Can't you just let it be?"

No, I can't. It seems I can't.

The lovely clothes do not matter. The reservoir of amusing stories is wasted. The pretty new necklace is not worn. The city seems to mock my efforts. If I can't find love in Spain in the spring, what is wrong with me?

What is wrong with me?

He flinches when I draw near. Tears sting in my eyes.

"It's not you," he says. "It's just how things are."

It is certainly how things are.

Early morning in Madrid, the sun is not yet up. I am stuffing lovely clothes in my bag to catch an early cab to the airport. He will not be seeing me off. I am crying again, humiliated and heartbroken, no touch, no kiss goodbye. I am untouched. I am untouchable. I cannot imagine how I came to be so thoroughly undesirable.

The plane takes off and Madrid is left behind in the cold spring sunshine. I am surprised how bleak the area around the city appears. When I was inside, all the tiny cheerful restaurants and crowded little streets made it seem as if there was a shortage of space for Madrid's many attractions. Yet from above, I see the city holds itself tightly together in a great barren space, with nothing to stop it from letting go and spilling out into the desert.

I sit on the airplane, holding myself tightly. For just a moment I wonder what would happen if I stopped—stopped trying so hard, stopped hoping so much, stopped holding so tightly onto all the things that made sense of my life.

What is stopping you? Nothing, I realize.

Nothing is stopping me but a paralyzing fear of open, lonely desert.

TERRIBLE CARELESSNESS

I returned to Lagos and a smashed-up car.

Despite specific instructions to the contrary, Precious had driven the car. Since he did not know how to drive, he drove it straight into the wall surrounding the compound.

It was too much for him, I realized after the fact. What had seemed to me like a minimum requirement for a decent life—a semi-livable wage, a clean and furnished place to live, a little respect—these were all new things to Precious, things he had likely never expected to have. To have them all—at once—and then be trusted with keys to a car, a car worth several times his annual wages, was as if he had won the lottery. Like lottery winners everywhere, he made poor choices with his windfall. It was too much to handle, too much at once.

After smashing into the wall, Precious apparently sensed he was now in insurmountable trouble and might as well go out in style. He invited not one, but four young female guests into the compound at once. Guests were not allowed in the compound, and certainly not while I was away. When an irate security guard tried to stop him from entering with his bevy, Precious punched him in the face and bloodied his uniform. I returned from Spain to a dented car, a furious driver, a beat-up security guard, and a hangdog Precious—who had made it impossible for me to do anything but fire him. I held Lucy as I stood in the concrete yard and watched Emeka drive Precious off the compound with his few possessions piled into my little Toyota, slightly worse for wear.

The compound now seemed even lonelier, if that was possible. I walked through my days numb. On Sundays, Emeka was gone all day.

I was alone with Lucy in the guesthouse, alone in the large compound surrounded by white concrete walls rimmed in razor wire. From my room on the third floor, I could see over the wall. The neighboring compound was a business of some sort. Monday through Friday, and occasionally on Saturday, people came and went. But on Sunday it was quiet. On Sunday, my neighbor was let out of her room.

She was the wife of the gardener, I was told. She was locked indoors during the week. But on Sundays, when there was no one around, she was allowed to go outside onto her balcony. Her room was on the second story of the boys' quarters, just a little below the level of my balcony and clearly visible over the wall. Her hair was wild and she was very thin. When she was let outside, she screamed. After she was through screaming, sometimes she sang—maybe in Yoruba, more likely in a nonsense language of her own. She sang a song of her own invention with only four lines. She sang the same four lines over and over.

The Sunday after Precious left, her singing made me feel as if I were going crazy. Her singing made me wonder if there was any real difference between our mental states. I came out onto my balcony and looked at her for a long time. After countless repetitions, I could stand it no longer and I sang her melody back to her, but with new words:

This is my Sunday song,
This is my Sunday song,
I sing it all day long,
Cuz it's my Sunday song.

She did not respond. Her singing continued. I sang to her again, louder. She suddenly looked up, mad and frightened eyes staring into mine, and appeared to notice me. She fell silent for the first time in hours. Then she began to sing again. I joined her again with the new words to our combined song. She stared at me intently, falling silent again. Then, feeling I had a captive audience, I sang another song, this one an old Adelaide Hall tune:

BLUE YARN

I'm in the mood for love
Simply because you're near me.

She was watching me closely now.

Funny, but when you're near me
I'm in the mood for love.

I looked across the balcony at this woman, wild-eyed and momentarily struck silent. She looked at me. I wondered what she saw when she looked at me — a phantom? A fellow prisoner? A reflection? I fell silent and, after a pause, she resumed her song as if I were not there. I closed my balcony door and went back into the guesthouse.

·   ·   ·   ·   ·

The writing was on the wall, but the wall was hard to see from across the ocean.

Emails started coming in daily: cash flow was tight, results were expected. Why wasn't the guesthouse finished, furnished, ready for visitors? Where were the contracts they were expecting? When would the cash begin to flow? And why did I need more money — again?

Each time a new email arrived, I felt a tightening in my chest. I sent replies. I provided updates. But I could not promise the quick cash my company so obviously needed. Nothing was quick in Nigeria. Everything took longer than anyone could possibly imagine — and then it took three weeks longer. Instead of buying proper furniture, I took to the streets. Beside the freeway or under the highway overpass, I found furniture makers who would craft wooden and cane furniture from local materials. I would see a bed or table or chair by the side of the road that looked serviceable and say to Emeka, "Let's stop and look."

Stepping over the small stream of wastewater, past the chickens, around a pot of something cooking on a fire on the ground, I examined the bed or table or chair that was not exactly what I wanted but showed promise. I located the man who made the furniture and told him, "If

52

you could make this part a bit taller and this part a bit wider and put a handle here..."

The man—Femi or Bola or Osondu—would listen and nod and promise to make it just as I described. I would order two of whatever it was and pay for one. For two weeks I wouldn't know if I had thrown away money but, at most, I'd have squandered less than a hundred dollars. Approximately two weeks later, I would get a phone call.

"This is Femi/Bola/Osondu, the man you ordered the beds/desks/chairs from. They are ready. Where should I bring them?"

They arrived. Some were better, some were worse. All were unique. In time, I had an actual desk, there were beds in all the uninhabited guestrooms, and makeshift tables in the office—all standing at a slight cant. Emeka and I continued the work of assembling documents on the lopsided tables. Shortly after I returned from Spain, another email arrived.

Subject: Pay cut
Carrie: Our financial situation is getting worse. It pains me but we must cut salaries of top managers by 20% to save cash. We also must recover International's projected loss of 2 million USD this year. I will rely on your accelerated efforts to get your marketing program underway and to generate cash flow.
Take care.

Did I contemplate leaving the company after this email? I have no recollection of even considering it. I was now paid no more for heading up a company in Nigeria than I had made as a manager in Minneapolis. I must have realized this was wildly unrealistic. I only recall thinking that perhaps, if I was paid so little, their expectation of rapid riches might be somehow tempered.

I slowly pushed projects forward. Some were lost, but others proceeded to the next level: more meetings, more documents. I kept a steady stream of paper going out the door, and Emeka delivered the paperwork. The proposal materials were complex and required close attention. There was a hypnotic quality to the work. I could lose hours at a time. I could go for an entire day without wondering what was happening in Brussels. We never missed a deadline. I never missed a meeting. This may seem like a small thing, but in Nigeria it felt like a noteworthy accomplishment. I continued to work on the catawampus wooden tables. It was good to be busy.

I tried to not go to the Yacht Club at night, as it invariably involved a lot of drinking. I woke one morning with a splitting hangover and realized, whatever else happened in my life, becoming a drunk in Nigeria was probably not a positive life choice. I vowed to keep running and keep eating—I noticed I had lost a lot of weight. My business suits were starting to hang on me, and my shorts required a belt to keep them up. On some level, I knew I was not doing well, but I decided if I could try to not get completely drunk at the Yacht Club, it would be a small step in the right direction.

The conversations between my husband and me tapered off to almost none at all. And still, there was no explanation of what had happened. There had still been no conversation about why our marriage was over. More often now he did not answer his phone when I called. Emails were returned a day or two later and offered no information to put my constantly spinning mind to rest. He was tired. He was working hard. He was not doing well. He didn't want to talk. I tried to think of questions he might be able to answer and spent days formulating what I might ask, if ever given the chance. But when he did answer the phone, I hesitated.

I wanted to ask, "Has anything changed?" This seemed like something he might be able to answer. He could say, "Yes," and I would be filled with hope because things had been really bad before and so, whatever had changed, it would have to be better. Or he could say, "No," and that would mean the unknown thing that had happened was still happening, and he still did not want to be with me.

But asking him anything was fraught with risk. I knew he would say I was badgering him. He would say I was asking too much. And I would remember he was depressed and I would realize I was (again) demanding things he could not provide. Then I would wonder how much was too much to ask of someone I was married to—depressed or not — and I would be filled with hopeless grief and confusion. So I waited. I waited because I was afraid to ask questions I did not want answered, afraid to do anything but wait for the inevitable.

He doesn't write. He rarely calls. I write. I tell him I'm okay. (I wonder if I actually am.)

A few days later he calls. He tells me he has started to collect corkscrews.

I ponder this for a long time, as I do all communication from him. I am sure it has some sort of significance, but I'll be damned if I know what it is.

Another day. More paper out the door, more greens for dinner, more email. And I am still in Lagos, still in my very white, very empty guesthouse, still trying to figure out what happened. Another month passes. Now he does not call at all, not even to update me on his corkscrew collection (which I imagine to be quite expansive by this time).

Finally, one night in June he calls. I get up my nerve and I ask him if anything has changed, and he says no, as much as he would like to say otherwise... no.

Then he says, "Should I see a lawyer while in the States?"

And I say, "Yes, I guess that would be a good idea."

He says, "Oh, God."

And that, I guess, is the end of that. A little early: he didn't require six months, but finished with a full month to spare. Nothing has changed. Everything has changed. No one knows anything — still. And I need to tell them — finally. But I am not ready. I am not yet able to admit what has happened to my parents and my friends. I am not yet ready to unleash the grief I have worked so hard to hold at bay.

•　　　•　　　•　　　•　　　•

More paper out the door, more greens for dinner, more email. At some point, I broke the news to my parents that my marriage was over. I don't remember what I told them. I tried not to think of how it affected them. My relationship with my parents had always been strong. I was a little girl who always sought, and invariably received, the approval of my loving parents. The oldest child of an oldest son, the oldest grandchild of doting grandparents, my earliest memory is from approximately age two when I stooped to smell a flower and my parents and grandparents all laughed. Noting their amusement, I did it again.

Even as I lived a life of my own design, it was of some essential importance to me that the narrative of my life's unpredictable trajectory was acceptable to my parents, that my life made sense and met with their constant surprised approval. I was buoyed by their indulgent acceptance and generous approbation of my sometimes-unorthodox life choices. I was sixteen when my father asked me if I knew what he admired most about me. Stymied, he answered before I could hazard a guess.

"Your tenacity," he told me. "I admire your tenacity."

Now I was filled with shame. I don't remember what I told them, but I know it was not what I wanted to tell them. I wanted to tell my parents I was ashamed I had lost this marriage, ashamed I had lost the only man I had ever loved, ashamed I could not have the kind of marriage they had maintained and nurtured with such grace for almost fifty years. I wanted to tell them I was sorry I could not hang onto my husband, sorry I was no longer the person I used to be, sorry I was insufficiently tenacious. I felt that combination of violation and culpability experienced in that moment when one realizes something irreplaceable has been lost forever. Losing my husband while living abroad felt like terrible carelessness: like losing my passport in a foreign city, like losing my house keys on a dark night.

•   •   •   •   •

It was nearing the end of our fiscal year, and the pressure to bring in cash had reached a fever pitch.

Subject: International plan to bring in revenues
Dear International team:
We are now approaching the end of our fiscal year. I want us to rally and put the bad performance of this year behind us and move forward with confidence and with a sense of resolve. The character of an organization and of its team members is most visible in time of difficulty and misfortune. We are

going through a transition period in which we must believe in each other and in the mission. I hope that you all are mature enough and have the understanding to follow my leadership and actually give even more now than before because the company needs you. I will do my absolute best on the front line to lead, to achieve, to care, and to plan for a better future.

And, hard as it is now to understand, I believed him, my hardworking, impetuous, never-say-die president. I didn't have much left to hang onto. He had pulled the company out of some tough scrapes in the past and, if we could just survive the endless Nigerian delay, I was certain the rewards would come. With nothing else to do, I worked. More paper went out, more meetings were held and, while a great many hopes did not materialize, I knew we were slowly gaining traction. A few of the contacts I made among oil service companies were solid, and I felt fairly sure they would result in something. But I also knew, even with a contract, it would take time to see actual cash—quite possibly more time than my company had.

One contact in particular looked promising and, after pre-qualifying for the contract, I brought Ismail in for a meeting, since no other engineers were available to me. We gave the proposal twice to increasingly influential employees of the company, a midsized Nigerian firm. They eventually asked for a formal proposal, which was produced and accepted. They then asked for more information and additional qualification materials.

After working on Nigerian projects for almost a year, it now seemed I might be able to finally bring something tangible—and substantial—to the company. I was really not thinking of my commission. I was not even overly concerned about the survival of my company. I think what I wanted more than anything was simply to be able to say my time had not been wasted. There had been so much loss. I wanted to point to one thing in my life that had not been a complete waste. Then another email arrived from Minneapolis:

Subject: Your Position
Dear Carrie: Due to continuing and mounting losses, your position with the company has been eliminated as of August 31. You should return to the USA before August 31. I will get back to you later today.

The funny thing is, in the moment I read this email, I didn't feel anger, I didn't feel panic, I didn't feel betrayed or grief-stricken. As the last recognizable part of my old life unexpectedly fell away, my first and overwhelming reaction was a heady sense of relief.

And, almost as quickly, I realized something I had not known until that moment: I was staying in Lagos. I didn't have any idea what I would do. I didn't have any idea how I was so sure this was right. But I knew for certain I would not be making my scheduled return.

How did I know this? After months of refusing to make any decision at all, why did this decision—to stay in one of the more inhospitable countries on Earth, away from family and friends, without a job or husband—why was this such an immediate and obvious choice?

I do not think I was saying "yes" to Lagos so much as I was saying "no" to every other possible alternative. The idea of returning home to the house under the maple trees was simply unimaginable. The image that came to mind when I thought of that life was a corpse, a corpse still warm. The idea of embracing it, returning to it, trying to make that dead life mine, seemed not merely difficult or awkward—it seemed grotesque and almost obscene.

"No," something deep within me said. "No." I will not return to my life as if nothing has happened when everything I know for sure has been proven false and everything I know about myself is no more.

I had always thought of myself as a person who was led primarily by reason. My practical, Scandinavian father told me from a young age, whenever I had a difficult decision to make, I should list all the pros and cons and balance them on a single sheet of paper (preferably on a clipboard) so I could dispassionately weigh the costs and benefits. When I was making a purchase or managing investments or pursuing a career, I made decisions in this way (with or without the clipboard). Yet when I look at the decisions that have had the most profound effect on my life, they have not been made using either the carefully honed reasoning skills my business education taught me or my father's clipboard. When I have had to make a life-altering decision, I have simply... leapt. Something deep inside me spoke and I obeyed.

"Get ready," She had said. "Get ready for the next big thing."

Lucy and I sat in the afternoon sun on the summer day I received the email that released me from my absurdly prolonged indenture and I knew nothing was or could ever return to normal. How did I feel in that moment, sitting quietly in the sunshine on the bed with Lucy? I don't know. I honestly cannot say. My journal is curiously silent on the subject. I don't imagine I was in the mood to write. Losing this job stripped me of the last excuse I might have used to continue pretending to be whoever it was I used to be. I seem to remember it was quiet for the first time in a very long time.

There was nothing left to hold onto and so I let go.

UNTETHERED

It was the following Wednesday when everything began to fall. I was employed until the end of August and had asked the CFO, an anxious man with a foul temper, if I could stay at the guesthouse a few weeks past the end of my employment to sort out my affairs. I did not mention those affairs included figuring out how I would stay in Nigeria. I was not sure how this news would be received, and I could in no way provide a rational justification for my decision, so I thought it best to keep the information to myself. The CFO told me I could stay as long as I needed. He assured me my health insurance would be extended. He told me the company would do right by me.

In those days immediately after my termination, I worked to tie up the loose ends. If asked, I would have said I did it because I expected to get a letter of recommendation for my next position and wanted to leave everything in order. The truth is, I would have done it regardless. My sense of culpability in the loss of my marriage had seeped into every aspect of my life. If I honestly didn't know what I had done wrong in my marriage, how could I possibly be expected to notice the myriad of other ways I might have failed or fallen short? And so I worked. I worked to try to make things right in the only way I knew how.

The "transition team" in Lagos was Ekpes. Ekpes was a Nigerian but not from Lagos. When he applied for a job in Minneapolis, I had suggested we hire him as a consultant rather than a full employee because I had serious doubts about his ability to read, write, or speak in public. The youngest son in a family without a father, Ekpes had a permanent chip on his shoulder and a voracious desire to succeed at any cost. He had worked his way into an oil contract with a Texas company a couple of years earlier, offering him the chance to leave Nigeria. Like most Nigerians offered the opportunity, Ekpes grabbed it.

Now, with my termination, Ekpes was charged with taking responsibility for the elaborate contract negotiations I had been shepherding through the lengthy process. I behaved as if it made perfect sense to hand over my detailed project and financial records to a man I knew would not have the slightest idea what to do with either. One by one, I informed our prospective clients I would be leaving and Ekpes would be following up on our proposals. The clients were not excited about the prospect of dealing with Ekpes. They were fairly blunt in telling me they didn't trust him. These Nigerians didn't know where Ekpes was from—in a literal geographic sense—which matters a great deal in a cobbled-together, former colonial country of uneasy factions and unstable alliances. Ekpes, a successful Nigerian working in America, certainly owed favors to someone. Without knowing what favors he owed to whom, my contacts did not trust him. I knew this but continued to assure them of a smooth transition—suspecting it would be nothing of the sort.

The company laptop I used in Nigeria by now contained all my personal records, so I arranged with the CFO to exchange the last month's car rental for my computer. Ekpes flew in from Minneapolis and spent the days running mysterious errands in my car with my driver, Emeka. Immediately upon his arrival, he ordered curtains and furniture for the office, and the guesthouse was a hub of activity, with delivery trucks arriving daily. I had no idea if Ekpes had approval for these purchases and I felt somewhat sheepish as I watched tailors and furniture vans come and go. As I organized documentation and records, cheap fiberboard furniture appeared and hideously ornate curtains were hung, blocking the sunlight out of this house already surrounded by concrete walls.

When I finally secured Ekpes' attention, he looked at the documents and then looked at me as if we were both utterly incomprehensible and dispensable. I stood outside his guestroom door while he stood in the half-opened doorway and I explained the current status of the work we were doing and the next steps to be taken. He squinted at me and continued to eat peanuts, roasted on the street and sold in a recycled gin bottle with the label still on it. He was glistening with sweat while his room air conditioner roared. As I explained what each of the documents required, his eyes glazed over with a combination of disdain and fear. I knew he would never read my carefully prepared reports.

Ekpes believed all business was personal. All deals were made based solely on the self-interest of the participants. Executing the actual work was a detail beneath his concern. If the right man received his share of the profits, if the right palms were greased at every step of the way, the deal would be done. Other people (people like me) could concern themselves with what the project was supposed to accomplish. There would always be fools who did the work and were paid in wages. Ekpes was not one of those fools. I don't know how this boy from a small village decided he was someone who would profit without work, close deals without understanding what they signified, make money with no concern if anything was accomplished. I handed over the documentation and continued to work. Even if it seemed to matter to no one but me, I would not leave behind an unfinished mess.

The weekend after my final day of employment, I completed the qualifications required for the gas project. I was astonished to see Felix, our long-absent Nigerian partner, appear at the guesthouse, and I was even more surprised to see that he and Ekpes (who had always regarded one another as rivals) now appeared to be friends. The writing completed, I printed and collated and hole-punched and assembled documents. Six huge binders held the assembled qualifications; they entirely filled one of the tables built by Bola.

Ekpes and Felix spent some of Saturday and most of Sunday sitting outside on Osondu's cane chairs, drinking beer and talking just out of earshot. Ekpes had hired a cook from Benin. The new cook patiently made trips back and forth, busing empty beer bottles and bringing more gin-bottle peanuts. Benin is a former French colony and many expatriates hire the Beninois, believing they are better cooks. Ekpes likely hired the cook less for his cooking ability than because he trusted Ghanaians and Beninois more than his fellow Nigerians.

It was nearly dark, that Wednesday evening when everything began to fall.

Something powerful and unpredictable was unleashed when I decided to let go of all the things that defined me and confined me until that moment of quiet in an echoing white guesthouse in Lagos. I didn't notice the tremors as the supports began to buckle. I didn't feel the foundation start to give way. The underpinnings of my identity would not hold much longer—now that I was no longer attached to this company I had come to despise, this marriage I could no longer deny was dead, this view of myself as a person in command of my life and my future—but I was oblivious. Living alone with Lucy, I didn't hear when the elaborately constructed, forty-year-old ideas of who I was began to fail. And I couldn't blame Lucy—Lucy was deaf.

I had been tentatively exploring my options in Nigeria. Ekpes had gone to the airport and, in his absence, I had invited a friend of Ismail's over to chat. Gozi, a cheerful Nigerian-American businessman, was building a housing complex and wanted me to assist in marketing his oil services business. Gozi brought his lawyer and the three of us were discussing his business plans. Just then, Ekpes returned unexpectedly.

Ekpes eyes narrow when he sees the two unknown men in the guesthouse.

"Carrie, I need to talk to you."

I say goodnight to the two businessmen and excuse myself to the living room, now festooned with garish pastel polyester lace curtains. In the living room, Ekpes is sweating heavily. He is obviously agitated. He has received a call, he tells me, from the company president, Viet. Viet is very angry and says I must leave the guesthouse immediately—tonight.

This cannot be true. Viet would not do this. "Why?" I ask.

"He heard you have been defaming the company. He says you've been working for a British competitor." Ekpes is mopping his face and neck.

This is so outrageous, I am stunned into silence for a moment. "It's not true."

"You have to leave right now. He says I need to take your computer and phone and have you escorted out of the compound now."

The computer I purchased from my former company contains all my financial records, medical information, the address of everyone I know, all the letters I have written to my husband, the only copy of my grandmother's eulogy... No.

"This is crazy," I tell Ekpes, the slow truth of what is happening slowly dawning on me.

Ekpes starts to complain he hadn't wanted to come back to Lagos; he had already bought his airplane ticket when Viet called him. He complains this was not his doing. He is just following instructions.

The sun is setting in Lagos. Through the awful lace curtains, I can see the sun is low in the sky.

This can't be happening.

"It's already night—where would I go?"

Something has gone terribly wrong. I don't know what it is, but I realize, for the first time since coming to Nigeria, how vulnerable I am. I am trying to think quickly as I turn my back to Ekpes and start walking back to the office where I had been meeting Gozi and his lawyer. They have left. My heart is beating loudly in my ears, but I pretend I am annoyed and impatient with the whole thing. My computer is on the table. All I know in that moment is I will not relinquish every piece of my personal and financial life to Ekpes.

I continue to talk. I don't know what I am saying, but it seems important I do not allow the sound of fear or silence to enter the room. I never stop talking as I walk into the office; I never stop talking as I slip my computer into my bag and casually put my bag over my shoulder.

Ekpes is becoming upset. He has the capacity to become irrational and I don't know what this means for me right now, but I know I do not trust him. He is standing in the doorway to the office, sweating profusely in his dark blue suit, his voice getting louder and angrier as he tells me he is just doing what he was told, tells me I had better do as I am told.

My computer and phone now in my bag, I take a deep breath and push past him, through the door.

Then I run.

I run up two flights of stairs to my bedroom and I lock the door behind me. The vibration of the door slamming wakes Lucy from her nap on my bed, covered by the bright batik cloth. I have the only two keys and I am now locked in my room on the third floor. From my balcony, I can see the sun is about to slip below the horizon.

Ekpes, who does not move quickly, arrives at my door well after it is locked. He is now very angry. He tells me I need to come out now; I need to hand over my computer and my phone and leave.

This can't be happening.

I start to call.

First, I call Viet. He does not answer his mobile phone. I call the office in Minneapolis. The secretary puts me on hold, then returns with the message that Viet cannot be disturbed. While I have been waiting for the call to be put through, Ekpes has summoned the security guards, who are now standing outside my bedroom door. Ekpes repeats his demand that the door be opened.

I call the CFO and reach him in the U.K. I tell him what is going on.

He listens in silence for several moments, then explodes, "I hate this fucking company!"

He says he will get to the bottom of it. I wait in tense silence as Ekpes and the guards stand outside. A few minutes later he calls back. He has heard the same message from Viet: I have been defaming the company and working for a British competitor.

Briefly, wildly, I wonder where this rumor came from and who these "sources" might be. It seems too incredible this hardheaded CFO would believe such an outlandish fabrication. I have a sick feeling in the pit of my stomach as I remember the former rivals, Ekpes and Felix, sitting on Osondu's chairs, drinking beer together for hours over the weekend.

They have heard this information from "three sources," he tells me. He says Viet is furious and I should get out now. Then he hangs up on me.

At this point the power goes out and my room is dark.

I hear the generator start up but, in an apparently unrelated piece of bad luck, the power to my part of the building remains off. There is no air conditioning and no power for the Internet. My phone has started to run low.

I call everyone on my phone from the Yacht Club, but no one answers. I remember it is Wednesday. Wednesday is a big night at the Yacht Club; most of the members are there and, as customary, their cell phones are turned off. Not one of my Yacht Club acquaintances answers. It will be hours before they do.

I reach my husband in Brussels and tell him what is happening. He is alarmed and calls my company in Minneapolis, demanding to speak with Viet. His call goes unanswered. He tries to find the number for the U.S. Consulate in Lagos and eventually succeeds. He gives me the number and I try it several times. Finally, someone answers. The man on duty at the American Consulate sounds concerned when I tell him my situation.

"What is the name of your company?" he demands.

But when he learns it is not a Nigerian company I work for, but an American company, he tells me there is nothing he can do. He gives me a number I can call in the morning.

"I can't wait until morning—they are forcing me out right now—tonight."

"Oh, don't worry," the American Consulate employee chuckles, "nothing in Lagos happens that fast." Then he hangs up.

Now the guards are pounding on my door, demanding I open it. Ekpes sounds increasingly agitated and tells me a locksmith has been called to break the lock. There is no deadbolt on the door and it would not take much to break into my room.

"I'm not leaving until I am packed!" I yell from behind my locked bedroom door. "This is my home and I have permission from the CFO to be here," I insist, trying to sound forceful.

I hear the sound of conferring between the guards and Ekpes and I seize the momentum. "I'll leave when I am ready. If you want to remove me by force, you better prove you have the authority to do so!"

The guards grow quiet; they do not like the sound of this.

I hear more muttered conversation. I can tell they think evicting the white woman who hired them on the orders of a Nigerian sounds like a risky proposition. I hear them talking to Ekpes, trying to find a way out of forcing the door. I keep calling. My phone is almost dead and the power is still out.

Finally, I reach Ismail. He is incredulous—and angry—and on his way. Ismail and Shirene live on the far side of Lagos, but in an astonishingly short time I hear his car in the drive and I watch from the balcony as Ekpes meets him outside. The guards open the gate to let him in. As I watch, Ismail pulls up one of Osondu's cane chairs and urges Ekpes to sit. Reluctantly, Ekpes sits. I cannot hear what they are saying, but I can tell Ismail is trying to calm Ekpes. Meanwhile, I hear the diminutive Shirene, armed with four-inch stiletto heels and a serious attitude, running up the stairs. She pushes the guards aside and comes into my dark room. I lock the door behind her and hug her fiercely.

"Good God, Carrie! What are they doing?!" I tell her I don't know.

Shirene begins to throw everything I own into boxes. I start to delete every computer file and "shred" it after it has been deleted. Delete and shred, delete and shred. With no air conditioning, the room is becoming hotter. Shirene is packing things in the bathroom and drops a bottle of perfume on the tile floor. It shatters. The room fills with the smell of musk. Excited by the frantic activity in the dark and the pungent smell, Lucy races in circles around the room.

Outside, I can see the light of Ismail's cigarette and I can hear the sound of Ekpes' voice, slowly calming under Ismail's patient influence. I know Ismail and he is not calm. He is a proud Lebanese man and feels responsible for the two women inside. But he is a shrewd negotiator, and so he sits, still as a snake, smoking one cigarette after another and letting Ekpes talk himself out. I also see my driver, Emeka, a slim silhouette standing motionless against the concrete wall, watching and listening to everything.

Suddenly, the gate of the compound flies open. A car with flashing red and blue lights drives into the compound.

Police?!

I cannot imagine Ekpes would call the police. But I could not have imagined I would be evicted in the middle of the night or accused of betraying my company. I could not have imagined my computer being taken or being thrown out of my house. Shirene and I run to the dark balcony and watch the car stop at the front door. A man in a black suit gets out. A woman in a black suit follows him. The man speaks a few words to Ekpes, then enters the guesthouse. Shirene and I run back into the bedroom and listen at the door.

Two sets of feet are coming up the stairs. We hear them coming toward the door. We hear them continue past my door and then up the next flight of stairs. Then we cannot hear them anymore. We exhale and continue to pack, delete, and shred.

At last, every file on my computer has been erased. My boxes are packed — the same two boxes that came with me seven months earlier, the same two boxes that tumbled in the snow at the airport. It is time to erase all traces of me from my company phone.

All these hours in the dark I have been focused on protecting myself, getting out without leaving behind the remains of my life. But now I have to scroll through the text messages saved on my phone, and it had a lot of storage. I have saved every note from my husband when he said he loved me and would see me soon, every time he said he missed me, every inside joke he sent while on a train or boarding a plane. I read each one and remember exactly when it was sent.

He must have still loved me when he sent this, I think as I delete each saved message. And now, finally, I am crying.

The empty computer and phone are left on my desk built by Bola. My boxes are neatly stacked by the door. Lucy is in her carrier, looking around expectantly.

I wipe my face with a washcloth still hanging in the bathroom, then Shirene and I unlock the door and Ekpes comes in. He is calmer but clearly uneasy. He orders the guards to open my boxes for inspection, as if I might be stealing the towels or the bedsheets. As Emeka and the guards load the boxes into Ismail's car, I see Ekpes' new cook come down the stairs carrying Osondu's small cane table with two empty

Coke bottles and two empty glasses sitting on it.

It is late when we pull out of the compound. I ride in the backseat of Ismail's station wagon with everything I own loaded in it and Lucy on my lap. Emeka follows in my car. We drive to Ismail and Shirene's house at the far end of Lagos. We do not turn on the air conditioning but instead let the night wind blow through the car windows. There is little traffic so late at night. There is little conversation.

I feel as if I have come untethered, as if the string that held me in place has suddenly worked itself loose. Lucy and I are floating now, floating up and away in the hot and humid night air.

PREPOSTEROUS MISFORTUNE

Ismail and Shirene lived in a modest and comfortable home in a gated community. Every day I walked from Ismail's green and shady neighborhood to the hot, virus-riddled Internet café near the entrance of the compound to let friends and family in America know I was "alright." I am not sure what my definition of "alright" was at the time. I was out of contact, out of a home, out of a job, out of a marriage, but essentially alright — for the moment.

There is a lot of dishonesty when we discuss making major life changes.

Maybe for some people it is really a case of going from strength to strength, learning from past mistakes, bursting with gratitude over the opportunity to begin life afresh. Not for me.

For me, change required a deep and terrible ripping away of everything I assumed was safe — love, career, home — all the things that combined to create my identity. In the first days after my eviction, only a couple of weeks after my firing, less than two months after the end of my marriage, I was not imagining what the next phase of my life would look like. I was not imagining anything at all. I was trying very hard not to think about my dizzying series of losses. In those first few days I was simply stumbling forward, steadfastly refusing to consider leaving Lagos or doing anything that would in any way resemble a return to my old life under the maple trees.

Ismail and Shirene were extraordinarily kind. They fed me and gave me space and politely ignored my dazed and disoriented appearance. My Yacht Club friends had never heard of an expatriate being evicted by his or her employer. When I finally made it back to the Club for a round of drinks by the water's edge at sunset, they were incredulous.

"It's not done!" my sailing captain, Don, shouted over a pint of stout, his face redder than usual. "You should sue them!"

Everyone agreed what my company had done was unethical and probably illegal, but, rather than being heartened, I was strangely embarrassed by these discussions. I could see my company's behavior was beyond outrageous. But rather than filling me with outrage, I was filled with an overwhelming sense of shame. How had I imagined I would be taken care of by a company so clearly off-kilter? Why had this not been completely obvious from the start? Why did I appear to be so utterly incapable of making a sound character judgment? I had believed my husband because he promised things were going to get better. I believed my company for the same reason. In both cases, my trust had been terribly misplaced. It was embarrassing and painful to realize Viet, the president of my former company, had accepted ludicrous lies about me without even speaking to me, without any apparent pause to consider if what was being said about me seemed out of character for this employee he knew rather well.

Viet was charming: a fiercely ambitious Vietnamese immigrant, he had traces of his original accent and knew a little bit about every imaginable subject. He could describe a new project idea and make it sound so real I was half-convinced it must already exist. He would dash off a quick sketch and send it upstairs to his bewildered draftsman, write a few words for me to embellish, fire off an email to the prospective client, and with no further ado we had another project "under development" listed in our catalog of accomplishments and touted in PowerPoint presentations. It seemed anything was possible with a business card, a good story, and a smile.

Founded on a shaky premise and dedicated to the improbable, we cheerfully boasted to clients that we were "doing well by doing good." I knew we cut corners from time to time. We presented the accomplishments of others as the work of our "team." We showed projects "under development" that were little more than pipe dreams. I knew all this, but I also believed as much as anyone in the power of a good story.

Believe a thing will come into being and it can—and often does. This was my experience. We were selling dreams, and while I knew much of what we promised was not possible (and some of it was simply not true), I also believed these projects had the potential to make a difference. If a few corners were cut in the attempt, I could sleep at night believing, given the opportunity, we would someday make the small lies true.

Once, while flying over the ocean, Viet explained how it was an advantage to be a woman working in developing countries where there were few female decision makers.

"Look at me," he said. "I hire these big white men and when I go into a meeting everyone looks at Dave or Henrik and they assume *he* must be the boss. Then I introduce myself and they find out *I* am the boss and they think, 'Wow! That little Vietnamese man must be really smart! He is the boss of those tall white men!'" Viet laughed. Then he turned serious: "This is the work you were meant to do." I began to believe him.

Felix never wanted me to come to Lagos. A smooth-talking fellow with hyperactive eyebrows, natty suits, and a background in banking, there were rumors Felix had not left banking entirely of his own volition. He had insinuated his way into my company by arranging meetings with prospective clients. One of these clients was a Nigerian prince whose father wanted to build a housing estate. Viet charmed the king with visions of an American-style complex filled with expatriates and we were awarded the contract. The project came at a time when my company was desperate for cash. Viet eagerly signed the small contract to build and promote the housing estate in hopes it would tide the company over—which it did.

Even in this small project, Viet was determined we distinguish ourselves by our creativity. I found an architect who was well known for his work in ecotourism and flew to London to promote the project. The complex was featured on a cable station catering to the large Nigerian population in London, and I was astonished to discover while walking the streets the next morning I had become a minor celebrity overnight among Nigerian expatriates.

The housing development promotion coincided with a visit from the kings of all four regions of Nigeria's Ogun State to London—the first time they had all appeared together outside of Nigeria. The kings spent the day sitting in the lobby of the Paddington Hilton hotel. They were dressed in embroidered robes and stiff hats, held tall staffs adorned with horsehair, and drank orange sodas. Throughout the day, Nigerian doctors and lawyers who had lived their entire adult lives in London, came into the hotel lobby to catch a glimpse of their traditional ruler. The lobby was not large and when these professional Nigerian men—most well over six feet tall, carrying briefcases and wearing expensive suits—stepped through the revolving doors, they immediately came face-to-face with their king and fell prostrate to the floor.

Boom!

When the first tall man in a dark suit hit the floor, the concierge leapt up in alarm. By mid-afternoon, it had become routine.

My first trip to Lagos was for the groundbreaking of this housing project. Once there, I learned Viet was delayed and would not be on hand to deliver the keynote address. He called to tell me I would be giving a thirty-minute speech to our client the king, two additional kings, the governor, assorted local dignitaries, and the Nigerian press.

I wrote a speech for the groundbreaking, then went to the building site and threw up—the side effect of nerves and anti-malarial medication. I gave the speech in the hot midday sun, the king seated with his three wives, all dressed in identical shiny blue dresses with matching starched confections perched atop their heads. When I finished, a brass band played, everyone applauded, and the king appeared pleased. I decided I didn't mind this place that was reportedly so hostile.

Nigeria, my fellow employees told me, was dirty, corrupt, dangerous, and no place for a woman. Nigeria was all these things (except, possibly, the last). Nigerians had little in the way of a functioning government or infrastructure but, like me, they believed anything was possible. Anyone could make it to the top, they believed, if they just found the right angle, the right connection—if they just kept trying. It was desperate, competitive, and completely unregulated. The police were corrupt and the politicians worse. But within this anarchy, a flamboyant brand of self-reliance flourished. I admired Nigerians for their ingenuity and reckless optimism. In this city where virtually nothing worked, every car bore a license plate that read, "Lagos: Centre of Excellence."

I could retrace but not yet explain the path that had brought me to Ismail and Shirene's, sitting every night before dinner with their three polite children as they finished their French homework in impossibly perfect longhand. Ismail's eight-year-old daughter, Megan, loved Lucy and Lucy spent her days getting wheeled about in a doll carriage festooned with jingling scarves Shirene had brought back from Dubai, like some sort of feline pasha.

"Carrie! You're not eating anything!" Ismail chided as I picked at the elaborate spread of Lebanese *meze* he had prepared, serving plates and bowls covering every inch of the table.

"You're too thin! You need to put on at least twenty pounds," he insisted.

I noticed I was losing more weight. Food in my mouth felt like an interesting sensation, but nothing essential to my survival. For several weeks, I did nothing but sit by the pool in large dark glasses like a movie star in rehab or an invalid at a sanatorium. I felt as if I were encased in bandages, immobilized, itchy, unable to move. I felt like some kind of freak, perhaps the survivor of a violent and grotesque accident. One particularly uncomfortable day the sense of immobility became intolerable. I felt the extreme edges of numbness wearing off and a terrible aching pain taking its place. Sitting by the pool, I wrote in my journal and noticed the date.

It was October 20th. Exactly one year earlier my husband had told me he didn't love me.

The man with whom I had shared more than half my life was gone. My former employer believed I was a liar and a traitor. I was without a personal or professional identity. A deeply painful curiosity forced me to look beneath the bandages at the violence of the preceding twelve months. I took a quick look at the still-fresh wounds and was immediately overtaken by a sick lightheadedness and disbelief as I caught a glimpse of how complete the damage to my identity had been and how little was left of what I used to be. I felt a little like the "before and after" picture paraded through Lagos traffic. "Look everyone! Here is the woman who, just a year ago thought she knew who she was and where she was going!" It didn't seem possible.

I slowly attempted to deal with the minimal requirements of my imaginary future life. I had not received my final paycheck and payroll deductions had not been deposited into my retirement account. I was pretty sure this was not legal, so I hired an attorney to see if I couldn't get my money. As long as I had an attorney, I asked her if she would file my divorce papers as well.

Sitting in the hot Internet café one day, I received an email from my new attorney. She had just gotten a call from my former company's lawyer telling her they had put out a warrant for my arrest.

Stunned, I immediately wrote back, "What can I possibly be arrested for? Living in Lagos?!"

Ismail was out of town and I was alone with Shirene and the kids. I had heard from my ever-resourceful driver, Emeka, that Viet was in town. Emeka was quiet and unassuming, but I had learned he was an unfailingly reliable source of information.

I called Ismail and he was calm.

"They're bluffing," he assured me. "They're trying to get you out of the country; they're afraid you will be competition for them. Don't worry about it."

Twenty minutes later he called back.

"Viet knows where we live. I'm going to be gone until tomorrow and Shirene and the kids are home alone… is it possible for you to find another place to spend the night?"

If Ismail was afraid, I knew I had reason to be.

Once again, I was packing quickly after dark. Shirene didn't tell the children why I was leaving. I packed a small bag and called one of my Yacht Club friends, an experienced Israeli businessman who seemed as if he had seen it all in his years in Lagos.

"I've run into a bit of trouble. There is a chance someone might try to arrest me. Could I spend the night?"

"Come on over," he said, without hesitation.

Just as Emeka pulled away from Ismail's house, I got a call from Shirene. Her driver said there was a Chinese man banging on the gate to their house, trying to get in. A Chinese man banging on the gate? Did he mean a Vietnamese man? Was it possible Viet had actually shown up with the police in tow? Shirene locked the doors and the gate and warned the driver and children that no one was to open the door. Eventually, the man left.

I arrived at my friend's house and told him the story.

"They don't want you to get a new visa," he said simply, opening a bottle of wine.

"They said they were going to have me arrested!"

He laughed. "It will never be served, but if there is an outstanding warrant for your arrest they believe it will delay you when you apply for a new work visa."

He handed me a glass. "It's an old tactic. Companies tried it with me all the time when I was headhunting engineers to work for me. The bogus warrants never stopped me, but they sometimes delayed the visa processing for a few weeks or months. They must believe you are competing with them," he said. "Don't worry about it."

Not knowing what else to do, I didn't.

Instead, as the threat of Nigerian prison faded, we had a wonderful dinner and drank a generous quantity of red wine. He had a funny and chic Ghanaian cook, Celina, who produced the best dinner I'd had since arriving in Nigeria. Celina heard of my plight and shook her head.

"Nigeria is crazy!" she said, pulling a tray of freshly baked wontons out of the oven.

In the morning, I returned to the hot, virus-riddled Internet café to collect more news. The warrant was in response to "unaccounted funds," I was told. Ekpes, my "transition team," had failed to turn over the books for the final month that I had given him. Fortunately (fearing ineptitude on his part more than actual dishonesty), I had emailed the financial records to myself, so I was able to email them to the CFO. The mystery of the late-night visitor at the gate was never solved. It may have been simply a lost Chinese gentleman with extraordinarily bad timing.

The CFO wrote back to say he was still not satisfied: I had not provided receipts for inter-company cash transfers—transfers I had made at his request. This money had been used to buy the building materials and pay the workers at the housing estate development. I had the emails from him instructing me to make these transfers, and there were records showing how all the money had all been spent, but no actual receipts showing the money had changed hands. He now said he regarded this money to be "missing." The absurdity of it made my head hurt.

Ironically, the tactics they were using to force my departure from Lagos made any contemplated return to the States more difficult. I imagined even my considerable gift for spinning straw into gold would be challenged in explaining (to a future prospective employer) how my previous position concluded when I was first terminated, then fired, then evicted in the middle of the night, and ultimately threatened with arrest in Nigeria.

"Fortunately," I would cheerfully conclude, "I am no longer being actively sought by Nigerian authorities and am therefore available to assume a position of responsibility in your company!"

While I worked to collect the money owed to me, Emeka, who seemed to have missed his calling working for the CIA, kept tabs on the daily activities at the guesthouse from the tradespeople and vendors who came and went. I heard from vendors who were instructed to raise their prices so Ekpes could take a cut from every transaction billed to the company—right down to the tacky lace draperies. I discovered most of Ekpes' furtive trips in my car had been to keep tabs on several mistresses he was visiting on the mainland. I learned how, after I left, teenage prostitutes were ferried back and forth to the guesthouse for Ekpes' friends, sometimes more than one shipment per day. I felt slightly sickened when I thought of Femi's off-kilter beds furnishing Ekpes' impromptu brothel: a handy place to meet a working girl in a nice, upscale neighborhood.

77

The mystery of the car with the flashing lights and the visitors in black suits on the night of my eviction was also solved. Even before I had finished packing, a room had been promised to one of Ekpes' colleagues to use with a high-end prostitute. The two sets of heels up the steps had nothing to do with me; they were just the first of what soon turned into steady traffic from Ekpes' associates. The muttered exchange at the door had nothing to do with an impending arrest; it was no more than a quick assurance the guest arriving by police car was supplied with condoms.

But much worse were the stories now coming in of computers, cars, and cash changing hands. I learned about the shadow company Ekpes had set up in preparation for his defection from my former company. While I never learned who had invented the story of my working for a British competitor, I understood why my removal as a witness to all this was so important. I had played an important role in establishing credibility for my company; now it was just as important I get out of the way. I began to appreciate how lucky I was to have escaped the downward spiral the company — through stupidity or simple greed — now appeared to be entering.

The more I learned about my former company, the more naïve and foolish I felt. While I certainly was aware corruption was pervasive in Nigerian business, and had seen some of it firsthand, I had no idea Ekpes and Felix were in the thick of it. I wondered what else went on that I was utterly oblivious to. I wondered why I had participated so long.

I think it was because I knew I was no less dishonest. Working for my imaginary company was not so different from saving for my imaginary retirement with my imaginary husband. The ability to overlook the obvious was not a skill I acquired overnight. It had to be honed. In my version of Lagos, I focused on the flower that pushed through the cracked pavement and not the growing feeling I had somehow willingly entered into a shadow world. In the shadow world, nothing was what it seemed — not my job, not my marriage, not the person I presented to anyone I met, not the person I saw when I looked in the mirror.

Alone in the guesthouse with Lucy, I had tallied every *naira* I spent on the vegetables I bought from the street vendor, but I never acknowledged the heavy price I paid that did not appear in the books. I did not acknowledge it because I didn't know what to do with the knowledge. It seemed there was nothing I could do with the growing certainty that every part of my life was a deception, that absolutely nothing was as it appeared to be. In the shadow world, we do not talk about how contracts are really obtained—how everyone, every step of the way, will inevitably be paid off, and how this is understood but never explicitly stated by anyone involved. I had willingly offered myself up to this world. I was in Lagos to lend legitimacy to a process that could not proceed without lies at every level, in every interaction. It was something I had been practicing for a long time.

How far down that path would loyalty have taken me? Where did the path of lies begin?

With me, it began by accepting a half-truth and not setting the record straight. It began when I allowed others to believe the exaggerations and deliberate misconceptions encouraged by my company. I believed the lies when I was hired. We had completed a hydroelectric plant in Greece! We had constructed more than 200 wastewater treatment facilities in Poland! I had the PowerPoints to prove it.

Slowly, I came to learn that what my company said about itself was not entirely true. Ultimately, I learned almost nothing we said was true. We had not done the projects we said we had done. We did not have the expertise or assets we said we did. We could not finance the projects we said we could. We were not what we claimed to be. We had only the flimsiest of agreements with the companies who had actually done the work we claimed was ours. Armed with a one-page "Letter of Agreement," we delightedly claimed the work of others to be our own. And I had stood at the front—in meetings, on television, with clients—and represented this company. We were no longer stretching the truth, but inventing things out of whole cloth. I had known it before my dismissal, and my presence made these claims more believable. I made the lies seem real. I was both deeply chagrined and enormously relieved to be free of a company I now saw clearly for the first time.

Sitting by the pool at Ismail's, I think I already knew I had been given an opportunity: although it didn't feel like much of a gift at the time, and I really had no idea how to use it. After the preposterous misfortune of being thrown out onto the streets of Lagos, I found myself living in the home of strangers who cared for me and about me. I had been given a chance at freefall. Without a personal or professional mask, who was I? With no husband, no career, no home, no country, what remained? Once all the lies were gone—the lies about the company, the lies about the cheerful husband and everything that happened in the farmhouse under the maple trees, the lies I had tried for years to make true (because I was tenacious, after all)—after all the lies were gone, what truth remained? What was left of me?

In my hurried glimpse under the bandages that day in October, I saw there was very little left of me. After months of remembering almost nothing, I sat in the sun immobilized, ate salty green olives, and began the slow and painful process of waking up.

HARDSHIP POST

My arrival at Ismail and Shirene's displaced their daughter Megan from her bedroom. Lucy and I woke each morning in Megan's pink room to the sight of Barbie and all her friends, glitter pens, and princess costumes. Every morning, I looked around me in surprise. I had seamlessly transitioned from one surreal setting to the next.

To get out of the house, Emeka and I ran inconsequential errands around Lagos. Nearly every day we drove around "puppy corner," the busy intersection where guard dogs and puppies were sold. Every time we rounded the corner I would ask, "Emeka, should we buy a puppy today?"

Every day Emeka would answer in his low, growly voice, "Not today, ma'am."

I tried several drivers before I hired Emeka. Most could not understand a word I said. I was saddened to learn that years of theater training had not enabled me to successfully conduct even a rudimentary conversation with a Nigerian driver.

"You talk too fast to the driver!" I was scolded by my Yacht Club friends who, regardless of what other languages they spoke, had all managed to master fluent pidgin English. "You need to talk more slowly."

"No, my driver needs to *listen faster*."

"That is *so* American!"

But then I met Emeka. Emeka was fast. He thought fast, walked fast, drove fast, and was quickly bored. Lagos has no proper exits, few turn lanes, narrow streets, a total lack of parking, and numerous one-way labyrinths. It also has deadly potholes that were often too deep to cross in my small Toyota and maniacal *okada* drivers darting between the lanes of traffic— "lanes" being a highly fluid concept that was entirely in the eye of the beholder. Every trip in and about town was an expedition requiring planning, strategy, cunning, and a bit of clairvoyance. Emeka was my trusted expedition leader. I told him where I ideally wanted to go if there was time, where I *had* to go no matter what, and if any one errand had to precede another. After that, he was in charge.

I had insisted on four rules as a condition of Emeka's employment:

1. *Don't be late.*
2. *Don't lie.*
3. *Don't get lost.*
4. *Don't tell people my business.*

To the best of my knowledge, he never broke these rules.

Emeka liked riding with Lucy and Lucy loved to travel. The *okada* drivers would careen between the tight lanes of traffic and Lucy would watch them, fascinated, face pressed against the window. More than once, an *okada* driver caught sight of Lucy staring directly at him just as he was about to execute a turn and nearly crashed. Emeka watched the startled drivers and laughed his deep, growling laugh. Lucy became his confidante and constant copilot.

Emeka was by nature as restless and impatient as I now felt. He was exceedingly thin, and I joked he would need to put rocks in his pockets on windy days. He had a low voice that was surprising coming from such a slender man, and he provided a running commentary as he drove. Muttering and grunting— "Ah! It is blocked!"—he verbally outlined how we would avoid a dreadful "go-slow." By executing a sudden U-turn, hopping a curb, taking a temporary sand road through a construction site, and going (briefly) the wrong way down a one-way street, we would avoid an hour's delay. He was not infallible. Driving through Lagos was a constantly shifting landscape of obstacles and surprise blockages. But generally, his clairvoyance came through and, by finding an imaginative new route to our destination, we avoided spending hours sitting motionless in Lagos traffic.

Along the way, I talked to Emeka in a way Ismail would never approve of. I told him my business (hence rule number four) and asked his opinion about whatever we encountered, constantly impressed by his opinions and wit.

"I haven't had anything to eat since breakfast!" I complained in one of our long-running jokes.

"You had *breakfast?!*" he answered indignantly. We laughed.

I would treat him in this thoroughly unprofessional way while we were together, and if Ismail or anyone else was in the car, we would conduct ourselves in an entirely different manner. Emeka would be quiet. I would not chitchat. I would tell him where to drive and he would say, "Yes, ma'am." It was our secret, this double life. We had one set of behaviors for Ismail and the Yacht Club expats, another for us — two strong-minded, opinionated, and slightly hyperactive people.

Emeka was not educated, but he could read and write. He was always working on various business plans and projects. He collected things that might be useful for the house he was building for himself and Rachel, whom he described as "the woman I hope to marry." There was usually something in my car — a half roll of wire, extra floor tiles, a broken but repairable appliance — he was collecting for his house. He showed me pictures of the house, a couple hours outside of Lagos, as he worked to complete it with the things he scavenged.

Emeka gathered information from all the drivers, guards, gardeners, stewards, and cooks, and he was a remarkable source of unexpected insights. His constant snooping provided a treasury of useful information about my former company and kept me abreast of Ekpes' latest shenanigans. Ismail did not quite approve of a driver who was always so busy, but I noticed Ismail went through a string of drivers who failed to show up to fetch his children from school or didn't make it back to work on Monday when it was raining. No matter how bad the traffic or how torrential the rain, Emeka was always there.

One day, as we rounded puppy corner, I asked as usual, "Emeka, should we buy a puppy today?"

He was silent for a moment then answered, deadpan: "We cannot, ma'am. Puppies are on public holiday today."

Oh, I liked Emeka.

Of course, I knew I could not spend my life driving around puppy corner. Somehow, I was going to have to make a living. While I had saved quite a bit in the short time prior to my dismissal, I knew I was nowhere near my "magic number" for retirement and would be miles away from it once I was divorced. While I was in no way yet able to think rationally about the hard consequences of my combined loss of marriage and career, I knew I would need some money coming in — soon.

Shortly after I arrived at Ismail's, I received a call from a would-be Nigerian senator whom I had met while working for my former company. The Senate-hopeful had an interest in securing two road construction contracts. Inconveniently (as is too often the case), he had no road construction experience. He called to tell me he had no interest in working with my "transition team" or my former company. He wanted me to work for him, to assemble a company to do the civil construction work.

Ismail and I talked it over. Ismail felt, since the two of us had done most of the work in Lagos for my former company, we might just as well do the same sort of work for ourselves. This seemed like a good idea, especially since I had no other ideas of any kind about anything.

I roused myself from the pool, put on a black suit, and flew to the capital, Abuja, to meet with the governor who would be awarding the contracts. I arrived after dark and was taken to the governor's mansion, where I waited in an absurdly oversized gilt-trimmed chair in an oversized room with an oversized flat screen television broadcasting a British soccer match. While I had been in these places before — the homes and offices of Nigeria's most wealthy — I could never quite get over my amazement. I fidgeted in the frigidly cold air conditioning and watched the absurdly ornate clock. Shortly before midnight, I was summoned in and I did what I had learned to do fairly well: take the limited facts at my disposal and construct the best possible story to conform to those facts.

Yes, indeed, we had the experience and the American know-how and could certainly fulfill the requirements of this road construction contract. I was on full autopilot and performed brilliantly. When performing, all other thoughts were necessarily crowded out. On stage, all I could see was the very bright light. I felt comfortable in this familiar environment. If I sensed the irony of slipping back into myth-based marketing with such ease, I have no recollection of it.

The governor was delighted with my performance, his aide informed me. Before I boarded the plane back to Lagos I was told we would be recommended for the contract. I flew back to Lagos, back to my Barbie room, and I hung up my black suit next to Megan's princess costumes. If my life had felt surreal before, I was now entering a new stage of unreality.

As Ismail coordinated the details of the road contract, which would be executed outside the city of Port Harcourt, Lucy and I spent long hours in Megan's bed with the pink sheets, sleeping much longer than seemed necessary or possible. I would wake late in the morning and startle slightly at the sight of myself in the mirror. Thin from not eating, brown from sitting by the pool, I looked nothing like the pale-skinned woman who had flown to Lagos only nine months earlier.

I never considered leaving Lagos once the decision had been made. I explained to my parents and friends in the U.S. my decision had to do with utilizing the contacts I had made during my time in Nigeria. I said I liked working with Ismail and I was headed off on a wonderful business venture with him. I told them I owed Ismail and Shirene a debt of gratitude for welcoming me into their home when I had been quite literally thrown out of mine. There was enough truth in all these reasons to sound plausible and everyone believed me.

But my reasons for staying in Lagos had nothing to do with senators or governors or road contracts or oil. My reasons had nothing to do with professional redemption or revenge or even, ultimately, making a living. Before I could seriously care about making a living or anything else, I had to see if it was possible to escape the shadow world and figure out who I actually was.

Weeks passed, while I was living at Ismail and Shirene's, the road construction project still on hold due to the usual Nigerian delays. One day, a public holiday was announced with little justification and no advance warning: the next day all banks, government offices, and businesses simply shut down. Another day, someone died and the death required everyone tangentially involved in the deceased person's life attend a three-day funeral. A week of work was missed and the funeral attendees were sent home with leftovers in plastic Tupperware-style containers emblazoned with the face of the dearly departed. Ismail and I waited.

While we waited, we talked about how this contract could be the beginning of the civil construction company Ismail had been dreaming of since coming back to Nigeria. I believed in Ismail. He had been there for me when no one else had. I admired his shrewdness in business and his gentleness as a father and husband. If I could help to make his long-cherished Nigerian dream a reality, it seemed like the most sensible use of my time when nothing else made any sense whatsoever. Mythologized marketing presentations notwithstanding, it really was the work he was meant to do.

Ismail had successfully led large construction projects in the U.S., had a master's degree in civil engineering, and perhaps most importantly, he was deeply enmeshed in the Lebanese community. Because Ismail was Lebanese, he was for all intents and purposes related to every other Lebanese person in Nigeria. Lebanon is a small country with large families, and there were more Lebanese living outside Lebanon than within that tiny struggling nation.

Nigerians criticized the Lebanese for being dishonest and paying their Nigerian workers too little. An indignant Nigerian driver explained to me shortly after I arrived, "Nigerians were honest before the Lebanese came here and taught us how to lie and cheat!"

But it was the Lebanese (and Indians and Chinese, to a lesser extent) who imported most of the consumer goods into Nigeria. It was the Lebanese who sold the furniture, the electronics, the appliances, the processed foods. It was the Lebanese who opened stores and beauty salons and service businesses of all types.

Americans, on the other hand, were generally loved by Nigerians. Americans paid well, had the best stuff, the coolest toys. But Americans did not invest in Nigeria. Americans came to fulfill their tour in this "hardship post." They got huge bonuses in exchange for tolerating Nigeria for a few years, paid no taxes on most of their salary, received a generous housing allowance and far more vacation than they would ever have had in the U.S., and had all their money deposited directly into their American bank accounts. After a couple of years, they left with a few souvenirs and stories of how they had survived Nigeria.

The Lebanese stayed. They said uncharitable things about Nigerians (and the Nigerians responded with comments in kind), yet the Lebanese forged friendships and business relationships with Nigerians that lasted for decades, long after the Americans had returned home and the next crop had taken their place in this hardship post.

Ismail did not have the equipment to execute the road contract. I knew this, Ismail knew this, everyone knew this. But Ismail was tied to a large familial community that could provide the infrastructure he lacked. Ismail carried a U.S. and Lebanese passport, had American children and American college degrees. He had not lived in Lebanon since he left at age fourteen. But to Nigerians, Ismail was and would always be Lebanese.

I was valuable as a partner to Ismail not simply because of my ability to tell tall tales, but also because I was that most desirable thing: American. Ismail had "American connections," as evidenced by the blue-eyed woman who made the whole deal palatable to our Nigerian clients. While I was uneasy with the credibility once again granted to me simply because I was American, I was happy if it could be used to help Ismail.

The would-be senator had the contract in hand; we knew mobilization monies would soon be made available. The governor said he wanted the project completed by Christmas and it was already November. Ismail was impatient. What were we waiting for? We decided not to wait. I was certainly not in favor of waiting, not if I could be doing something—anything—other than facing the painful and uncertain reality of my new life. Action of any kind seemed better than inaction.

BLUE YARN

The road project was just outside Port Harcourt. Since we were charged with overseeing operations, we decided I would move there preemptively to get to know the people we would be dealing with in Port Harcourt and be on hand when the inevitable word came to begin operations. I loaded my possessions (many of them still in boxes from the night of my exodus from the guesthouse) into my car for Emeka to drive across the country to Port Harcourt.

Ismail insisted there were too many police on the roads for me to ride with Emeka. The police were even more corrupt in Port Harcourt than in Lagos (a fairly high standard to surpass), and the road to Port Harcourt passed through a series of smaller communities, each of which had police and occasional military stops, each stop with its own makeshift and unpredictable agenda. The closer it got to Christmas, the hungrier the police and military men would be for money to bring back to their villages. Ismail knew bribes were an unavoidable cost of doing business. His quick calculation was an American woman in the car would result in additional bribes far exceeding the cost of a plane ticket to Port Harcourt. Even without me in the car, we budgeted a couple hundred dollars for the bribes Emeka would need to travel cross-country. Since Lucy would not be allowed to fly on the small domestic aircraft, it was decided Lucy and Emeka would make the long drive to Port Harcourt alone.

I watched Emeka and Lucy head out to the car just before dawn and felt a twinge of worry. Emeka carefully counted out the cash Ismail had given him to cover the inevitable bribes. He slowly counted it back to Ismail before putting it in his pocket and recording it in his little receipt book. Emeka kept meticulous records. Then, with a more than usually serious expression, he picked up Lucy in her pet carrier. Lucy looked out through the black screen, excited as she always was when she knew she was going to travel. Emeka and Lucy got into my little Toyota loaded with my few possessions and headed down Ismail's driveway. I watched them leave in the predawn light, headed to Port Harcourt.

PUBLIC HOLIDAY

Port Harcourt is not a nice place. You will not find anyone to tell you it is. Apparently, years ago, Port Harcourt was just another city — before the Niger Delta burst into violence, before the environmental devastation was complete, before there were shootings and kidnappings in the street, before Port Harcourt became synonymous with everything dirty and unsavory and irresponsible in the oil business, a sort of cautionary tale for other countries to look upon and try to avoid.

Lagos is a relatively new place. But Port Harcourt, located in the jungle at the mouth of the Niger Delta, has been a trading post for centuries. Shirene and her family lived there before it became the hellhole it is today. She and her neighbors dug dozens of slavery-era bottles out of the silted-up creeks that ran through town — heavy blue lead-glass bottles which, filled with rum, had once been traded for palm oil before the new, more profitable oil was discovered. Palm oil was good for making candles and used as a lubricant for machines. It was especially useful as an inexpensive source of nutrition to keep slaves alive on the long journey across the sea.

The international news covered very little of what happened in Port Harcourt or outside in the Niger Delta, where the earliest Nigerian oil and gas resources were discovered, in part because it was so difficult to report, but primarily because it was not really news anymore. Smog from burning oil and gas hung over the sky of Port Harcourt even when there was a breeze off the ocean. The jungle was filled with arms smugglers and oil spills. A combination of industrial greed and governmental malfeasance had resulted in a textbook environmental horror. The foreign oil companies left behind a wasteland in the delicate Delta ecosystem. The water was undrinkable. The fish died. The children grew hungry and all the money promised to the villages disappeared into the pockets of village leaders who built houses in Europe.

The young men who lived in the jungle became angry. Weapons were procured. So many foreign oil workers had been kidnapped and released for an agreed-upon ransom that it was a completely unremarkable event unless the kidnap victim was American, Canadian, or British — or if he was killed. The kidnap victim was almost never killed because that would complicate what was a very lucrative business. Instead, he was provided with his preferred brand of cigarettes and beer while he waited for the ransom to be paid by his oil-company employer, which viewed this expense as just another cost of doing business in the Delta. There was a formula for how much each worker was worth. Americans were worth the most. Nigerians were rarely kidnapped.

Oil pipelines are broken into, oil is taken. The oil is ferried out to sea, where it is sold to someone who sells it to someone who ultimately sells it to the refinery — the same refinery that refines the rest of the oil, regardless of where it was stolen from or who stole it. This is not a business where asking questions serves any useful purpose. The oil companies try to repair the oil pipelines as quickly as they are broken into in an endless game of cat-and-mouse. Often the pipelines are not repaired for a very long time. Sometimes the released gas catches fire. There are gas wells that have been burning for years. I heard (but was not able to verify) a story about an ornithologist who studied birds near one of these perpetually burning wells. Generations of birds had never experienced the dark.

I was not particularly alarmed by the prospect of moving to Port Harcourt. To be afraid would have meant I felt something, when I really felt nothing but a vague and reckless impatience. Moving to Port Harcourt provided momentum. Whatever was going to happen next, I wanted it to happen sooner rather than later. Living in Port Harcourt seemed preferable to living quietly inside myself. I wanted to put that off as long as I was able.

Early the morning after Lucy and Emeka left, I said goodbye to Shirene and the kids. Shirene gave me a huge hug, smelling of the spicy perfume she brought back from Dubai. She gave me a pile of slightly dog-eared thrillers to read and told me to be careful. Ismail drove me to the airport—he preferred to drive than trust whoever was driving for him that week.

As Ismail negotiated the early-morning traffic to the airport, he told me about the cousin, Hassan, who I would be staying with until we began operations. Ismail called Hassan his cousin, although I have no idea exactly how they were related. Ismail said they were good friends. It wouldn't be long before we were ready to start, he assured me, and it would be good to be there and get to know some of the folks at the various ministries ahead of time. Ismail hugged me as I got out at the airport. I had been with Ismail and Shirene the entire time since my eviction, and I was surprised by how vulnerable I felt as I said goodbye.

I landed in Port Harcourt and was picked up by Ismail's cousin and taken to his house. Hassan lived in a compound of about thirty small bungalows built in clusters and surrounded by a tall wall topped with razor wire; in the front stood a guard shack manned by a friendly guard named Friday. Hassan showed me to my small, slightly damp room with a private bath. I deposited my suitcase and walked around the compound of modest cement houses populated entirely by Lebanese Muslims. Arabic was spoken by the children bouncing balls on the sidewalks and the women with head coverings gathered together in the backyards.

Hassan's house was in a cluster of four houses owned and occupied by a group of middle-aged men who shared some obscure familial relationship. The men were able to send their families to more habitable cities—some in Nigeria, some in Lebanon—while they stayed in Port Harcourt for most of the year to do business. These men were merchants and traders and small business owners. They had come to Nigeria as young men and stayed. They had been in Nigeria for decades. I met them as they returned from their offices and job sites. The "uncles," as I came to think of them, masked their polite surprise at an American woman taking residence in the guestroom, greeted me warmly, and went about their business. In their high-waisted dress pants and short-sleeved dress shirts, they looked very much as if they had stepped out of an American sitcom from the 1960s.

The night I arrived, Emeka was still on the road. I had not expected him to arrive ahead of me, but when I received a tense, hurried call, I found he was nowhere as far along as I had hoped. The reception was poor, but he let me know he had already been stopped dozens of times and his license had been taken by the police.

"I will call tomorrow, ma'am!" he said before we were cut off mid-conversation.

I wondered how his money was holding out. I wondered how Lucy was faring. There was nothing to do but wait.

The next morning, I wandered out of the compound to a roadside stand and bought a melon and freshly roasted peanuts in a recycled gin bottle. When I returned, Hassan gave me a stern warning, telling me it was not safe to wander outside the compound on foot—even in broad daylight. I had no other transportation until Emeka arrived, and I realized I was essentially trapped in this small compound with strangers. I joined Hassan's neighbors for a late-afternoon dinner; they rotated houses and shared their evening meals together. Dinner was served by a Nigerian cook on a long table covered with an oilcloth. The meal included a lot of meat, which I don't eat, so I ate some rice and salad and then went to my room, where I ate my gin-bottle peanuts.

At sunset, the uncles gathered outside. It was the only time of day the generator they shared was shut off, as there was almost never electricity in that part of Port Harcourt. They sat outside and played backgammon, drank strong sweet tea, and smoked sweet tobacco out of a water pipe. Emeka called again, but I couldn't understand what he was saying. I gathered there had been more stops, perhaps many more. I thought I heard him say where he was, but I couldn't be sure. He said something about a police station. After sunset, I went back to my room, where through the thin door I could hear Al Jazeera in Arabic on the satellite television. The old air conditioner roared and the room smelled dank.

The next day there was still no sign of Emeka, and my calls to him did not go through. The uncles told me not to worry. "He's Nigerian. He'll manage," they said.

I worried anyway. I didn't mention Emeka was also traveling with a small deaf cat, as that would have been difficult to explain with or without the benefit of Arabic.

Finally, on the third day, Emeka arrived without warning. The guard, Friday, threw open the gate and Emeka drove into the compound with Lucy proudly perched on the dashboard.

Emeka was exhausted. His license had been taken and he had been unable to get it back. He had almost expended his supply of bribe funds, and he carefully counted out the remaining money for me. But he was smiling as he told me the story of his last two days on the road.

At every stop, he told me, the police wanted to know what was in the black carrier sitting in the passenger seat.

"It is a cat," Emeka replied.

"Why are you traveling with a cat?!" the policemen wanted to know.

In most of Nigeria, cats are traditionally feared and avoided. It is safe to say no police officer had ever seen a cat traveling in a car. Eventually, Emeka said, he started to realize how uncomfortable Lucy was making the police and decided to use this to his advantage. The next time he was stopped, the policeman asked what was in the bag at his side.

"Miss Lucy," Emeka answered.

"What is Miss Lucy?" the policeman asked.

"Miss Lucy is a cat."

"Why does the cat have a *name?*" the policeman wanted to know.

"That is what she is called: *Miss* Lucy," Emeka replied. This seemed to spook them, Emeka told me. They didn't want to get too close to this mysterious carrier, and his fine was decreased a bit.

So Emeka told me at the next stop, he took it a step further. He let Lucy out of her carrier so she was looking out the window. When the policemen saw this cat looking out the window at them, Emeka said, they were reluctant to approach the car. This became the new protocol.

BLUE YARN

When Emeka saw a police stop, he made sure Lucy was in the front seat, peering out the window. Several officers, when they saw the cat looking through the window at them, waved Emeka on with no fine whatsoever.

The final stop was just outside Port Harcourt and the police were determined to get a bribe from every car. As Emeka pulled over, the policeman demanded he come to the police station.

"I cannot!" Emeka replied. "The cat will jump out of the car if I open the door!"

The policeman stepped back from the car and eyed the cat warily. "How do you relieve yourself?" the policeman demanded.

"I have not relieved myself since I left Lagos!" Emeka exclaimed, sounding desperate. "Let me get to Port Harcourt, I beg, without further delay!"

Emeka told me he slipped a 200-*naira* note (about $1.50) through the barely opened window and was allowed to go—a bargain thanks to Lucy.

The next day was Sunday and Emeka rested. I came out of Hassan's house and discovered a small goat had been delivered to the compound. It was tied in back of one of the uncles' houses next to the clothesline. I had no idea what to make of this until I saw one of the cooks approach the little goat and cut its throat. I beat a hasty retreat to my room. When dinner was served less than an hour later, the goat's flesh was being run through a meat grinder on the oilcloth-covered table, mixed with herbs and spices, and eaten raw on pita bread while still warm. I skipped dinner in favor of more gin bottle peanuts (wondering how long a person could live on peanuts and the occasional salad), but at sunset I joined the uncles outside again as the generator was blissfully silent. Lucy and I joined them for their nightly gathering. The uncles were delighted with the appearance of Lucy. While dogs are considered unclean by many Muslims, the uncles reminded me (just as the moneychangers in Lagos had) Muhammad himself reportedly had a cat.

I looked around me in the light of the rapidly setting sun. The uncles had graciously accepted the sudden appearance of a blond American woman and her small gray cat at their evening tea, although I was fairly certain it was a first. I drank the very sweet tea and watched

Lucy sitting on the lap of one of our adopted uncles. He spoke to the tiny deaf animal in Arabic and smiled. Lucy looked up at him, her head bobbing, and purred. She appeared to be perfectly at home.

I wondered what on earth I was doing here.

Port Harcourt made less sense than Lagos and living with my newly adopted Arabic uncles made considerably less sense than living in the princess room. There was a justification for my decision to be here, but I think I knew even then my justification was simply that—a screen I had erected between myself and any serious contemplation of my life. The idea of being alone with myself, without the benefit of any of the supports that had comprised my sense of self, was somehow bearable as long as my life bore no resemblance to any life I had ever lived in the past or any life I could imagine in the future. As long as I remained in a sort of sustained limbo, all thoughts of how I might "end up" could be forestalled. The terrible work of reconstructing a life could wait. Literally locked within concrete walls, there was a safety here that had nothing to do with being protected from corrupt police or armed robbers. The safety I had found within the walls of this compound was protection from the fearful and unthinkable task of beginning life anew at middle age.

On some level (although I was not ready to admit it yet) I knew the deals I had made with myself to stay in a deeply unsatisfying marriage, the ethical compromises I had accepted to be a loyal employee, the most fundamental ideas I had of who I was as a person and what I wanted out of life simply made no sense anymore. I had known, in the moment I decided to stay in Nigeria, I was not going to be able to find a rationale to try to reconstruct myself as I had been before all of this occurred.

But, for a brief, sweet moment, I rejoiced in the unexpected peculiarity of it all. I rejoiced I was alive in this unlivable place with people I did not know and with whom I had virtually nothing in common. Drinking tea in the sunset, I experienced the curious feeling my life had been temporarily suspended. I had been given an impermanent reprieve from painful reality—a brief public holiday from my life.

PART TWO

UNREMITTING OPTIMISM

Still in Port Harcourt, I was trying not to see something had gone seriously wrong.

With Emeka and my car back in Port Harcourt, I could now leave the compound, at least during the day. I met with the folks Ismail suggested in the various ministry offices, but with no actual project underway, after a few pleasantries, there was not a lot to say.

"It will be good to be here when we are finally ready to start," I assured myself as we drove back to the compound. But when would we start? The delays were worrisome. Calls from the would-be senator were becoming less frequent.

"Don't worry, Carrie!" he assured me in one of his sporadic communications. "You will soon be busy enough!"

There was virtually nothing to do in the compound. I nipped outside on foot one day just to orient myself in town and was chastised again by one of the uncles.

"This is not Lagos!" he insisted, in one of the few instances I heard Lagos serve as a favorable comparison to anything.

Any ideas I may have had about going running outside the compound were immediately dismissed. Instead of running, Emeka and I drove to a hotel called the Bougainvillea, where I was told I could use the pool. The hotel, surrounded by the ubiquitous concrete wall topped with spiraling razor wire, was owned by yet another relative of my new uncles. I was introduced to the manager of the hotel and his twentysomething-year-old brother, Bassam. Emeka and I would stop by the local market to buy some pineapple or peanuts in a recycled gin bottle and then go to the Bougainvillea, where I swam laps in the outdoor pool. Bassam, who seemed to have few duties at the hotel, sat at the bar under a *palapa* roof and flirted with me when I came up for air.

"You are an *excellent* swimmer!" he told me when I came up.

And you are young enough to be my son, I thought every time he did.

In time, there was nothing left to say to anyone at the ministries and little more I could do but make my daily trip to the Bougainvillea and swim laps. I waited for business to start and I swam: back and forth, back and forth, back and forth. The constant motion helped me to ignore the growing recognition that moving to Port Harcourt had been a big mistake.

Even on our short excursion to the Bougainvillea, Emeka and I drove with caution. One day, Emeka came to a stoplight and a policeman began to harangue him, saying Emeka had stopped too far into the intersection. Emeka was unprepared, I suspect, for a functioning stop light, as this would require that the city's notoriously unreliable electrical supply be operational. Emeka opened his window to argue with the officer and, the next thing I knew, the policeman had jumped halfway into the car. Emeka took off at high speed, trying to shake the policeman loose. The policeman was demanding we drive to the station and trying to grab the steering wheel while Emeka tried to grab it back. The car swerved and careened through traffic as the two men fought for possession of the steering wheel, threatening to collide with oncoming vehicles and vendor stalls selling fruit and refurbished mobile phones along the side of the road. I sat in the backseat, hanging on for dear life, and tried to reason with the officer.

"Where can we drop you off?" I asked, trying to sound friendly, as though we were providing a friend with a lift home.

The policeman eventually realized the futility of his efforts and Emeka deposited him at a corner in town. We then sped off and locked all the doors.

"We do not open the window again for anyone," I told Emeka.

"At all!" Emeka agreed. We looked at each other and started laughing.

There was no Yacht Club in Port Harcourt. The few places where expats gathered were usually within an oil company compound. I saw no one but my Arabic uncles. I went nowhere except to the Bougainvillea once a day to swap a few pleasantries with Bassam. My swimming improved. I was now doing fifty laps across this half-Olympic-sized pool, back and forth, back and forth. It made me tired — and being tired felt good.

I received an email from my husband a few days after I arrived in Port Harcourt. My heart pounded when I saw his name in my email inbox. He wrote to say he was annoyed with the young couple who were supposed to be taking care of our house. Car repair was reportedly occurring in the barn. Some wood had not been stacked over the winter and now, he wrote testily, it would probably rot. He said nothing to indicate he ever thought about our former life under the maple trees.

A couple days later, I received an email from the Nigerian Field Society, run by an endlessly energetic Canadian couple who had fallen in love with Nigeria. I had never attended any of the Field Society events while in Lagos but, through the Yacht Club, I had been put on their mailing list. They were hosting a concert by Jimi Solanke on December 6th at a small hotel in Lagos. I knew I would not be able to attend, but for some reason I wrote it in my calendar anyway: "December 6th, Jimi Solanke." I felt certain I should be there, and just as certain I wouldn't be. I would be in Port Harcourt, and certainly by December our work should be underway.

As soon as the sun set and the tea drinking was over, the compound would quickly grow dark. The generator started up again. I sat in my room and the claustrophobia became overwhelming. Port Harcourt is low and wet and the compound was not new. My room was damp. The carpeting was old. The ceiling was stained. My only window was filled with a decrepit air conditioner that wheezed and coughed all night. My few belongings were stacked in boxes along the damp plaster walls. In the evenings, I read the pulp fiction Shirene had lent me. I tried to remember to be grateful for the hospitality of these kind men who had welcomed a strange blond woman into their lives, but it was difficult not to find the atmosphere oppressive.

BLUE YARN

There, in Port Harcourt, I found myself in a self-imposed solitary confinement with nowhere to hide and nothing to do but face the dark thoughts I had successfully fended off until now. Lying in my bed in the damp room, I wondered how I had managed to get so far off track. But as I looked back from my holding cell in Port Harcourt, I saw what an exceptional job I had done in disregarding all the warning signs.

My marriage had not been good for a very long time.

Admitting this obvious and unremarkable fact felt like an act of treason. I sat in a damp borrowed room in Port Harcourt, Nigeria, and for the first time in my life was forced to examine the belief that had sustained me: that reality was merely a temporary inconvenience that could, with sufficient imagination and tenacity, be rendered obsolete.

As a young child, I remember sitting on the edge of my bed in the summertime, my feet dangling just over the floor, overwhelmed with the possibilities of what I could do with the day ahead. I directed plays and holiday pageants and elaborate puppet shows in my basement. I organized the neighborhood kids in the collection of roadkill off the streets: we identified the cause of death for the salamanders and frogs and occasional chipmunk we found (cars and lawnmowers were the chief culprits), cataloged the deaths on three-by-five cards filed in a recipe box, then buried the unfortunate victims in the backyard with appropriate fanfare. I staged carnivals on the hill with ponies and fortune-tellers and clowns, and we raised money for the local rehabilitation center. It seemed whatever I saw while sitting on the edge of my bed was easily made real. Eventually, the neighborhood kids simply showed up at my back door in the morning to find out what they would be doing that day.

In fifth grade, I imagined what it would be like to see the entire grade marching away from school waving pom-poms in a parade. Captured by the image, I invented a reason for a parade, lobbied the teachers, and created more than sixty crepe-paper pom-poms so every student would have one. On the day of the parade, I watched from the end of the line of fifth graders. We were headed down the hill to personally thank the school volunteers. One of the teachers pushed a rolling metal cart loaded with gifts to show our appreciation. (And who

100

could argue against the worthiness of the enterprise?) It was a sunny day and the pom-poms were wildly colorful in the hands of the fifth graders as they marched out of school and down the street. I saw my heavily pregnant teacher waving her pom-pom, all my classmates marching in a long line ahead of me, and I realized that I had made this happen and no one in the parade knew they were doing it only because I had imagined it. No one knew they were waving pom-poms simply because I thought it would be a wonderful thing to see.

There were no repercussions. I overheard two adults in the elementary school supply room discussing the fact that an entire year's worth of crepe paper had mysteriously gone missing and my heart leapt to my throat, but no one tracked the missing supplies to my beautiful parade and I learned an important lesson about what was possible if I didn't ask permission.

I remember that beautiful spring day and the sense of wonder that filled me. I didn't know I had just created and executed a business plan, but of course I had. I didn't realize this was controlling behavior, but of course it was that as well. All I knew was I wanted to make magic happen, to see the pom-poms waving in the breeze, to make something so unusual and unexpected and exciting occur that it would alter the outcome of a moment, a day—maybe a lifetime. I never verbalized what I wanted. I just knew on the day of the parade it was a deeply satisfying thing to watch an ordinary day altered beyond recognition and to know I was responsible.

As time went by, I became more and more skeptical anything was outside my sphere of influence once I had decided upon it. I learned to never assume a thing could not be done. And probably, none of this would have been problematic if I had confined my desire to control reality to my artistic and professional life. But staking my life to a version of reality that did not exist had become so habitual that, as my marriage began to disintegrate, I instinctively directed my considerable skill in turning straw into gold toward the relationship itself and began the incremental process of reinterpreting the reality of my marriage to suit my beliefs.

Living under an illusion is not easy. Because it was not easy, I assumed it must be a noble endeavor. Feeling I had control over my life in this way, feeling I could, through force of will, make things something other than what they were, took tremendous effort. Every piece of data concerning my marriage had to be screened to determine how closely it conformed to my worldview. Every piece of discouraging news was one more obstacle I would have to overcome. Nothing unpleasant could be allowed to simply exist. My job was to make the world—my world, the world of my marriage, the world at large—a place better than, and fundamentally different from, what it was.

A woman who cannot state her needs, accept the consequences, discuss what is painful and possibly irretrievably lost, is not someone with whom you are likely to share your deepest intimacies. A woman like that has her own impenetrable agenda. It is the Happiness Agenda, and it is as deluded and potentially damaging as any other mad fixation. Never did I allow the thought to enter my consciousness that my unremitting optimism was a malignant force in my marriage, a force that did not provide hope and consolation, but rather pushed my husband more into himself and further from me. Never did I acknowledge that a partner who is unwilling to see an unpleasant truth and name it for what it is might be difficult to be close to—even if she were on the same side of the ocean. It never occurred to me he might be tired of the parade.

Complicating matters further, the justification for my optimism never completely disappeared. We never stopped being friends. We never stopped laughing at the same jokes. We never had a shortage of stories to tell one another. We stayed in touch through a stream of text messages sent while boarding planes, checking into hotels, and hopping on taxis. His travel became so constant and erratic that at one point I received a text message more than a month old, mysteriously resent, saying he was in Idaho.

"Idaho?" I answered. "What are you doing in Idaho?"

From then on, no matter where in the world he traveled, I would receive periodic updates that read simply: "Still not in Boise."

If I had been able to see the truth, I would have realized this wonderful friend of mine had ceased to have any interest in remaining my lover. But because I could not acknowledge such a deeply painful reality, I continued to push my unremitting agenda of optimism on him, causing him more guilt. In the face of such an impenetrable wall of cheery conviction, what can a man do but feel worse and worse about himself and his much-maligned version of reality? Surely, he must have come to dread my invincible assurance. I became his adversary through my insistence that nothing was broken when it lay in pieces before us. By the end, I became the thing he desperately needed to escape.

When exactly did he leave?

It was hard to tell at the time. He had gone away from time to time almost since the beginning of our marriage. In the early years of our marriage I didn't have a name for his depression: when he would become angry all the time, when all he would want to do was spend hours sleeping or sitting on the couch staring into his laptop, when he would not want to touch me or talk about what was happening.

"What do you want for dinner?"

"I don't care."

"Do you want to go for a walk?"

"No."

"Do you want to talk about it?"

"No."

He did not want to talk about it with me. He certainly did not want to talk about it with a therapist. It was his problem. He was dealing with it. Except he wasn't.

Questions angered him and upset any delicate peace I might achieve when he was this way. There was less pain, less yelling, less angry silence if I pretended I did not notice he had, in every meaningful sense, taken another indefinite sabbatical from our marriage.

"Don't give up on me," he said, "I'm coming back."

I believed him. I believed as I had never believed anything in my life. I believed in the way one believes when one must, when there is no other hope, when any other option is a denial of everything that has given life shape and meaning. It was during these times I perfected the art of deliberate blindness. The trademark rose-colored glasses I wore had become so deeply tinted they no longer let in the light of day.

The last time he went away was the longest. I insisted he see a therapist. I made an appointment. He went. He took pills. He became, if possible, more withdrawn.

"They do nothing. The pills make my head feel hollow."

"Try again. Try something else."

He did. It did not work. Nothing worked. Nothing broke the gray stillness, the silence that lay between us. The nights that became months of no physical contact when I would reach for his shoulder, hungry for a touch, any touch, and he would flinch. In that moment, that moment when he pulled from my touch, he looked as if I had hurt him. In that moment, for just a moment, he looked as if I were his enemy, intent on doing him harm.

"Don't give up on me," he said, "it's not a lack of love."

I remember with the clarity of a snapshot one afternoon about two years before he left me. He was deep in his depression and I was sitting alone in the bedroom of our old farmhouse. It was very quiet and the sun was shining through the French doors. I was looking out on the sunny canopy of maple leaves when I suddenly asked myself, "If this is what I get in this marriage and nothing more, will I stay?"

And I knew I would.

That afternoon, alone in my bedroom, I grieved for the life of passion and laughter I would never have often or easily with him. In that moment of clarity, I knew I would regularly trick myself into believing our life together would get better in order to avoid despair. I would tell myself comforting lies in order to preserve my vision of what our marriage was. Like two young trees that had grown too close together, I was joined to him; my bark covered him. To leave him would be to split myself in two. I looked out on the maple trees swaying together in the sunshine and I knew I would stay.

I held fast to a view of the world my rational mind would have tossed out in an instant, but I held on tight. I held on out of loyalty. I held on out of love. I held on because I believed in the power of belief.

More than anything, I held on because I had perfected the art of doing so.

But now, in Port Harcourt, it was the end of November and every day there was yet another delay. The would-be senator, who used to badger us constantly, was now unavailable to take my calls for days at a time. The plans to open the office seemed to be on indefinite hold. It was getting harder and harder to maintain the illusion things were going according to plan.

Ismail called me nearly every day: "Carrie, have you heard from him?" No. I had not heard from him. Something was very wrong. I sat in my damp room with the roaring air conditioner fighting back suspicions of the worst Nigerian kind.

Finally, the inevitable news reached us. We had, in fact, been used in the worst Nigerian way.

Once the would-be senator had landed the road contracts, he suddenly became much less interested in road construction. Ismail and I had been brought in to lend our credibility and secure the sizable contracts, but now the would-be senator was no longer interested in founding a construction business with us. In fact, once he had the down payment in hand, he no longer felt the need to build anything at all.

Ismail called, his voice shaking with rage, to tell me the would-be senator had already sold the contracts for a fraction of their value to someone who would sell them again until there was no money left to build a road of any kind. The money would be used to finance the would-be senator's campaign. The phone went silent. I sat in my damp room. There was no reason for me to remain in Port Harcourt. There had never been any reason to be here at all.

I said my goodbyes to Hassan and the uncles. I went for a final swim at the Bougainvillea Hotel and said goodbye to Bassam. I made a few calls. Gozi, the cheerful Nigerian-American businessman I had met with on the night of my eviction, was back from the U.S. He was surprised to hear from me.

"What happened to you, Carrie?" Gozi asked.

"Oh, it's a long story." He would still like to work with me. I was suddenly available.

I packed my boxes into the car once again. I watched Emeka pull out of the compound, waving goodbye to Friday, heading back across the country to Lagos with a glove compartment stuffed full of small bills and Lucy running free in the front seat to intimidate the local constabulary.

IN TRANSITION

With Lucy running free in the vehicle, Emeka made it back to Lagos with considerably less police interference. I returned to Lagos on the first of December and was met at the airport by Gozi's driver, a quiet fellow who drove me to Gozi's home on the mainland. As we rounded the corner into a shady, tree-lined neighborhood, I saw a man laid out on the sidewalk, motionless.

"Is he alive or dead?" I asked Gozi's driver. The driver glanced in his rearview mirror as we passed, then back at the road in front of us.

"He is in transition, ma'am."

Gozi was a buoyant American businessman of Nigerian descent who had been raised in Los Angeles. A big man, he had traded in his sweatpants and Lakers T-shirts for traditional Nigerian robes and deftly navigated an intricate cross-cultural dance with one foot in Nigeria and the other in the U.S. In his floor-length embroidered *agbada* with a matching *kufi* perched on his plump shaved head, he claimed many of his prospective business connections thought he was Nigerian until he opened his mouth, when his pronounced California accent betrayed him, and this momentary deception amused him to no end.

"I really had him going!" Gozi chortled.

Gozi was easily amused. A small joke would make him throw his head back and laugh until tears ran down his chubby cheeks. I made Gozi laugh regularly, and he was familiar with the work I had done for my former company. In the U.S., Gozi could not have afforded the services of a full-time marketing person, so it seemed like an act of providence when an MBA, desperate for some cash and a place to live, washed up on his doorstep.

He wanted me to refashion his marketing materials and assist in presentations to oil companies who might use his American anti-corrosion technology. I readily agreed — as I had no other plan of any sort and no place to live. Ismail had introduced me to Gozi, whom he had met while working on some roads near the apartment complex Gozi was building. The small eight-plex was riddled with construction delays, but Gozi had a "model" apartment I could live in once it was finished — which he insisted would be very soon. When the entire complex was complete I would need to move out. But until then I would live and work in a nice flat on the second floor that almost had a view of the ocean.

In the meantime, while Gozi, his wife, and his two daughters were back in Los Angeles, Lucy and I moved into Gozi's house on the mainland and stayed in the room of his youngest daughter, once again surrounded by Barbie and her pals. In the family's absence, Lucy and I were not the only guests. Without fumigation, huge cockroaches and worse quickly moved into the house. I worked on Gozi's marketing brochure in the dining room and kept a wary eye trained on the kitchen, where I knew there was a rat of enormous proportions. I planned to move into the apartment before I went home for Christmas. The worst was over, I thought. It had to be.

Those bleak days of staring at the damp walls in Port Harcourt and the crushing recognition my marriage had not been what I imagined were behind me. Yet I was still not ready to go back to the U.S. on any permanent basis because I was not ready to resume anything that looked or felt like a permanent life yet. Not yet. Maybe not ever. The thought of creating a new life in a familiar place without my husband was not imaginable. Somehow, I needed to find enough of a living here — in this inhospitable place — to justify the decision to my father and my friends and possibly myself. Gozi had provided that justification. If he did not strike me as the most natural of businessmen, I was untroubled. I was beginning to more than suspect I was not the ideal marketing MBA. Providence had provided.

It was the 6th of December and I was returning from visiting the as-yet-unfinished apartment. While the model unit I was going to inhabit was nearly finished, work on the rest of the complex had barely begun. The walls were bare concrete; rubble filled the hallways. Driving back from the apartment complex, I was thinking construction would take longer than Gozi imagined—perhaps much longer. I felt, for the first time in Nigeria, time was on my side.

It was a late, hot morning in Lagos. The traffic was terrible, as the traffic always was. *Okadas* wove their way between the lanes of cars and the sun pierced through the fog of exhaust from stalled buses and diesel generators. I was going to buy a new journal. The journal I had started a year ago in the autumn, a month before my husband returned from Brussels with the news that he no longer loved me, was now almost full. I needed a new journal and was on my way to buy one at a small shop run by a brusque and industrious Swedish woman who sold Nigerian crafts. My phone rang. It was my husband, calling for the first time in many weeks.

"Can you talk?" he asked. The reception was bad in this part of town, and his voice crackled in my ear. "It's really important," he said, "I have something I need to tell you."

"Call back in twenty minutes," I nearly shouted over the interference.

I found a parking spot under some trees behind the small craft shop. Emeka parked the car and I asked him to go outside for a bit as I waited with my phone in my hand. My heart was beating in my ears.

There is no reason to hope for anything, I tell myself.

I know this, but my heart will not stop beating loudly in my ears. The sunlight makes patterns through the trees on my hand holding the phone. It is unusually quiet for Lagos.

He wants to talk, he says. It is important, he says.

I am not thinking or guessing or hoping. I am listening to the sound of my heart and watching the patterns of leaves dancing over my phone, waiting for it to ring, terrified it will ring. Exactly twenty minutes after his last call, my phone rings.

"Can you talk now?" he asks. I can. I tell him I am in a parking lot and it is a nice day in Lagos.

"How are you?" I ask.

"I'm feeling better," he says. I feel my heart, already loud in my ears, grow louder still.

There is no reason to hope for anything.

"Oh, God, this is hard," he says. "I never thought I would be making a phone call like this to you."

I listen for his next words. All I can hear is the sound of my heart beating in my ears.

"I have met someone who is important to me," he says. "She lives here in Belgium and I didn't want you to hear it from someone else."

Spinning, spinning, the world is spinning.

He tells me they just met two and a half weeks ago. He tells me their meeting was an accident and he doesn't know if it means anything yet, but she makes him laugh and he hasn't laughed in a long time. He tells me they are going to spend Christmas in Germany.

"Don't hate me," he says. "I think, under different circumstances, you would like her a lot." I wonder if this is true. He tells me her name is Azi, short for something I do not catch.

"She's a strong lady like you," he says.

She is a political refugee and apparently spent some time in prison for something or other. I realize, despite one close call, I have not been incarcerated—yet. As he speaks, I wonder (briefly, wildly) if this was the one thing I overlooked when trying everything I could to be more attractive to him.

He asks me if there is anything I want to know. I can think of nothing except the obvious, so I ask it.

"What was wrong with me?"

"Nothing," he says. Nothing was wrong with me.

I tell him I love him. But I suppose he already knows that. There is nothing else to say.

The phone goes dead and I step out of the car and blink. The sun seems unnaturally bright. I suddenly remember why it was I came here and walk across the parking lot and into the small shop. I look at a shelf on the far wall full of colorful journals covered with hand-dyed fabrics and I find two that are nice. The paper in one journal is lined and in the other is not. Caught between the two, I am stymied. I take them both to the counter.

The Swedish owner, dressed in a deep indigo blue print, is waiting behind the cash register. As I stand with a journal in either hand, staring at this woman in the deep blue dress, silent tears begin to stream down my face. I cannot speak and am incapacitated for several long moments.

"Can I help you?" she asks, looking worried.

"I just cannot decide," I finally say, "whether the next phase of my life will require lines or not."

●　　　●　　　●　　　●　　　●

Emeka drove me back to Gozi's house. It was locked. Apparently Gozi's driver had the key. There was nowhere to go, so I took a small blanket out of my car, spread it in the grass, and lay down under a tree.

I had lost my marriage and my job and my home. I believed I had nothing left to lose. But now I had lost my story of why it had all happened. I had been hanging onto this last idea: my husband's depression was so profound he had lost all interest in romance. My over-the-top optimism and denial of his reality had strained our relationship, but I never doubted—if somehow he were to feel better, if he were able to banish the demons once and for all—I would be the woman he wanted. This story has now crumbled.

I believed this story about my husband and the reason for my divorce. When I finally told my friends and family about our split, I told them this story and urged them to be sympathetic towards him. But now, it seemed, he was perfectly capable of love and affection and desire. He was perfectly capable of it—with someone else.

The pain of this realization made it hard to breathe. I felt insanely foolish, impossibly naïve. I lay in the grass and wept until there were no more tears left.

The sun moved from afternoon light to twilight. Gozi's driver had not returned with the key. I filled the last page of my journal, recording the events of the day. When it was finished, I read the first page, written just over a year ago. In it, I am lying in bed beside my husband in our farmhouse in Wisconsin, three days before our twenty-second anniversary. I am full of hope and excitement. I read the entire first entry, dated the last entry, then closed the book.

It would be a good night to self-destruct, I thought.

It seemed to me it would be easy, as there wasn't much left to destroy. I realized, with an odd sense of detachment, I couldn't think of any real reason to go on living. But I also noticed, as if observing some other life form, I was not a particularly self-destructive person. I felt as though I had entered a void and had no idea who I was or what to do next. I was not even entirely sure, for a moment, where I was. But because I had just finished my journal, I did remember the date. It was December 6th. There was a concert I was going to go to tonight, I suddenly remembered. I had learned about it in Port Harcourt when I was sure I would not be able to attend. Now I was not sure of anything at all, but this concert had seemed important enough at the time to write in my datebook. I no longer remembered why it had seemed important, but the house was still locked and there was nowhere else to go.

I picked up the blanket from the grass, folded it, and put it in the car. Still without a home, everything I owned was packed in boxes in the car. I took fresh clothes from the boxes and changed in the boys' quarters outside the house. I rinsed my face with cold water and I got back in the car.

"We're going to a concert," I told Emeka, who had said nothing to me all this while. He looked at me seriously and nodded. We headed off in the twilight.

The roads were uncongested heading onto the island at night. We drove to the small, Nigerian hotel where Jimi Solanke was playing and I bought a ticket to the concert. It was a Wednesday night. The concert was a small affair, with a tiny stage under palm trees and folding chairs set close together in the front lawn of the hotel. Nigerian paintings covered the walls inside and sculpture hung from the walls outside. Nigerian Field Society members were handing out programs and selling refreshments, and a small backup band was playing as Jimi took the stage and began to sing.

I took a chair and again had the curious feeling I was observing myself while floating out of my body. My eyes were raw from crying, but it was dark, so I doubted anyone could see. The music washed over me and I saw stars flicker in the humid Lagos sky. I thought about Christmas in Germany, with Tannenbaum and schnitzel and carols sung in German by cherub-faced boys' choirs, Christmas trees covered in perfect Christmas snow. The images paraded by me, but most of the pain was dulled by fatigue. I was tired of thinking.

Instead, I listened to the music, exhausted yet curiously alert, the suspicion growing stronger there was a reason I was supposed to be here — exactly where I was.

A Nigerian man entered and looked around. There was a vacant chair next to mine. He spotted the seat and sat beside me. Watching him out of the corner of my eye, I noticed he had nice shoes (not the pointed ones so many Nigerian men favored), and while he was not classically handsome, his face was strikingly animated, his body well sculpted, and he moved with a remarkable grace. I also noticed he was closely watching me while pretending not to.

We pretended not to be watching one another for a while. Finally, he asked if the program (the program under my chair) was my program. This struck me as a particularly inept icebreaker, but it served the purpose.

"Do you like French literature?" he then asked, apropos of nothing. I laughed and told him I loved the plays of Molière.

"I'm right in the middle of reading the most wonderful story by Balzac — do you know Balzac?" he asked, and I confessed to a lamentable ignorance of Balzac. The conversation languished for a moment. Then I told him I'd just come back from Port Harcourt and related Lucy's usefulness in reducing bribes.

"Do you teach literature?" I asked, and it was his turn to laugh. No, he was a public health scientist, recently returned from Cambridge, but he made his living as an art dealer, and somehow it came up in conversation he used to be the Lagos State Ping-Pong champion, which I found inexplicably funny. Then the concert was over, and I saw he wanted to contact me and did not know how to do this.

Then, before I really knew I was going to do it, I said, "Send me your Balzac story," and handed him my program (the program under my chair) so he could write his name on it, which he did. His name was Azu; he wrote his email address on my program and I told him I would let him know what I thought of his story by Balzac.

I left the small hotel and climbed into the car with Emeka and Lucy. Driving home on the nearly empty roads, I had never felt so empty. Every explanation of what had happened to me now appeared to be untrue. Any clarity I had glimpsed in the past fourteen months had vanished. For the first time, I realized how fully loving this man had defined who I was. A middle-aged woman without a job or home or credit card in her own name was painful but manageable. A middle-aged woman without a big life-defining love left a frightening void. I could no longer say he would still love me, "if only…" No. There were no mitigating circumstances to comfort me. He did not love me because he did not love me. It was a dead end, a full stop.

My love for him was not yet dead—it was in transition—and I honestly didn't know how to end a love that had lasted half a lifetime… or who I would be when I did.

PECULIAR COINCIDENCE

The concert was over; the day was over. The following days were filled with little food and less sleep. I was still staying with Barbie and numerous other uninvited guests. I did not want to go into the kitchen and face its occupant, and I was not hungry anyway. While Lucy chased cockroaches, I lived on nothing but white wine and the peanuts sold on the street in recycled gin bottles. I had dropped more weight I noted, with the same detached interest I now employed to observe so much about myself. By day, I finished up Gozi's marketing materials. At night, the story of my marriage replayed itself in my head, an endless loop of images and memories that would not rest, like a melody that cannot resolve but always returns, again and again, to its refrain.

I met my husband in Alaska the summer I turned nineteen. I was a college freshman on summer break, a theater major who had somehow failed to get cast in summer stock. It was the first major setback in a virtually disappointment-free life. With no backup plan for this unforeseen miscarriage of justice and no idea what else to do, I was momentarily confounded. I wandered into the cafeteria and picked up a copy of the student newspaper where I saw an ad for "Jobs in Alaska." While I was not especially interested in the opportunity to stand knee-deep in fish entrails in an offshore cannery, in the absence of any other tangible plan for my immediate future, the idea of Alaska suddenly seemed irresistible. Denied the right to perform Shakespeare, I decided going to Alaska was my only available recourse.

I bought a map of Alaska. Alaska is a large state and the map nearly filled the floor of my small dorm room. My roommate from the "Show-Me State" looked on skeptically as I charted a bus route to Alaska by means of an intricate series of layovers in the Northwest Territories and the Yukon. My father got wind of the scheme and bought me a plane ticket to Anchorage.

I arrived by train from Anchorage through a tunnel leading to a small town at the mouth of Prince William Sound. The train finally emerged into the light in sight of the tank farm, the city dump, three taverns (until one burned down), and rubble left from the aftermath of the 1964 earthquake. I got a job cleaning rooms, then waiting tables, and then working on a boat for a man who snorted my meager wages up his nose.

My husband always said I met him waiting tables. He had just gotten back into town with his brother-in-law, Tom, whom he described as a man with two of everything and a boxcar to store them in. Tom went into Anchorage for a vasectomy and my future love traveled along to get his wisdom teeth extracted. After their respective procedures, these comrades in medical adventure went out drinking to anesthetize their injuries.

A trip to an Anchorage tavern usually involves a tavern brawl, with fists and colorful invectives thrown and considerable glass broken. In the cruel justice of tavern brawls, my love ended up with a fist to the jaw and Tom ended up with a knee to the groin. My husband said I met them both the next morning as they nursed their wounds over breakfast. I was holding a coffeepot and serving eggs. That's not how I remember it, but it may be so.

What I remember is a smoky bar and my new love leaning against a pole with a green corduroy hat pulled down low. I told him I was an actress and he asked me, "If you're an actress, what are you doing here? Why aren't you in New York?"

My husband and I talked all night about everything that had happened to us in the nineteen and twenty-one years we had been alive. It's funny how little I remember of what we said those first nights together. But I did not sleep at all for one night, and then for a second, and on the third night I slept deeply in his arms.

My husband had shaggy hair and shaggier jeans. He had a slight build, green eyes, and looked younger than his twenty-one years. There was wistfulness in him, a little anger, and a lot of poetry. He liked Bob Dylan and Kurt Vonnegut. He wore a yellow mackintosh and had a stack of well-worn paperbacks and a ceramic jug of Platte Valley Corn Whiskey tucked under his bed.

I returned to Chicago and, a few months later, he followed me.

"Will you love me even when I'm old?" I asked him.

I had moved to an off-campus apartment and we were curled together on my small twin bed, the wind off Lake Michigan rattling the leaky window.

"I will always love you," he said. "I can't wait to see you when your hair is white."

"Will you love me if I get fat?" I persisted.

"Well, I'd rather you didn't get *really* fat," he chuckled, "but I will always love you."

When I finally did go to New York, he waited for me in Chicago. He climbed telephone poles and wore a tool belt and lived with a group of men in a partially heated house with a skating rink of frozen beer on the kitchen floor. I attended dance class and speech lessons and ran around Washington Square in peasant skirts, leotards, and floppy boots.

We wrote dozens of letters back and forth. We wrote every day and sometimes twice a day. He mailed his letters in envelopes made of grocery sacks with whimsical return addresses. When we finally married, we tied those letters together with heavy blue yarn and stored them in an old steamer trunk he had inherited from his grandmother. He told me he loved me and I made him happy. I continued to believe him long after evidence to the contrary was unmistakable.

Alone with Lucy in Gozi's dark house, I spent the nights imagining my husband as he had been when he was a young man, when he would reach for me, when he was not always tired, not always stressed or jet-lagged or whatever the reason was. My hair was not white. At forty-four, my hair had not yet started to gray. Instead of growing fat, I was now threatening to disappear altogether. But now he reached for her. Now, I knew, he held her in the way I had ached to be held for years.

"Two and a half weeks," I said aloud. They met two and a half weeks ago.

And somewhere in those days of blackness, I read the story by Balzac. I read it as if my final grade depended upon it. There was so little left to hang onto. There was so little that mattered at all. Completing my Balzac assignment gave me a focus that was otherwise utterly lacking.

The Cambridge-educated, art-dealing, Balzac-loving, Ping-Pong-playing public health scientist called me a few days after receiving my review. (Apparently, I had passed the exam. The perennial student in me was pleased.)

"Would you like to go to a nice bar with me?" he asked. (I didn't remember him as being handsome. I worried he might have a lisp.)

But we did go to a nice bar and he was nicer looking than I remembered and only had a slightly sibilant "s" that nicely complemented his Cambridge accent. We talked about movies and politics and art and everything under the sun and a few things that weren't. I quickly realized he was one of the smartest people I had ever met. He was quick-witted and wonderfully funny and much too young — twelve years my junior — but somehow, he didn't seem much younger than me. He did not seem to feel I was too old for him. And when he kissed me goodnight (which he did), it was very nice.

I was still not sleeping. I was eating fewer peanuts and nothing else. I was so very tired. I saw, in the peculiarly objective way I now had, I was spiraling downward. This nice, professorial, Ping-Pong-playing public health scientist-turned-art dealer seemed the only thing worth rousing myself for.

We went out to dinner and then I met him one afternoon in his office. He said he had something to tell me. Seated behind his large desk in a small room crowded with stacks of beautiful art, I feared the worst.

"My living situation is a bit unsorted," he told me. He was still living with the Dutch mother of his child. They had tried to make their relationship work but it was not working. She was a good person and a wonderful mother to their child, but they no longer had a relationship. They were, however, still living under the same roof, sleeping in separate rooms.

"So, things need to be sorted out…" he told me, before he could enter a relationship.

I looked at his beautiful hands fidgeting slightly on his desk. "I'm not divorced yet," I told him, "I shouldn't really be in a relationship either."

We would "sort ourselves out," we agreed, and see where we might go from there.

The sun was shining through his office window as he walked around his desk toward me. He held me very close. I liked the feel of him, firm and sinewy. But more, I liked the smell of him through his starched cotton shirt. It was a smell something like coconut, and it was nothing at all like the smell of my husband. It was a new smell entirely.

A few days later, my husband called again. I was looking for furniture for my unfinished apartment that almost had an ocean view, so I stepped off the bright noisy street and into a dark furniture store filled with heavy mahogany to talk. Again, my heart was in my ears; again, I felt tears beginning. There were no customers in the store, just two wide-eyed young Nigerian salesgirls.

"How are you?" he wanted to know.

"I guess I've been better," I told him.

I watched a gecko emerge from under a sofa and explore the store as we talked. I tried to relate the soul-crushing effect this sudden revelation of his new love had on me but realized, as I watched the gecko, this was probably not of much interest to him. Realizing how uninteresting I was to him, I started to cry in earnest and saw out of the corner of my eye the salesgirls hanging behind large mahogany desks, enthralled by the drama this white woman had unexpectedly visited upon them.

We decided we would get divorced after Christmas. (*After he has gone to Germany*, I thought, *with all its snow and schnitzel and carols and — stop, Carrie, stop.*) There were no disagreements between us. I would divide our assets down the middle and we would hire one attorney to file the papers. I would not ask for spousal support. I knew this instinctively. The idea of being supported by someone who no longer loved me sounded repugnant—even if my plans for supporting myself were nebulous at best.

My husband called a third time, shortly after my meeting in Azu's office, as I was preparing to fly back to the U.S. for Christmas and my divorce. I had gotten a few hours of sleep, although still not much food. I took Lucy outside and sat in the sunshine. He was giddy, I could tell. This new love had raised the register of his voice, quickened his speech. I was shocked by how much he sounded like a younger version of himself.

"I never thought I would be dating someone named Azi!" he said incredulously.

"I never thought I would be dating someone named Azu!" I almost replied—but didn't.

I didn't tell him because I really was not dating anyone, not until things were "sorted out." But I also didn't tell him because the peculiar coincidence of their names struck me as almost too implausible to be funny.

He hung up and I sat on Gozi's stoop, looking at the tree I had cried so long beneath.

This marriage, which had not been officially declared dead but which had certainly not been alive for some time, would now finally end in divorce. I had no job, no home, no idea of a future. I had an appointment in a courtroom I could not think about too long or too hard. On the bright side, as far as I knew, I was no longer wanted by the police.

It was time, I knew. It was time to take some steps forward, however tentative, time to start taking care of myself. Married at twenty-one, at forty-four I had no credit card or bank account in my name alone. After my divorce, I would have no health insurance. My passport was about to expire. Although I didn't own a scale, I imagined I must weigh less than I had since middle school. There didn't seem to be much of me left to care for.

I sat on the stoop with Lucy in the sunshine, thinking of our trip back to the U.S., back to where it all started. It didn't seem possible a year had gone by. It seemed as if it was either a few days at most — or a lifetime.

"Oh Lucy, what happens next?" I asked, not really expecting an answer this time — not sure I even wanted to know. Lucy raised her head so I could scratch her chin and began to purr.

LOW MAINTENANCE

I was back in the U.S., surrounded by the familiar.

My husband and I spent the evening talking in what used to be our home under the maple trees. The books were still on the shelves, the art still on the walls. The house was now sitting vacant; a new house sitter would be moving in shortly. Over the holidays there was no one in the house, so we built a fire and ate cheese and drank wine and talked.

Azu called at one point during the evening. His combination of accents, Nigerian and British, sounded odd here in the familiar Midwest. "How are you, my dear?" he asked.

"I'm spending the evening with my husband. My divorce is in the morning."

I listened to him struggle for something to say. "Ah, well.... Good luck, then." He hung up hastily. He was probably embarrassed, I thought, sorry he called. But really, what was there to say?

My husband wanted to talk about his new love, Azi, and instead of asking him to stop, I asked snide questions about her (disguised as polite interest), questions I knew he would have difficulty answering.

"Does she like to go camping?" (I knew she almost certainly did not.)

"Does she want to live in the U.S.?" (I was sure she did, and just as sure he did not.)

I asked these questions because I wanted to see if he cared enough about me to get upset. He got upset and I apologized, as I always did. Then he gave me good advice about moving on and taking care of myself. He seemed very calm and sure of himself. He promised we would always be friends.

"Our friendship is nonnegotiable," he said. "No matter what happens, we will be friends."

I looked at this man who had been — and technically was still — my husband and I wanted to believe this was true. Even if all the rest had turned out to be false, it was somehow terribly important I was left with this one thing to believe in. And so I did.

"Yes," I said, "our friendship is nonnegotiable." Then I went out to the porch and fell asleep in an instant. Somehow, even my poor attempts at politeness were exhausting.

•　　•　　•　　•　　•

His phone rang early in the morning.

The sun rose and it was the day of our court appointment, the day we would tell the world our marriage was irreconcilably broken. I hoped no one would ask me why. But then I thought perhaps it would be good if someone did ask us why, because then my husband could tell them and a court reporter could write it down and I would then know for sure, because you cannot lie in court.

I heard his phone ring. It rang and then it rang again. Azi was calling from across the ocean at regular intervals because she was upset, apparently.

I was not feeling very empathetic. She was apparently upset because I had just spent the previous night talking with my husband on the last day of our marriage. She was upset because he spent this night talking to me within the same four walls. She was upset and she was now calling and calling on the morning of our divorce to tell him how upset she was.

I picked up glasses and listened to him patiently explain what time the court appearance would be and I wondered if she would be watching the clock. I wondered if she would have champagne ready — but I doubted it. I did not know this woman, but I somehow already sensed she was not someone who looked for reasons to celebrate. I was still washing dishes when, inexplicably, he asked me to speak to her.

I felt a headache growing in the back of my skull as I picked up the phone.

"Hello, this is Carrie."

There were no pleasantries; her German-accented voice was immediately intense.

"I understood your marriage was long dead," she told me. I felt my eyes stinging but I kept listening.

"I understood you had not had a real marriage for years."

I wondered when he told her this. I wondered why he had not told me.

"I am not a person who would ever break up a marriage, but I was told you had not been together for a very long time. I do not want you to think I am a person who would ever become involved with a married man. I am not a homewrecker..." She talked on and on, growing more and more upset.

I walked into the dining room with a dishtowel still in my hands. I wondered why my husband was so sure I would be kind to this woman, so sure I would try to make her feel better. Then, inexplicably, I heard myself trying to calm her, trying to make her less upset. I knew this was somehow very funny and probably very wrong, but I found myself saying the words she wanted to hear.

"No, I never thought of you that way," I said. "No, you had nothing to do with this. Of course not." I felt very tired. I felt my headache getting worse. I wondered if there was something terribly wrong with me that I did this, that I felt I must do this for him, on this particular morning.

"I would like to speak to him again," she said abruptly, her tone formal and crisp, after I had done what I could to allay her concerns, after she had what she wanted from me.

I handed the phone back to the man who would be my husband for a few more hours and he left the house so he could have some privacy to talk to her. I saw him outside on this cold January day, pacing in the yard, speaking urgently into his phone. I went back into the kitchen and I watched the clock and I washed the dishes and I wondered if I should have a picture taken of us at the courthouse, as you would at a wedding or a graduation. I wondered what I should wear. I thought of the photos I had seen that used to be taken of the dead and it suddenly made sense that we would photograph the dead in their coffins. It made sense to me because people do need to remember. They need to remember all the things that matter most in their lives.

I decided to wear the new clothes I'd bought for Christmas. I wanted to look nice, even if there were no pictures. I didn't know who would be there (should we have invited guests?), but whoever was there, I didn't want them to say, "Well, no wonder. He could certainly do better than that."

He finally returned to the house.

"Would you like me to iron your shirt?" I offered.

"No, no, you don't have to do that," he said, looking embarrassed.

Then *I* felt embarrassed, but I was not sure why. In offering to do this routine domestic chore, which I had done for so many years, I had apparently broken some rule for the about-to-be-divorced.

Because the court appointment was not until early afternoon, we had time to take Lucy to get her shots. Our local country veterinarian, a kind man who had seen us through the death of our dog and two previous cats was, as always, loquacious and happy to see us.

"How are you doing?" he asked when he saw us seated together in the waiting room with Lucy on my lap. "Are you still in Nigeria and... wherever you are?"

"Yes..." my husband said, and then faltered.

"Yes, we are still wherever we are!" I offered, hoping this would bring an end to the inquiry.

"So, are you ever getting to see each other?" he inquired jovially.

I saw my husband's jaw tighten slightly and I thought briefly of Italy and Greece and the imaginary white curtains flapping in the Mediterranean breeze.

"No, actually we're getting divorced today," I said cheerfully. I saw our kindly vet's face fall, and for the first time in recollection, he was without words.

Lucy had her shots and finally we went to the courthouse. We had to fill out forms in one room and then wait in another. I had not prepared myself for the waiting. The courthouse was a new building, filled with blond wood and modern carpeting. It felt empty and large. Once I no longer had papers to focus on, I started to feel I might begin crying again, and I was certain, if I did, I would not be able to stop for a very long time. I wondered what I might do to prevent this from happening when, fortunately, we were called into the courtroom and I was distracted again.

I was asked to stand in the witness box; I had not expected that either. The judge began asking me questions. It was hard to concentrate on what he was saying as I felt the familiar sense I was leaving myself again, and I had to try very hard to focus on what I was supposed to say.

"Do you understand," the judge asked for the second time, "that you are permanently forfeiting the right to maintenance?"

"Yes, I understand."

"Do you understand, once this decree is final, you will not have the right to pursue maintenance?"

"Yes, yes, I understand," I answered again. But I almost said, "I have always tried to be low maintenance."

This seemed very funny to me and I wanted to laugh, but I knew I could not start laughing any more than I could start crying because I wouldn't be able to stop and I had to concentrate. I had to try very hard to assure myself this was real; this was really happening. I needed to remember this, and it is so hard to remember the things that matter most as they are happening. It is so hard.

The decree was finalized and we left the courthouse.

"Would you like to get some dinner?" my now ex-husband asked. I wondered why his phone had stopped ringing and then realized it was the middle of the night in Europe.

"Yes, I'd like that," I said, although the idea of eating actual food sounded preposterous.

We drove to an Italian restaurant we used to go to. He told me more about Azi. He told me what a brave woman she was. She had escaped Iran and lost custody of her young son in the process. He mentioned she was, like me, not particularly busty. (I was not sure I needed to know this.) He told me she had a slightly big behind, but he said it in a way that made it clear this did not present a problem for him.

I wanted him to stop talking about her. I wanted him so badly to say one thing about us; I was hoping he would say something to indicate the last twenty-three years of my life had not been a terrible, sad joke. I wanted to hear he had some good memories, that I had not been a complete failure as a spouse, that he might harbor some kind thoughts about the more than two decades we had spent together. But he kept talking about her and I could not ask him to stop talking about her for fear he would stop talking altogether. The sound of his voice seemed like a precious resource I might need to store up for the future. Besides, we were friends now, he had said. I wanted to act like a friend if I could.

After dinner, he dropped me off at my parents' condo and I do not remember if he came inside to say goodbye to them. I somehow think that he did not. But perhaps he did.

Perhaps he came into my parents' tidy condominium and stood stiffly on the rug by the door in his winter coat, making sure his snow-covered boots stayed on the little rag rug, and exchanged pleasantries with them. If he did this (and it does sound like him), my now ex-husband would have remembered the day more than two decades earlier when he had stood in the yard talking to my father. My father, five inches taller than my ex-husband, had been standing on a ladder at the time, fixing storm windows while my ex-husband craned his neck and asked for my hand in marriage. My ex-husband had done this not because he had to, but because he was that kind of man. He was not the kind of man who would divorce his wife, he would have wanted my father to know up there on the ladder, despite his somewhat threadbare jeans and longish hair. He would have wanted my dad to know he was the kind of guy my dad could trust.

If my ex-husband stood on the little rug by the door of my parents' condominium, he would have known he had disappointed my parents in the most profound way. He would have known he could no more explain it to them than he could to me. I would have seen the pain this caused and wished it would end. The habit of caring about his pain was so deeply etched in me I wouldn't want to see him suffer like that, and if he did, I wouldn't have wanted to remember it. I would have wanted to forget this scene — as, in fact, I have.

RAMBUNCTIOUS LOVE

For the next couple of weeks, I stayed with my parents, applying for a credit card in my name, finding health insurance, getting a new passport. I was alarmed by the photo I had taken for my new passport. I had not imagined I'd changed as much as I apparently had. I looked gaunt and rather frightening. The friends I visited all had the confused and sympathetic reactions I was afraid they would. This was the first time I had seen them since the dissolution of my marriage, since my firing, since my eviction, since my divorce. (I typically didn't mention the warrant for my arrest, figuring that might be just a little more information than my nice Midwestern friends could digest.) I had no real explanation for the end of my marriage and was deeply uncomfortable with any disparaging remarks about my ex-husband. I could offer no indication of my future plans and was prone to breaking into tears for no apparent reason. I was not a great dinner guest.

I attended a New Year's Eve party with a group of friends I hadn't seen since moving to Nigeria. My expectations for New Year's Eve were low. While it had never been a favorite holiday of mine, the previous New Year's Eve had been particularly bad, I recalled, spent weeping on the cold floor of a farmhouse in Wisconsin.

I was with a group of schoolmates and friends of friends from high school. It was the first time in a long time I had been surrounded entirely by people of about my age. I was looking forward to hearing old stories, catching up on news, toasting good friends, good health, and a little more peace on earth. I was eager to say goodbye to the year. No matter what this New Year would bring, I figured it had to be better than its predecessor.

I was surprised by how old everyone seemed. Surrounded by the familiar drinks and snacks, the familiar Midwestern accent in my ears, as midnight approached, the usual discussion of resolutions began.

"I'm going to quit smoking," said a friend who had smoked intermittently since high school.

"Twenty pounds!" said another woman. "I'm going to lose twenty pounds!" I thought of suggesting the peanut and heartbreak diet but thought better of it.

As midnight approached, the party showed signs of breaking up.

"I'm getting too old for this!" said another friend — someone at least a year younger than me — with a heavy yawn.

What has happened to everyone? I wondered. What happened to the years between high school and this evening? I'd met my husband the summer I turned nineteen and did not feel I was a fundamentally different person tonight. The intervening years had folded over on themselves until here I was, surrounded by peers who were clearly middle-aged.

More resolutions were offered up — to exercise, to eat better — the same promises that had been broken the previous year and likely in each of several years before that. I realized I wasn't ready to make any kind of resolutions just yet — I hadn't yet come to enough resolution to resolve anything. But I also felt a building frustration with all this premature maturity.

"Carrie, do you have a resolution for the New Year?" the woman determined to lose all the weight asked me.

"Yes," I announced, without forethought, "I'm going to be painted in the nude." And I somehow knew — unlike most of the resolutions made that night — mine would be kept.

·　　　·　　　·　　　·　　　·

"Get up," She says, this voice that has been silent for many months.

It is the same voice I heard in the woods on the day my husband told me he no longer loved me. I have not heard it since. But now it is back, as quiet and inexplicable and inescapable as it was the first time.

I am not a person with a religious framework to accommodate insistent voices that seem to come from nowhere and brook no contradiction. But then again, I am not a person who actually requires an explanation because, when it comes to spiritual matters, the only thing of which I am completely certain is my inability to know anything for certain. All I know is on this morning a voice that does not appear to be my own seems considerably more certain of anything than I am, so I listen.

"Get up," She says.

"You've been gone a long time," I say ungraciously, putting on my boots and coat and mittens — all the swaddling I had forgotten about in Africa. I quietly leave my parents' condominium in the soft darkness and walk to the woods.

It is still early January. I am still staying with my parents. I come from Scandinavian heritage, which means we hug a little less than others and are leery of big emotions. It's not that we don't have them. We just figure a powerful emotion is like salt: if you use it all the time, you'll no longer appreciate it when it's needed, get high blood pressure from using too much, and die early of a heart attack. Or so the thinking goes.

But now, really for the first time, I feel anger.

My now-former husband has flown back to Brussels and I feel an anger building inside me that has not been there before. Angry, stomping through the snow, I cannot pinpoint the source of my anger. I am angry with my ex-husband's new woman, angry with her history of drama and intrigue. He told me more than I wanted to know about her: how she was a political refugee and the subject of a documentary, how she was twice married to an allegedly arms-dealing Iranian billionaire. When she divorced her husband for the second time (a point which annoys me as well), she lost custody of her son. She tried unsuccessfully to escape with the boy illegally and was captured in Turkey and thrown in the slammer for three weeks.

I am unreasonably infuriated by this plotline straight out of Sally Field's *Not Without My Daughter*. I am furious with her for having such an over-the-top story, a story I know will make him feel like a hero, make him feel special and romantic and extraordinary simply for showing up at the right time. As I stomp through the woods, I start to speculate how much of my ex-husband's attraction to this new woman is the result of his sublimated desire to play Errol Flynn.I know this is nonsense. I know losing custody of a child, regardless of the country or screenplay-like circumstances, would be a terrible and painful thing. To start quibbling that people lose custody of their children every day without attracting the interest of documentary filmmakers is to deny the real and inescapable pain.

No, I am not angry with her story, but with my own.

To a large degree, my love and my ability to love defined who I was, what I had become. Love made me larger. Loving in the face of difficulties made me stronger. The big story in my life—the only story I was sure of—was that I was unconditionally loved by the man to whom I had given my whole heart.

My big, unconditional love for the man in my life had made me proud. Love for him had brought out the best in me. I was good at loving and had grown better with time. Now, I realize, I must grieve again. But this time I am grieving for my lost self. My love for him was an essential part of who I was. I am angry—not so much for the loss of my life with him, which is gone—but for the lost love I was convinced we shared and the meaning that love gave my life.

I'm not sure if I'm angry at his new woman for taking his love away from me or angry at him for not having it to begin with. But as I stomp through the snow, I feel like I've been robbed and I'm damned angry.

"You can keep it," She says quietly.

"Keep what?" I snap.

"All of it."

I stop walking in the frozen woods.

Yes.

I start walking again. And stop again.

Yes.

Then I begin to cry.

Because I have made a terrible mistake.

I have not lost love. The loss I am grieving, the loss of this love—

this love defines me. The love that makes me proud and strong and happy, the love that has given my life meaning—this love belongs to me.

This love did not come from him. This love has not been taken by her. This love did not fall from the sky. I made this love myself, from scratch, every day for twenty-plus years. It is the product of my life, my accomplishment, my gift from the divine, and I get to keep it. I get to keep it all. The strength love gives me, the understanding, the patience, the humor, the compassion, the empathy, the insight—all the gifts of love—those gifts belong to me.

I suddenly remember a story I heard a woman tell years earlier about how her mother died when she was a young girl. She said she learned then the heart is like any other muscle: once broken, it grows back stronger and larger than before. My perfectly serviceable heart has not been destroyed; it has simply been returned to my possession a little larger. I had come to believe the gifts of love could be taken from me. I thought my ex-husband was getting custody of my oversized, rambunctious love. Now I see how ridiculous this idea is. I feel like taking out a newspaper ad: "Strong heart, slightly used, free to a good home."

The sun is coming up and making a fantastic show of crystals in the snow-covered trees. I am still crying, but I don't care if I stop today. I am flooded with light and filled, for the first time in far too long, with gratitude.

My love is not lost. Love is who I am. Love is what I am made of. No power on earth could separate me from the strength and power of my own love.

She is silent now, but present. I feel Her smiling at me, smiling at my foolishness, smiling at my stubbornness. I feel the sun warming me and I feel a small reprieve from the ache that had become an inextricable part of me.

I walk back through the snow in the early morning light to my parents' home. They are up in their bathrobes and slippers, taking early-morning pills and making a first pot of coffee. They are talking quietly, thinking I am still asleep when I walk in the front door.

"Good morning!"

"Where have you been?"

"Walking and thinking."

"Thinking about what?"

"Do you really want to know?"

"Yes." My father looks directly at me with blue eyes the color of mine, eyes that don't see as well as they used to. My mother glances back and forth from me to the television news and the highlights of the Vikings' football game the night before. She looks as if this might be a little more information than a person really needs before morning coffee — or possibly ever.

I tell them what I have just learned: how I get to keep my love, my capacity for love, my experience of love, the growth that only comes through love.

"I think I've just started on a journey, and it might take me a while to figure out where I'm going."

My parents look at me a little worried.

"I'm not sure where I'm headed, and I might not end up being exactly the same person I was."

My dad continues to meet my eyes.

"I don't have all the answers right now, but I want you to know I love you."

"We love you too, Bird," my dad says, looking relieved.

Then my mother exclaims over last night's football game and we all have our coffee.

•　　•　　•　　•　　•

"Why do you have to go back to Africa?" my four-year-old niece, Isabelle, asked me, and I didn't have a ready answer. She had already learned to cross-country ski and we were skiing in circles around the loop my parents had created in the snow outside their condominium. I knew I would miss seeing her grow up and it saddened me.

Maybe I imagined telling the house sitter to leave, retooling my resume, jumping back into business. Maybe I briefly entertained moving back to live with my family and friends, reentering a life that looked and felt familiar so I could become the full-time sister, daughter, and auntie I sometimes wished I could be. But I don't think I did. In fact, I am almost certain I did not.

I remembered the black suits I put on every morning in my house under the maple trees and the long drive into the city in the dark. I remembered how, on Sundays when he was away, I spent hours calculating the growth of our investments, imagining there was a number (a number!) that would free me from a life that never seemed to fulfill my heart's longings. I thought of that woman sitting over her spreadsheets, growing older every day, and I wanted to weep. The spreadsheets, the hope, and the life under the maple trees that contained them — all of these things were irretrievably gone. Nothing had taken their place. Only Lagos and its utter confusion and chaos seemed to make any sense at all. Lagos offered the ideal refuge for a woman living in a void.

I packed my two boxes to go back to Lagos. The size was immaterial to the airlines, but the weight was crucial. So, my father first weighed himself alone and then again holding my box while I added and subtracted items to reach the optimal weight. (The process took so long my father insisted on weighing himself a second time without the box, fearing he may have lost weight through his exertions.)

Finally, I was set to go. Deep in the bottom of one box I had stashed all the love letters my ex-husband and I had written to one another while we were courting. They were tied together with heavy blue yarn.

Before I left, I'm sure I told my parents I had a grand plan to support myself. "Wonderful opportunities," I probably said. "I'm looking to leverage my expertise in the Nigerian market," I might even have said if I was feeling especially full of myself, or if they looked especially worried. None of this was true.

It was not what Nigeria offered I was flying to, but rather what it lacked. Nigeria contained both a wealth of things I had never seen and experienced and a wonderful absence of everything familiar. Nigeria had everything I needed.

FLOATING

I returned to Lagos and found something had changed.

"Where are the Nigerians?" I asked Don as we sailed his leaky fourteen-footer around the harbor on a Saturday afternoon. "Aren't there any Nigerians who sail?" I was trying to attach the spinnaker and take my mind off my stomach, which always rose to my throat when I tried to fasten the colorful sail to the tiny carabiner in the tossing swells.

"We try to get them interested," Don said, "but you know, Nigerians don't like the water. Most of them are scared to death of the ocean."

I knew the stories: how Nigerians didn't like the water, how Nigerians claimed they couldn't swim.

"Why don't you swim?" I once asked a young Nigerian man.

He laughed. "We don't float," he assured me. "White people float."

The easy camaraderie of the Yacht Club and the easy explanations for why this club was filled almost exclusively with foreigners now seemed forced. The Yacht Club had been my escape from the guesthouse; it had been my refuge in the early days in Lagos when everything was new and strange. Now, coming back to Lagos for the first time, I felt as if I were seeing it anew. The Nigerians who did sail were very few and very reserved and nothing at all like the brash, opinionated Nigerians I had come to know. I was struck by how this venerable institution, left over from colonial days, remained so very white. I started to hear more of the comments made in the Club by longtime expats.

"My driver is such an idiot," a ruddy British banker laughs.

"My steward is so filthy, I won't let him come into the house until he's showered," the blond wife of a Texas oil executive complains.

"You know how they smell," the South African manager says under his breath.

"Of course, they'll all steal given half a chance," remarks a Swiss importer matter-of-factly.

In the evening, I heard the men discuss one of their members who had married a Nigerian woman. "Why would you marry what you could buy for 200 *naira*?!" someone said in a loud whisper. Pink from the tropical sun, all the men laughed together on cue.

I was sitting at the polished bar, invisible, listening. I was part of this, I realized. I had joined the club. If there happened to be a Nigerian member present, the conversation would be different; the comments would cease. But there were so few Nigerian members this was rarely a concern. The only Nigerian in earshot was the bartender, dressed in white, towel in hand, eyes fixed on the bar, carefully wiping the glossy surface and silently refilling the drinks.

I had a queasy awareness I no longer belonged. Surely not every person in the Yacht Club was racist. A great deal of good work was done by Yacht Club members in charitable organizations of all kinds. But there seemed to be an impenetrable divide between the Yacht Club and the rest of Lagos. The Yacht Club existed in a separate world, and I was growing less and less comfortable with the distance.

But if I no longer belonged in the Yacht Club, where did I belong?

My apartment that almost had an ocean view was in fact marginally habitable when I returned after Christmas. Azu was out of the country; he had been very quiet since my divorce. I had no idea of what would happen next with him, but I was grateful for this time alone. I needed to create a little space that was mine and I needed some time to regain my equilibrium. My expectations were low, but as long as the small apartment was clean and secure, I hoped I could put the feelings of homelessness and fear of eviction behind me. I didn't know how much time I would have in it, but I was determined to make this little home—the first since my divorce—a comfortable place, even while there was rubble and construction all around me.

When the construction workers were away, I was alone in the

compound with Emeka, Lucy, and a security guard named Buba who ran a little store out of a shack on the corner made from discarded concrete forms. He usually wore a used T-shirt, which had somehow found its way from the U.S., with fuzzy lettering that read: "Too much farting causes blindness." Buba sold dried noodles and tins of tomatoes and washing powder and toilet paper and cigarettes and anything else people didn't feel like walking five or six blocks to buy. When not operating his store, he did odd jobs around the neighborhood while keeping an occasional eye on my gate.

With money I could not really afford, I bought a beautiful painting on metal called *Peace Lady*. Peace Lady had doves woven into her hair and held doves in her hands. Every morning and evening, when her metal surface reflected the low light in the sky, I felt an unfamiliar taste of peace. I had sheer copper-colored curtains made and hung them from heavy, hand-wrought iron curtain rods. I bought a small desk and a bed. Everything I had brought with me to this country easily fit in my corner bedroom with sheer iridescent curtains blowing in the breeze.

Each night, I took my run through the neighborhood. Like the Stations of the Cross, I passed the same people each night on my run, greeting them as I passed. A Muslim family with five young boys all waved together. The gatekeepers and guards offered the usual, "You try-o!" (which sounded faintly condescending, but was not intended that way). A little girl dressed in finery, a princess in a poor little shop, smiled shyly in her fancy dress as her proud parents waved to me. Laborers insisted they wanted to run with me and every day I replied, "You talk the talk, but no walk the walk!" Or: "Many try, few succeed!" Or just: "Come on!" But no one ever joined me. Instead, I was followed by gales of cheerful laughter, laughter at this absurd, big-mouthed American woman in the bright blue running shorts.

A woman appropriately named Happiness sold grilled sweet potatoes and fish. I paid her fifty *naira* (about forty cents) so I had credit for several weeks to steal a piece of hot sweet potato off the grill as I ran by without missing a step. Happiness would smile and wave. The hot, charcoal-tasting sweet potato in my mouth, I ran through the faded fuchsia bougainvillea petals piled on the pavement and headed back to my apartment just as the sun set, brilliant pink across the sky. The wind lifted a cool breeze off the ocean that was just out of sight.

Lucy was there, always pleased to see me, and the buckets of water were there that Emeka had carried up for my bath, and *Peace Lady* was enjoying the evening light.

And, after a while, Azu was there as well.

When Azu called to say he was back in town, I nervously put off seeing him for several days. This man who, before my divorce, had served as a bulwark against despair now appeared in front of me as a real person to be reckoned with, and I had been far too preoccupied with my divorce and its repercussions to think of what (if anything) would be expected from me. I needn't have worried. Azu stepped out of his small car in a crisp white shirt and designer jeans, a slow, sly smile spreading across his face as if we shared a marvelous secret. When he put his arms around me, I was jolted by the electricity of his touch.

Azu moved with a nonchalant grace and stayed exquisitely fit without ever seeming to exert himself. He had the cat's trick of appearing to never be caught off-guard, and a Cheshire cat's grin to match. Azu met me at my apartment and informed me he had "sorted himself out," and he did appear to be making an effort to do so. He had moved out of his baby mama's house and into his brother's hotel—the hotel where I heard the music, the hotel where I met him.

"I've waited long enough," he said simply as he took me to bed.

I felt strangely at ease with this young, very experienced, utterly sensual man. Making love to Azu was like everything Azu did: well-orchestrated, enormously satisfying, and accomplished with inimitable style. My body, famished for touch, quickly remembered all it had been missing and needing. I was suddenly hungry again—for food, for sex, for everything I had been without for so long. I felt as if I were waking from a long and troubled sleep.

After lovemaking, we would lie awake in bed till all hours. His interests were wide-ranging and his enthusiasms intense. He would ask me to read Tolstoy and P.G. Wodehouse to him and laugh aloud at his favorite passages. We would listen to recordings of Nigerian jazz great Fela Kuti and choral music from Minnesota's St. Olaf College Choir (a musical combination I believe may never have been heard before).

Almost every night he would join me in my little apartment that almost had an ocean view. If he was running especially late, I would perch a stereo speaker on my windowsill facing out so he would hear "Great is Thy Faithfulness" sung by the St. Olaf Choir as Buba pried open the huge metal gate to let his car in. He would make his way up the stairs filled with rubble and enter the little sanctuary I had carved out: where there was food and wine and candles burning and *Peace Lady* taking it all in. I would fall easily and happily into his arms and wake in the morning knowing I had begun to heal.

No longer interested in public health, Azu's passion was now the Nigerian art he collected, sold, and exhibited. He drove around Lagos with piles of artwork strapped to the roof of his car. He was always working late, bringing a painting to the wife of a Lebanese business owner or a British oil company manager. He would loan dozens of paintings out at a time, a strategy that worked on several levels: it provided him with free exhibit space and, while the painting was in residence, Azu would have no compunctions about asking if a stranger might come by to see it. The person who had a work on loan in his or her home was invariably flattered by the visit ("Really? Someone from the Austrian embassy wants to stop by?") and immediately thought more of both the art and Azu.

When he felt the time was right, Azu would phone the folks who had been so proudly displaying the work and tell them "someone might be interested in it" and he would have to come by and pick it up. By then they had usually bonded with the work and wouldn't consider relinquishing it. Azu would make another sale.

One morning I was listening to Azu on his phone trying to persuade another artist to paint. I heard him slip from English into Ebu (his traditional language, which he spoke only occasionally), into Yoruba (the dominant language after English in the southern part of Nigeria), and back into English. I toasted bread and chopped tomatoes for breakfast as Azu told the artist he believed in him. Azu promised to get money and more canvases to him while he painted.

Azu's relationship with the artists was complicated and necessary. Many had little experience selling their work. Most had no idea about the market. They alternated between believing their every work was a masterpiece and believing they were wasting their time completely. Azu encouraged and charmed, bribed and flattered to keep them painting. I listened to his normally Cambridge-perfect accent slip into Nigerian vernacular and street slang as he joked and cajoled. He found artists whom no one had seen and displayed them side by side with some of Nigeria's acknowledged masters. He gave young artists hope and provided aging artists with new inspiration.

He bounced on the balls of his feet as he paced around the apartment. I stopped chopping tomatoes long enough to hear him encourage whichever artist was feeling down that day.

"What is it you really want to do?" I asked him when he was finally off the phone.

Azu sat down at the kitchen table and leaned back in his chair. He was silent for a moment, focused on a point in space in front of him.

"I want to start an arts organization to assist artists from all over Nigeria and eventually the continent, a foundation that will provide African artists with a wider audience for their work, and healthcare, and a pension fund, and support for women artists..."

"Wait," I had stopped chopping again. "Stop. Let me get this down." And I started to write.

Azu didn't need a feasibility study to know what the artists needed to be successful. He knew them personally and had a gift for recognizing raw talent. What he needed was an organization behind his efforts.

"Where do you see the foundation in five years?" I asked, and his face lit up as he described a permanent gallery and international exhibits and classes led by master Nigerian artists, artists from throughout West Africa touring their work in Europe and the U.K. Azu's mind was so quick and his vision of what was possible so huge I couldn't take notes as fast as he spoke. He described the future of the foundation with such excitement and in such detail, I half believed it was already built and prospering.

And, almost before I knew it, we were drafting mission statements, putting together marketing materials, writing press releases, assembling budgets, and courting board members. We worked all day, turning what had only lived in Azu's mind into a reality. We talked late into the night about the foundation and the plans we were making for it to grow. He would describe his ideas, I would draft something, then he would edit what I had written until it was impossible to tell where one of us picked up and the other left off.

"This is our child," Azu told me. "This will be the child we made together."

And for someone who had never had a child, this felt like it might be a good time. I decided I might like to make a child with this creative, quick-witted, passionate man who was just so happy to create this important new thing with me.

I encouraged Azu to find an impressive location for the foundation's first exhibit and suggested the newly completed Lagos Civic Center, built on the waterfront and designed to look like a ship at full mast. Azu doubted an unknown organization would be permitted inside, and if we were, it would certainly exceed our (virtually nonexistent) budget. I made an appointment with the executive director and nearly laughed aloud when I learned she was an African-American woman from Chicago. We made polite conversation for a few minutes, commiserating about the challenges of living in Nigeria.

Then she abruptly sighed and said, in a familiar Midwestern accent, "I assume this would all be *pro bono* on our part."

I knew we were in. Azu was ecstatic.

Now we had a fixed focus to our efforts. A date was set for the first exhibit. The artists needed to be lined up. Experienced artists had to be persuaded to participate. New artists had to be flushed out of the woodwork and encouraged to produce more work. Sponsors were needed. Advertising and fliers had to be created. I immersed myself in foundation work. After years of voluntary confinement in my respectable job, doing practical work, I was remembering the joy of working on something for the sheer love of it.

One day Azu asked, "What will happen if we build this organization and, years from now, the foundation is doing well, we have a six-story building, but we are no longer seeing each other?" He was not expecting this, he said, just asking.

"I will burn the building down," I told him.

His eyes grew large and he said nothing. I held his gaze for several seconds.

"Just kidding." And I was.

Although this "child" we were making was everything to him now, I knew he was in many ways a traditional Nigerian man. A woman beyond the age of having children would never be his wife. I knew this, and I also knew I was growing more and more fond of him. I was so grateful for this chance to feel alive again. I felt my creative spirit, long in hibernation, beginning to wake.

Azu taught me things about Nigeria I could not have learned on my own.

"I don't like going to the market," I told him, where I was the only white face. "Everyone yells, 'Oyibo! Oyibo!' at me." They were saying, "Hey, whitey!" I told Azu it did not feel friendly or polite.

"No, no, that's not what they mean," he told me. "Try this: when they say, 'Hey, oyibo!' yell back, 'Hey, dudu!'" Dudu meant "black" in Yoruba.

"I can't do that!"

The idea of walking the streets yelling, "Hey, blackie!" nearly sent my Midwestern sensibilities into apoplexy.

"Try," he said.

The next time I went to the market, the calls began, as they always did. "Hey Oyibo!" a young smart aleck hollered at me as I entered the long aisle of vegetable stands.

"Hey, Dudu!" I answered cheerfully. His face changed in a moment and he broke into laughter. I was not the clueless white lady anymore. I was giving it back. I got it. I belonged.

I could never be Nigerian, but I could befriend Nigeria. I could take solace in it and comfort from it. I had been standing on the shore; now I was stepping more deeply into the country and seeing it as my own:

flawed and corrupt, struggling and hurting—but also funny and compassionate, open-hearted and forgiving. I was filled with an overwhelming gratitude to this country. When my husband and my company no longer wanted me, this most inhospitable of places welcomed me. This country embraced me.

I felt myself stepping away from solid ground and any lingering notions I controlled my future. As I waded deeper into Nigeria, I felt myself letting go of all the things I had clung to so tightly to keep myself from sinking. I wanted to know how it felt to go in deeper. I wanted to see if I would float.

THE NEXT BIG THING

A friend forwarded an article from a local newspaper in Wisconsin that mentioned me and stated I was "on a mission in Africa." This both amused and saddened me: apparently no one from Wisconsin went to Africa for any reason other than to proselytize. But it also got me to thinking about what my "mission" in Africa really was. I remembered when I was last back in the States in January, my mother and I were taking advantage of post-Christmas sales when I saw a towel rack I thought would be good for my new apartment that almost had an ocean view. As we checked out, I mentioned to the cashier the towel rack was on its way to Nigeria.

"Oh!" she said. "Do they need towel racks in Africa?"

The question was so innocent and well-intentioned. I imagined an organization of do-gooders taking up the cause: toothbrush holders for the homeless, bathmats for the destitute, towel racks for the great unwashed… No. I knew my mission was not to bring better bathroom accessories to the Dark Continent. But as I felt the arms of Nigeria open to hold me, I wondered if there wasn't a reason I was in this country after all.

Plans for the foundation were taking off. Azu and I had created the legal entity with the help of a local attorney who had never worked with (and had possibly never heard of) a Nigerian nonprofit, and I was already making presentations to potential oil company sponsors.

"Hello, my name is Carrie and I'm with a new arts foundation here in Lagos. We'll be holding our first public exhibit in the Lagos Civic Center and I was wondering if I could speak to someone about the possibility of corporate sponsorship."

The response was almost universally positive. These foreign-based businesses had an obligation to philanthropy and gave generously to other types of charities. But the arts had simply not been organized in a way that would permit them to contribute: they had no idea where their money went or whether it did any good. Being provided with an opportunity to contribute to an actual organization—with a mission and a board of directors—was almost a relief.

After a successful day of meetings with oil companies, I returned and shared the news with Azu. He was amazed at how having an organization behind him made such a difference. He was excited by the future and, as always, optimistic.

"My dear, this could be the next big thing!"

I looked at Azu's earnest face. He had a high, broad forehead, a strong chin, and a huge smile. I watched his face as one would watch the sky, thoughts moving across it like clouds, forming quickly and dispelling. I loved the lax and careless way he draped himself across a chair while on his phone or laptop. I was amused by how he kept his money wadded up in untidy piles in his pockets and how it was forever spilling out onto the floor. I would pick up the contents of his pockets, smooth the bills, and return what he had left scattered about. Was this my role, I wondered—picking up whatever fell from Azu's pockets? Caring for this careless, brilliant, and charming boy? Could this be the next big thing? The thing that made sense out of the loss of everything else?

I did not know any white women who had come to live in Nigeria permanently, but I knew there were some. The few white women I knew were "trailing spouses," safely ensconced in an oil compound or a foreign embassy. They worked to replicate the lives they left behind. They ordered foods from their home countries so the menus could remain the same. They kept their homes frigidly air-conditioned so they could sleep under familiar blankets and wear the clothes they were used to. They grew nonindigenous plants in gardens their gardeners maintained and they watched the latest American television series on Netflix.

But I had seen other foreign women, women who had stopped

living as if they were from somewhere else, women who were not simply surviving a stint in a hardship post. There were not many of these women, and they did not seem to congregate, but they lived their lives on the mainland surrounded by their new Nigerian families and Nigerian friends. I saw them shopping in local markets and heard them speaking pidgin English: laughing with vendors, carrying the ubiquitous plaid "Ghana-must-go" shopping bags of woven plastic in the crooks of their elbows, wearing simple flat sandals on their feet. I saw them driving older cars with the windows rolled down. They wore clothes made of bright Nigerian fabric and wide-brimmed hats to protect their white skin from the brutal equatorial sun. Was I one of them? I thought of my closet full of black suits and my briefcase full of business plans. I wondered if I would ever feel alone surrounded by laughing Nigerians. I wondered if I would ever feel at home.

I was still looking at Azu's smiling face.

"What? What is it?" he asked, his face turning serious.

"I'll tell you later."

Between appointments for the foundation, I continued to help Gozi build his business in exchange for my apartment that almost had an ocean view. I would provide him with the documentation he needed when he competed for a project. This bit of work provided me with a place to live, but I knew I would still need to make a living. I continued to see Ismail and Shirene. I met them for long dinners of Ismail's homemade hummus and grilled fish and told them about the foundation and the things I was doing. Ismail distrusted Azu. Azu was Nigerian and "artistic" — two strikes against him to Ismail, the practical-minded engineer.

"Carrie, you shouldn't work for free!"

But he also saw I was happy and I had put on weight, both of which pleased him.

"What would you think of working together?" he asked me one night after dinner, "Doing something for ourselves this time?"

After some investigation, Ismail informed me there was a chronic lack of dump trucks in Lagos. Construction of new housing was at a fever pitch as the oil business boomed. Most of Lagos is at or just above sea level. Thousands of truckloads of fill were required to raise the elevation of the building sites so the residential developers could ignore the advice of Jesus and build more houses on the sand.

Despite our fiasco with the would-be senator, I could think of nothing that made more sense, so Ismail and I each invested some of our savings and acquired a few used dump trucks. (Except in Nigeria they are called "tippers," which sounded much nicer.) We painted the trucks bright green and blue and I kept the books to monitor the progress of our small fleet. The trucks broke down regularly. The customers almost always paid late. I set up a special account to track the bribery expenses we incurred every day just to get past the police. (This budget category was not in the QuickBooks template.) Slowly we started to make a little money. Ismail proudly sent me the first 20,000 *naira* we made (about $150) in an envelope with a kind note and wishes for many more to come. I decided my new motto would be: "When life dumps on you, buy dump trucks."

Because I really had no idea how this business worked, one day I went riding in one of our trucks to the sand quarry. The driver, an elderly fellow who knew the streets of Lagos like the back of his well-worn hand, served as my guide, pointing out where the police were stationed to collect bribes, noting how we might elude some of the delays. The other drivers gaped and laughed when they saw a white woman riding shotgun in the bright blue and green tipper. I smiled and waved back.

We arrived at the sand quarry and a serious-looking female gatekeeper declared, "No women allowed in the quarry."

I laughed aloud and told her this rule would now have to change.

"This is my truck now," I explained. "Surely, my friend, you cannot make me leave my own truck?"

The woman, wearing a uniform and sitting in the small guard shack, looked at me sternly for a few moments as she processed this new information. Then a slow, knowing smile broke across her face. She waved us in. The truck came to a stop at the edge of the lagoon and I hopped out of the tipper and stood in the morning sun, watching the bare-chested quarrymen fill the truck bed with clean white sand dotted with seashells. I thought of the incredibly fortunate life I had lived—to have been all the places I had been, done all the things I had done, and hear "no women allowed" for the first time that day.

In the months since my return to Lagos, I had heard nothing from my former employer. It was only through my rapidly growing grapevine I learned the outcome of the last bit of frantic work I had accomplished for them in the days right before my eviction, while Ekpes and Felix sat outside drinking beer in Osondu's cane chairs. The project I had initiated had gone through several transformations and expansions and had ultimately been awarded to my former company in the form of a contract worth $144 million. I had never been paid my final week's salary and, of course, received no commission.

Instead of infuriating me, this information somehow pleased me. Some of the shame I felt in being tossed out of my home was relieved. The contract settled the question (if it had ever existed) as to what my real worth to them had been. It was somehow perversely good to know, even though I would never receive a dime, I *had* been effective.

My ex-husband called at least once a week. Sometimes he wanted information of some sort, or at least he used that as a pretext for calling. Once, he called to get a recipe and I thought how strange it was he was cooking for her. I didn't remember him cooking before. He told me little of his life in these calls and he called when she was not around, as she did not like to know we were in communication. But it was good to hear his voice, good to know he was doing well. There was no more talk of collecting corkscrews.

•   •   •   •   •

One night after making love, Azu was sleeping and I was wide awake, a candle burning. I looked over Azu's shoulder at *Peace Lady* reflecting the candlelight, serenely watching me from the far wall. Since I no longer went to the Yacht Club, mine was the only white skin I would see for days at a time. In the dim light, my white arms and legs appeared almost alien-looking. (Azu described me as "lithe," which pleased me.) As I looked at my pale limbs wrapped around his dark body I knew any lingering notions of what my life was going to look like were now gone.

The copper-colored curtains lifted and the candlelight flickered in the breeze. In that moment, I was viscerally aware I wanted to be nowhere but exactly where I was—and also aware I had not felt this way in a long time. I buried my face into the nape of Azu's neck. He kept his hair long for a Nigerian man—which was not very long, but long enough for me to rub my face into the back of his hair and pick up the scent of him. He smelled like the perfect combination of Palmer's Cocoa Butter Formula and Azu. Wrapped around this sleeping man, I was as peaceful as I could remember being.

And something inside me stirred.

How long had it been, I wondered, since I had really done as I wanted to do? I had lived in a world of making do. I had struggled—and won—my battle to make peace with the idea that caring for someone who I thought needed me was enough. Somewhere in that time, I had stopped enjoying art. I had stopped inventing things. I had stopped creating. I had stopped playing. Instead, I had learned how to make money. I had learned how to save and invest. I had acquired a collection of dark suits and sensible shoes and amassed a lot of miles in an airplane. This beautiful six-foot ebony man, so full of ideas and visions and smelling slightly of coconut, had awakened something within me besides my sleeping sexuality. This man felt like my muse.

Now, more awake than before, I held Azu tighter. *Peace Lady* was looking at me intently. I met her eyes and thought of my young self: the girl with all the ideas and the dreams and the inventions and the life filled with fun. The necessary dishonesty of living in an unhappy marriage had silenced the noisy racket of my honest, creative soul—and now I wanted that girl back. I wanted my lost curiosity and fearlessness. I knew it would not be the same and I didn't care. I wanted to be that girl again so badly it hurt.

Until that moment, I had wondered how I would recover from the loss of my marriage, the loss of my career, the loss of everything that looked like my life. In that moment, wrapped around Azu, holding Azu, I did not want any of it back. I wanted to throw it all away and replace it with something new and brave and more honest than I had known before. It had taken all the pain and all the loss to recognize I wanted a hell of a lot more than what had been.

"I'm going to do it," I said softly and certainly to the sleeping Azu.

I didn't know what I was going to do. I only knew an essential part of me had been silenced for a long time and now she was awake, rattling at the bars, awakened by this unlikely muse and demanding something be done.

The next day, after making our usual breakfast of tomatoes on toast, Azu left to meet with a prospective art buyer. After he was gone, I sat on the floor of my little apartment and thought about what it was I wanted—what I wanted to do next—perhaps consciously for the first time since everything fell apart. I approached the job of reassembling a life like a small child playing with blocks: I had no instructions and there was nothing left standing, so I sat on the floor and puzzled for a long while.

The room was quiet. I could hear the hum of diesel generators and the din of horns in stalled traffic around a corner. I heard a truck rumble and the sound of my heart beating as I thought: *What do I really want?* For a long time, nothing came to mind. All the things I had wanted with my ex-husband in my former life bubbled up and floated away. What was it I now wanted? If I was going to build something, I figured, I'd better start at the bottom. I picked up an imaginary building block for my new imaginary life.

"Freedom from fear," I announced.

I put this block in front of me and I thought some more. What would I want if I could live without the fear of being suddenly left alone, if I could be free of the fear of losing my home, free of the constant nagging fear I had somehow lost my identity and the meaning in my life? What would I want then? I picked up another block.

"A creative outlet."

Another pause. I didn't know what that meant, but I knew the girl inside me who had been kept quiet so long was awake and wanted things she had been denied. I had been filling journals at a furious rate and was now starting to write other things as well. I wasn't sure what they were or would become, but I knew something had started that showed no signs of letting up. What else would she want if she could be brave enough to dream of a new life without fear?

"A healthy body." Yes.

"Travel." I was picking up steam.

"To see my family."

"A home."

"Someone to love."

It was not exactly a life plan. But my little tower of blocks, entirely in the abstract, looked promising. Because I had not played with them in so long, I had forgotten how easily a pile of blocks can be toppled.

SAFFRON LAUGHTER

Azu and I spend a Saturday night with a group of journalists, drinking and dancing until all hours. He seems distracted and a little remote. We get home late and he does not have much to say. I wonder if he is feeling stifled by our domesticity. Before I fall asleep, I curl up behind him and tell him I do not have long-term expectations. I wrap my arms around him.

"You are the sweetness in my life right now," I say. "And my life has been a little of short of sweetness lately."

The next morning the sun is shining. It is Sunday. I lie in bed as he dresses, admiring the long lines of his body as he puts on the white shirt he wore the night before.

"I need to tell you something," he says.

These conversations never turn out well, I think.

And he tells me about his "Spanish ex," a woman he dated while at Cambridge more than a year ago, after his baby mama. She is a midwife and they have been talking. She has decided to come to Nigeria to see if they might make their relationship work.

"She casts a shadow over my life," he says. "I think she is my destiny."

"Your destiny."

"Yes, I think so."

"When did you know this?"

"It just happened."

And I see how fragile my pile of blocks really is.

All the things that had filled my heart and mind for the last three months—the arts foundation and dreams for our "child," P.G.

Wodehouse and Balzac in bed, Fela Kuti and the St. Olaf Choir, tomatoes on toast in the mornings: the little bit of a life I have assembled — all of it was somehow built with him as the foundation. I think of *Peace Lady* smiling on us in bed, my newly awakened creative self, how safe and brave I felt when I held him, how alive I was in his presence. Without him, the page is blank again and I will have to begin anew.

But at this exact moment, I can't imagine how that can be done.

At this exact moment, it is just too much. I am flashing back to the guesthouse with the empty white walls and Lucy and I are alone again.

I can't do it, I think. *I can't do it all again. I'm too tired, too fragile. I cannot fight anymore.*

Azu hurriedly gathers his phone and the pile of bills I assembled the night before that had fallen out of his pockets in their usual way. He gives me a brief kiss and looks concerned.

"What do you want me to do?" he asks.

"I want you to leave," I say.

"You do?"

"Yes."

He does. I hear the door close and his car start. I hear Buba open the giant steel gate and I hear the gate close. It is Sunday and Emeka is off work. There are no construction workers. Everyone is in church. The complex is silent. I don't go to church. Where do I go when I want to go to church? I wonder. Where do I go when my blocks have been knocked over once again?

I can think of nothing. I can think of nowhere to go, no one I want to talk to. My mind races, looking for a place to rest. And all I can think of is, more than a year earlier, traveling to the small fishing village in Mexico with my now ex-husband. I remember how I swam far out in the bay and around the small islands. I remember finding peace as I spun slowly round and round like a compass. I want the tranquil sea.

I will go swimming, I decide.

The sky has clouded over somewhat, but the sun is making occasional celebrity appearances. There is only one real beach in Lagos, across the bay, not easily accessible by road. To get there, picnickers line up at a dock along the harbor to board rickety fiberglass boats that ferry them across the bay to the beach. Since Emeka is not there to drive and I do not want to leave my car alone at the dock, I decide I will take an *okada* to the dock. The *okada* flies through the quiet Sunday traffic and leaves me at a dock where I pile into a blue fiberglass boat filled with Nigerians loaded with picnic baskets and cold boxes. Soon the boat is full and we race across the bay to the beach. I pretend I do not notice the looks directed at me, the lone white woman on the boat, as I stare at the water flying by and dip my fingers into the waves. Nothing else matters. To be on the water now is what I need.

When I arrive, the beach is packed but I know no one. I wander along the long line of umbrellas until I see a group of French bathers who seem to have a little more room than absolutely necessary. I slip in between the French group and three cantankerous middle-aged Lebanese gentlemen lounging about with their young Nigerian girlfriends. I am not looking for company; I am here to swim. I put my clothes in my bag and tuck it under my chair to make it less inviting and wade out into the ocean.

No one else is swimming. The beach is for picnicking and socializing, but I am here to swim. The sky has clouded over but I do not mind. I swim out past the boats, away from the noise of the picnickers, and I float, motionless in the water.

I can float for a long time in the ocean. The salt keeps me up without any movement. I don't know how long I am out there but it is good to be floating, lying still in the sea.

I am tired. I am tired of trying to understand, tired of rebuilding, tired of the painful and tentative steps to becoming whole. I am tired of the journey and the daily decision to make this day better than the last. I feel so tired and so very alone. I float in the water for a long time.

Suddenly I become aware the sky is much darker than it was.

When I lift my head out of the water, I see the shore is a long way away. I don't understand how this is possible, as it is a sheltered beach with a huge breakwater on either side. But somehow, in spite of the breakwater, I am being carried out to sea.

I look at the sky and see along the horizon a band of black. A huge storm is coming and it has created a riptide with strong sea currents pushing away from the shore. I try first to swim toward the shore until I see what is happening. I have never been in a riptide, but I remember what I have read and try to swim across it, perpendicular to the current. I make no headway at all. The shore continues to retreat.

It begins to rain. The wind picks up and I see I am now approaching the end of the breakwater and there are whitecaps just beyond. It is raining harder, and with the rising waves and the heavy rain, I am inhaling water as I swim. I wonder what I should do.

I notice with a sort of detached curiosity I am not panicked. I don't think I will drown because I don't think I will sink for a long time, but I also have no idea how to get back to shore and I can see I am getting closer to the open sea.

I wonder if anybody would see me. I wonder how far I would go. I wonder how long I would float.

How long would it be before someone noticed I was missing? Azu would think I was avoiding him since he told me about the midwife, his woman of destiny. He would leave me alone for a couple days, annoyed I did not take his calls. Ismail might think I just wanted some privacy with Azu, although he would worry. I still have friends from the Yacht Club, but we all take impromptu holidays and go away on business. Emeka would notice sometime on Monday. Emeka would worry. He would be the first.

I continue to swim and, while I am aware there is a good chance I will eventually drown, at that moment all I can think is how sad it is no one will notice I'm dead until Monday.

The storm has gotten worse and the boat owners are clearly worried. One by one the boats are racing out of the little harbor. Since I cannot come back in, I figure my best chance is to be seen by one of these departing boats. Most are like the one I rode over the bay to the beach: open fiberglass boats with bench seats to accommodate as many people as possible. One after another they race out of the harbor into the storm. I wave and yell, but soon I stop yelling as my voice is worthless against the wind and waves get into my mouth, making me choke. I wave my arms over my head, but I am now surrounded by great waves and I doubt my arm can be seen above them. The entire sky is black and pouring rain. The boat drivers do not see me.

Soon all the boats that have decided to leave are gone and there are only two private yachts with engines running, preparing to spirit away their owners while it is still possible. Since the drivers of the open boats did not see me, I doubt one of these enclosed cabin yachts will spot me in the water. A large yacht is pulling out now.

Amazingly, the Nigerian driver sees me.

He turns the boat and heads toward me. When he is close, he idles the engine and I awkwardly scramble aboard. I perch on the bow; it is cold. Rain is pelting down and the wind is howling. The driver heads towards the shore. As I am getting ready to jump off the bow, the owners of the boat come wading in from shore, hurrying to get back on their boat and away from the storm.

"Carrie!" one of the men coming to board the boat yells.

"Bassam?"

It is Bassam, the brother of the hotel manager all the way from Port Harcourt who flirted with me as I swam back and forth. I thank him profusely, perched on the bow of his boat in my black bikini and ridiculous tinted swimming goggles. I tell him I nearly drowned and his boat rescued me.

Bassam shakes his head disbelievingly and explains to his friends as they stand hip-deep in the waves, "…and this woman is an *excellent* swimmer!"

They tell me to come along, they will give me a ride back, but my shoes and my clothes, my phone and the key to my house—which has no other occupant and no security besides Buba—all my things are on shore. Bassam cannot wait; the storm is now here in earnest. I dive off the bow and they power away.

I come onto land and discover on shore there is a sandstorm. The rain has let up for the moment and, in its place, the sand is coming in sideways. All the umbrellas have blown away. All the chairs have either been removed or toppled. Everything that was left is under mounds of quickly drifting sand. The sand stings my skin and I can only see because I am still wearing my round black swimming goggles.

The last of the beachgoers are running with all their possessions in their hands, frantic and yelling, herding into some sort of shelter farther up shore. I go to where my pack was. Everything, including the chair, is gone.

I am grabbed by a pair of strong women, nearly the only ones left on the beach. "Come with us now!" they yell over the wind and start pulling me toward the shelter. It is difficult to shake off these strong women insisting I go with them, but I do and I begin to walk up the beach, looking for where my bag may have blown or been taken. I find two young boys hiding from the storm on the leeward side of a bamboo shack. I tell them what I am looking for: "There is only small money in my bag but I will give you big money if you find it."

The beach is now deserted except for an unfortunate group of Indian men who somehow missed the exodus. The rain starts again. It comes in a torrent and is ice cold. The Indian stragglers gesture for me to join them. They have found the wall of a bamboo shack that has blown away and are trying to hold it over their heads for shelter, but it is useless against the powerful cold rain.

They also have a length of fabric, bright saffron in color, that they must have used to shield them from the sun earlier. It is wrapped around the whole group, which now includes me, and we are all standing in the torrential rain, these six or eight Indian men and me, under the remains of the bamboo wall, all wrapped up like a bright orange package.

The rain finally subsides, but the wind is still strong and the sky is still black and there is another wave of storms on the horizon. I am shaking uncontrollably, my teeth chattering. The Indian men give me the bright saffron cloth to wrap myself in and I imagine I look like some sort of odd Hindu monk with my round black goggles and the saffron cloth all around me.

The last of the boatmen come running down to the beach. They seem to have decided now is the time to leave, before nightfall, before the next wave of storms hits. The Indian men move as a group, like some many-legged animal, to the edge of the water and queue up for whatever vessel may be leaving next.

Just then I see two small figures running toward me, two small boys in raggedy T-shirts, and in the hands of the younger of the two is my blue bag. They run to me and they give me the bag. I open it and my shoes, my clothes, my phone, my key, and the little money I brought are all there. I grab each small boy in turn and kiss him on the cheek. They are surprised and embarrassed and I give them my phone number on a piece of paper and tell them to call me for the promised reward.

The boat is leaving now. I wonder if this is a good idea—the waves are still very high, but the decision seems to have been made. The Indian men and a number of Nigerians who have come running from the shelter all climb on board until I know we are more than the sixteen that would completely fill this small, fragile boat.

And we are off, riding low in the water. Once out of the breakwater, the wind is strong and the boat is pitching. I am riding in the bow of the open boat like the figurehead on a ship's prow, bright saffron cloth flapping madly about me, shaking from the cold. Someone offers me one of the few life jackets and I shake my head and laugh, knowing I may well be the only one of the passengers who can swim on this decidedly unseaworthy vessel.

But we are headed home, headed into the storm on a rickety fiberglass shell of a boat powered by an ancient outboard motor and loaded with twice as many people as the boat was ever meant to hold, with perhaps five life jackets on board. We are all pressed together as protection against the wind, the boat is being tossed about like a toy, the rain is pelting down again, and I wonder if I might be getting hypothermia.

I turn to one of my Indian companions and yell over the wind, "What the hell are we doing in this country?!" He looks at me, startled, and I start to laugh.

The saffron cloth is blowing all about me and I laugh and laugh and laugh.

OCCASIONAL VIOLENCE

Azu's Spanish Midwife of Destiny never made it on the plane. I wasn't terribly surprised. Lagos is not for everyone and it is the destiny of very few.

I continued to help Azu from time to time with the foundation, and I learned to admire his gift for finding the wounded heart in the room, the one sad girl in the crowd, and for a few days or weeks, or maybe just a night, filling her with hope and a bit of joy. The hope may be misplaced and the joy short-lived, but the sad girl would usually forgive him for being a bit of a rake. He was inherently kind and provided short-term relief of long-lasting misery, which did not seem like a fundamentally immoral practice to me, and we remained friends through his complicated and frequently overlapping relationships.

I missed the curves of his lean body lying next to me, his witty and invariably stimulating conversation. More than anything, I missed not being alone.

I returned to Lucy and my little apartment that almost had an ocean view and, over the next couple of months, the pace of construction accelerated noticeably. Gozi was running out of cash and anxious to get a lease signed with the typical two years' advance payment. He was now lowering his sights, no longer imagining he would get an American or European company but actively courting Chinese and Indian firms. One afternoon, Gozi showed up at my apartment, breathless and jubilant.

"I've signed a contract!" he informed me in a singsong voice. A new Indian oil services company was coming to Lagos and Gozi had just received a large down payment.

"Oh, man, I thought this project was gonna kill me," he said, dropping heavily into a cane chair and mopping his forehead, which was crowned, as usual, in an embroidered *kufi*.

I noticed he had put on weight. The stress of endless delays, missing materials, and dishonest contractors had taken a toll on his health. He told me he would be taking his family back to Los Angeles for some well-deserved time off and I had just over a month before the Indian employees arrived. Gozi paid me some money I was owed for marketing work I had done and wished me well. Once again, I needed a home.

Emeka, always patrolling the neighborhood for gossip and information, found a building under construction just a few blocks away. I met with the landlord and he was excited about having an American as a tenant. Since the building was to be completely gutted and remodeled, he agreed to let me design the apartment as I saw fit. I began to design a layout for my imaginary new home, excited by the thought of finally having a place where the threat of eviction was not looming. The landlord said I could have a small rooftop terrace and I imagined dinners on the roof where I might almost catch a glimpse of the ocean.

Returning from my run one Friday evening, I found an officious-looking Indian gentleman with an oversized mustache making himself comfortable in my living room.

"Good evening, madame," he said brusquely.

"Um, good evening." I was in my sweaty running togs, trying to make my way into my bathroom.

"I was wondering when you will be vacating the premises."

"I understood from Gozi that I had until the end of next month."

"No, actually, my men will be moving in immediately."

I hated this man's mustache. It was enormous and looked as if it had been oiled. He was sitting in one of my cane chairs, one leg crossed over the knee of the other. The apartments were nowhere near ready to be inhabited and wouldn't be in a month's time. There was still rubble in the halls. The plumbing fixtures had not been connected. Even if the complex were habitable, it was highly unlikely enough Indian workers would arrive at once to completely fill it. But as my uninvited guest sat there, nervously bouncing his knee, I knew none of this mattered. Gozi had delightedly taken his down payment and flown to Los Angeles. I had no lease and no legal standing in the apartment.

"I see. When would you like me to be out?"

"I would like you out by Monday. If it is convenient."

It was not convenient.

Lucy and I began packing again. I put my possessions into the same well-traveled boxes I had brought with me to Lagos. Lucy hopped into a box; I moved Lucy and put more things in the box. Lucy jumped back in the box and we continued until it was full. Then we started on another box. (Lucy always enjoyed the packing game.) The renovations to my new flat with the as-yet-imaginary rooftop terrace had barely begun. Lucy and I were homeless again. I thought of asking Ismail if we could move back into the princess room. The thought was not a happy one.

Then Nora called.

Nora was a drilling engineer for a major oil company. A rare woman in an almost entirely male field, Nora was in her mid-thirties and had just finished working on an offshore oil rig in the North Sea. She was licensed to use large explosives and drive heavy machinery. She was also an amateur geologist, a student of crystal healing, and a competitive ballroom dancer from Vienna with long red hair that fell to her bum. I had met Nora a few weeks earlier when I was publicizing the foundation's first exhibit. Nora loved art and promised she would come and round up some fellow Austrians to attend with her.

Nora called me out of the blue. She knew I had Lucy with me in Nigeria and she told me she had just adopted an abandoned Persian cat named Bernie. Now she was flying home to Vienna for a week. "I'm wondering if you would be willing to take Bernie while I'm away."

"I'd be happy to, but there is a problem. I won't have a home after this weekend." I explained my sudden eviction and my as-yet-unconstructed new flat.

"No problem. You come stay at my place while I am gone. I have plenty of room."

Nora needed a cat sitter and I needed a temporary home. It was perfect. Her apartment was the typical housing provided to expat oil workers. She lived alone with her cat in a three-story, four-bedroom, five-bathroom flat in a gated compound with a swimming pool. Lucy and I moved into Nora's spacious flat. Lucy loved chasing the languid Bernie around the house and I reveled in the novelty of hot running water and nearly constant electricity.

When Nora returned from Vienna, my flat was not yet completed.

"Stay," Nora said. "Stay here until it's finished."

A couple of weeks later, I received a terse text message from the landlord of my new little flat; he was changing the floor plan to better suit Nigerian tenants who might rent it in the future. The spacious open design had been discarded in favor of a warren of windowless hallways and cramped bedrooms.

"I think you should stay here—for good," Nora announced.

She liked our little two-woman, two-cat household, and Lucy and Bernie had become fast friends. While she had been living alone in the large company flat, Nora's naturally reclusive nature had been exacerbated by the chaos and occasional violence of Lagos. Even the commute into the oil company office where she worked was fraught with risk of encountering something dreadful, so Nora had devised a system with her driver so he would distract her whenever there was anything she would not want to see outside the window.

There is a lot of dreadful in Lagos, so Nora spent a lot of time looking intently to the left at the giant billboards selling local beer ("Shine Shine Bobo!") or to the right at the small commuter bus pulled off on the side of the bridge, the roof piled high with baskets and Ghana-must-go bags, passengers patiently waiting by the guardrail as the driver looked under the hood.

Nora followed her driver's instructions, and looked where she was instructed, so she would not see again what she saw one day on her way into work, the day before she negotiated this strategy with her driver. She wouldn't see the thief caught by the irate crowd, caught by people who knew Lagos police were too busy collecting bribes and protecting important people to worry about the thieves who steal from the poor. The crowd had stacked automobile tires around the thief's body and set the tires on fire. Nora arrived just as the fire was dying, the remains of the thief clearly visible in the stack of tires still smoldering directly in front of the international oil company where she worked.

Nora had retreated further into her shell, spending most evenings reading paperbacks and watching her impressive DVD collection. She needed company. I was tired of living alone. We decided on a six-month trial, and I hung the ever-tranquil *Peace Lady* in an upstairs bedroom.

It was peaceful at Nora's. I was not sharing a bedroom with Barbie and her pals. There was no danger of being tossed out on the street. With the threat of firing, eviction, arrest, and princess costumes removed, I experienced my first extended period of peace since moving to Lagos.

Shortly after moving into Nora's, Emeka announced he was going to leave me. I no longer really needed a driver and he wanted to start his own business. I wished him well. I would miss his frantic energy and stream of insights into all things Nigerian. But I knew he would never be content as a driver and I was learning to drive around Lagos myself. I wasn't going anywhere fast, but I was in the driver's seat. He handed me the well-worn Toyota key and Lucy and I watched him leave, the large compound doors closing noisily behind his skinny frame.

Nora adopted a second Persian cat; this one had been rescued after a group of drunken Norwegian oil workers attempted to give him swimming lessons in the pool. After he failed the class and was fished out in the nick of time, they decided to give him a haircut. He was rescued a second time and brought to Nora's because someone knew she already had a Persian. The beleaguered animal arrived with bloody scissor nicks and a choppy coif, but he surveyed Nora's house as if he were conducting an inspection and was uncertain whether we would meet his exacting standards. Apparently, we did.

After observing his imperious manner and nonchalant grace, we decided to name the cat Azu. Azu (the cat) and Bernie soon became inseparable, a pair of sleepy lions slowly prowling around the flat. Lucy raced in circles around the two magnificent Persians, trying to rouse them from their languor like a feisty personal trainer. She was largely unsuccessful. The Persians, recovered from their traumas, spent their days eating cat food imported from Austria and basking in Nora's kind attention until they became substantial creatures covered with long, flowing coats. Lucy remained the same scrappy five-pound spitfire she had been the day I adopted her.

I continued to work with Ismail and mind our tippers, but they now required less attention. I bought another work by the artist who had made my *Peace Lady*. It was called *The Women* and depicted a long line of female faces with the moon on either end. I found, for the first time in my life, I was making a number of female friends. I joined a book group and met a lively and opinionated group of women who hotly debated the merits of a new book every week. Originally formed as a means for wives of foreign diplomats to meet educated Nigerian women, the club had morphed over its fifty-year history into a diverse group of British, American, European, and Nigerian women—some trailing spouses, some professionals, some entrepreneurs—who gathered every week to discuss books about Africa and books written by African authors. We rarely agreed on anything but had a wonderful time disagreeing.

Through Azu (who seemed to have a gift for meeting every unmarried expat woman in Lagos immediately upon her arrival) I met Angel—another redhead like Nora. Angel was a beautiful and wickedly funny French journalist originally from Australia. Azu and Angel had an extended affair with predictable results. Like me, she remained friends with him after he moved onto the next (we both agreed) completely inappropriate conquest. Angel and I became fast friends. While European foreign journalists were not paid a great deal, Angel had worked all over the continent and had friends from virtually every country. She received regular deliveries of French champagne and endlessly interesting dinner guests from countries around the world.

Now, instead of simply housing her collection of DVDs and well-worn paperbacks, Nora's house became a meeting place for parties and nights of conversation with Angel's large and varied circle of friends, with members of the book club, with artists and art collectors we met through Azu and the foundation. We hired the amazing Ghanaian cook, Celina, who had been baking wontons for my Israeli rescuer on the night of my threatened arrest. The always-funny and ever-chic Celina would commandeer our kitchen for an evening: grilled fish, apple strudel, and, of course, her famous wontons would emerge, bottles of wine would be consumed. We'd talk till all hours with people from around the globe, then stay up laughing a bit longer as we helped Celina clean up the kitchen. Nora's horrific visions from her car window began to recede.

And as the weeks passed, I found myself caring less and less about business and becoming more and more honest about what was now most important. I was not pursuing Great Nigerian Opportunities. I was healing. I was learning. I was not going to be rushed. There, in the peace of Nora's house, the time had come to make healing my full-time job.

Nora and I decided we would take a week's vacation to São Tomé e Príncipe, the second-smallest country in Africa: just a sprinkling of volcanic islands lying along the equator off the west coast of Africa. A new flight service had just been started and each day a single small plane departed from Lagos, returning passengers a week later. A neighbor minded Lucy, Bernie, and Azu (the cat) while Nora and I arranged with a new ecotourism outfit to spend the week — the first two days climbing the mountain in the center of São Tomé. The mountain was a very tough climb. For much of it, the grade was so steep we had to grab onto saplings and tree roots for leverage.

"How're you doing, Nora?" I inquired nervously as Nora lay panting on her belly on the nearly vertical incline.

"Oh, fine!" Nora said, snapping a photo of a tiny jungle plant from her position prostrate on the jungle floor. While I was still running six days a week in Lagos, Nora was not very physically active, and this was a far harder climb than either of us had anticipated. Used to parks in the U.S. that labeled hikes "challenging," when they were not, I had paid little attention to the warnings that this was a "challenging" climb. While I struggled, I worried it might be more than Nora could manage. Every time she was near collapse, Nora took out her camera and captured whatever was in her line of sight until she was able to continue climbing. By the end of the day she had taken hundreds of photos from her unusual vantage point.

We made it just short of the summit well after dark and camped on one of the few places level enough to pitch a tent. The next morning, we climbed the final few hundred yards and then stood at the top surveying the ocean in all directions.

"Beautiful!" exclaimed Nora, snapping yet another photo (one of the few taken from a standing position). She had not complained the entire way up.

To recuperate, we had planned to spend a few days on the beach in a cabaña. But when we arrived at the resort, we found there had been a breakdown in communication since last year's hurricane. The cabañas, we were told in broken English, were in ruins.

"You cannot stay," the staff insisted.

Nora and I conferred. We had a tent and sleeping bags. We only needed food and water to "manage," as they say in Nigeria. I began to negotiate in my poor Spanish with the Portuguese-speaking staff. A few minutes later, a Jeep was taking us down the long, rutted road to the place where the resort had been. We came to a clearing and saw a breathtaking beach and little huts ripped to bits by the hurricane. The Jeep dropped us off and disappeared into the jungle. One of the huts still had two beds and a roof, so we rolled our sleeping bags out and listened to the ocean as the sky grew dark.

"I wonder if they will remember we're here," Nora worried.

"I'm sure they will," I said to Nora.

I hope they will, I thought to myself.

But we were tired from the climb, and tired from life in Lagos. Nora fell asleep almost immediately. I listened to her breathing and the night sounds of birds in the trees, the waves on the shore, the palm fronds overhead. The utter quiet was so different from Lagos.

• • • • •

I woke to the sound of a tiny engine in the distance.

It was eight o'clock and I heard the engine winding its way over the badly rutted road. I jumped out of my sleeping bag and pulled on some shorts. A few moments later, a little motorbike came into view. The man driving it waved when he saw me, parked the bike, and removed the large wicker basket he had strapped to the back. In it was fruit, freshly baked bread, four hard-boiled eggs, and a thermos of coffee. He deposited the basket on a picnic table, waved again, and disappeared.

"Do you suppose he'll come back?" Nora wondered aloud as she peeled an egg and listened to the little motorbike retreat into the jungle.

After breakfast, we wandered along the beach until we came to a protected pool bordered by a wooded peninsula and sheltered from the waves. We stripped off our clothes and waded into the warm salty water. At precisely twelve o'clock we heard our friend coming down the road. He quickly located us. Nora threw on some clothes and retrieved another basket. This one contained a salad and cheese, more bread, and a bottle of wine, all neatly wrapped in a white linen cloth.

"I think this is going to work out," Nora declared as she worked the cork out of the bottle.

For the rest of the week, we swam and ate and drank bottles of nice Portuguese wine. Nora got a sunburn. As the week came to an end, I knew we were both, in our own way, a bit stronger, a bit better able to face whatever lay ahead. Sitting on the equator, life pared down to its essentials, these quiet days were a necessary balm for the occasional violence Lagos delivered.

"Thank you, Nora," I said, "thank you for everything."

BLUE YARN

In the accumulation of emails waiting for me when I returned, I learned my ex-husband had married Azi. I sent him a note wishing them well. He replied, saying he would no longer be in communication with me. Our nonnegotiable friendship had apparently been renegotiated. Even with all the losses that had proceeded it, the loss of his friendship was surprisingly painful.

There is nothing original you can say about healing a broken heart.

As I read the latest curt correspondence from this man I had loved so hard for so long, I felt like the survivor of an earthquake. The first shock does the most damage because it is so unexpected. Everything that can break comes crashing to the ground and shatters in an instant. But after the first wave passes, there is another, and then another, and these aftershocks are often stronger and more prolonged than the first wave. Even after there was nothing left to break, the aftershocks still came. They continued until hugging the earth became a way of life.

Finally, I accepted the inevitability of more aftershocks. I realized I would survive the next tremor and the one after that. I also realized I wanted to take something from all the destruction. I wanted to sift through the detritus that had once been my life. I wanted to take more time than was perhaps absolutely necessary because I did not want to overlook anything. Some part of me believed there might be treasure buried in the remains of my former life, and I wanted to claim whatever belonged to me. Maybe it would provide fare for the next journey.

And so, while I no longer longed for my lost marriage with its long silences and deep depressions, I was still troubled. The question that continued to trouble me was whether I had ever been loved at all.

Always and until the very end he had said he loved me. Then, suddenly, he had not. What happened? Where had the love gone? It seemed terribly important to know if my entire adult life had been some sort of delusion, if I had been living a lie from the start. Now, with no chance to learn anything more from him, the only clues I had were the letters he had written to me, and I to him, when we were courting.

I decided I would untie the heavy blue yarn that still tied them together and read them. But more than that, I had a plan for my healing — a plan that, in the absence of any reasons that made sense, seemed as if it might provide the closure I longed for. I would transcribe the letters. I would read and type those words — all of them — to see if I could find the love I had believed in for more than twenty years. I would sift through the rubble and see if I could find something of use.

I told no one but Nora what I was doing. It was a big project. He had written dozens of letters to me, tens of thousands of words written on yellow legal paper, stationery, and brown paper bags. Based in large part on these words, I had given my heart and more than half my life to this man. I typed all day every day for more than a week. I cried. I kept on typing. I read the frantic, slanted writing, the whimsical return addresses on homemade envelopes, his passionate stream-of-consciousness letters. I read pages and pages of love and laughter and longing and loneliness.

Nora would return home from work and I would cry into her T-shirt and wonder if what I was doing was even healthy. I felt all the emotions anew. I remembered it all. The next morning, I poured myself a cup of coffee and started typing again. Transcribing those words allowed me to own them. Like my love, those words belonged to me. They had been written to me. When I was through, I read them all from start to finish. With more than two decades' perspective, I read the letters he had written. I saw clearly for the first time he was not a happy young man; he had never been. But he had loved me.

Then I started again. This time I typed my letters. This took a bit less time; it was easier to read my own quarter-of-a-century-old handwriting than his. I laughed at my own jokes. I cried for the girl who had written them. When Nora came home, I again cried into her T-shirt, but I no longer felt unhinged. I felt I was meeting someone new and wonderful. I was meeting a nineteen-turning-twenty-year-old girl overflowing with love and excitement, ideas and plans. She was funny and endearing (and a little naïve) and I wanted to be her friend. When I was through, I read them all from start to finish. With more than twenty years' perspective, I read the letters I had written. I saw I had always been a happy person and I had loved him deeply.

Then I did the hardest thing: I took all those letters, his and mine, and I put them together in order. Sometimes the sequence was a little off; we were writing so constantly that often a letter would be sent before the previous one was received. But a duet emerged, a song sung by two people in love. I laughed—and I cried again—when I read this combined song. I saw all the love, but I also saw the boy's deep unhappiness, his yearning for something not quite seen or understood, his hope this love would provide a happiness that seemed always just out of reach. I read the girl's responses. She was nearly always happy. She read all his sad words and saw them as proof of how much he loved her. She believed him when he said she would make him happy. She believed it because she was so happy, simply loving him.

A contract was made. The unspoken contract said she would save him from his unhappiness and, in exchange, he would love her forever. They both succeeded for a while. In the end, they both failed.

Again and again, I had wondered what it was that made him stop loving me. I wondered whether I had changed. I had not become needy or unattractive or dull. I had accepted him and all that he was in sickness and in health. I never spoke ill of him to anyone. I never stopped believing in his potential. I loved him and believed in him every day for more than twenty years.

But perhaps I *had* changed.

There was a slow shift in our relationship as he sank into depression and I tried to save him from his own black moods. I assumed too much of his life as my responsibility. I deprived him of the opportunity to care for me, to nurture me, to love me. In response to the lack of caring, the lack of nurturing, and ultimately the lack of love, I became someone who imagined she could do without all three.

And I did.

And as I became more and more self-supporting, he must have known I no longer expected his emotional support. I saw him as integral to my life—yet I required nothing of him. There was no give-and-take. Ultimately our relationship atrophied and died from lack of use.

The project took almost three weeks to finish. I was exhausted but, at last, I had something resembling an answer. In the absence of any kind of explanation, any plausible story, or any truth-telling, I had found a way to reconcile my loss and find a story within this blue yarn sufficient for my healing, sufficient to move on. Because, in those letters, I saw we had both found what we were looking for nearly twenty-five years ago. While it ultimately had not lasted, it was not an illusion and it was not a tragic mistake. There was no power on earth that would have made us see or do things any other way.

●   ●   ●   ●   ●

I am lying here naked, trying very hard to be still. Being still has never been a specialty of mine.

It is almost midnight. I have a ruby-colored champagne flute in my hand that matches exactly the big red bird-of-paradise flowers in the vase positioned directly behind me. There is a lovely shimmery cloth of cerulean blue thrown over a cane chair and I am lying back in it, my eyes half closed. I am listening to the sound of the artist's brush on canvas and a recording of Fela Kuti is playing softly. It is July 12th, the eve of my forty-fifth birthday, and because I am a person who consistently does what I say I will do even if it no longer makes a great deal of sense (a habit I freely acknowledge is more a liability than an asset), I am lying here on this iridescent blue cloth and a simply gigantic nude painting is being made of me by one of the better artists in Nigeria. I am welcoming my new year exactly as planned six months earlier on New Year's Eve.

Angel is hosting the event in her apartment; she has piles of Jollof rice and drink on hand. Nora is here, taking photos and watching the artist work. (Nora paints, in addition to everything else.) Azu has arranged for the artist and materials and is here making sure all goes well. I'm watching them all through half-closed eyes. Angel shoots me a devious smile as she offers the artist a drink, Azu adjusts the lighting while Nora snaps more photos of the artist and of me and, I confess, I'm having a few second thoughts…

But this is not a bad idea, I remind myself, lying in the altogether on Angel's cane chair. Not a bad idea at all.

I didn't tell a lot of people after the New Year's Eve announcement that I planned to be painted in the nude. One of the women I told said, "Well, yes, it makes sense, as you certainly won't look any better as the years go by."

But that's not what this is about. This is not about winning a fight against aging or capturing a souvenir at a stage in life when I feel good about myself, with or without clothes. No.

I think Nora explained it best as I struggled with some trepidation after having made the arrangements. "Of course you want to be painted in the nude," she assured me. "This was the year you were stripped of your marriage, your career, your country, your future, and most of your identity. The only fitting way to conclude a year like that is with a painting of yourself in the nude!"

Nora is *so* smart.

Because only now did I realize how tied I had been to this blue yarn: this story of depression and longing and fated romance. The story held in the blue yarn had been a beautiful one; I was not going to replace it with anything less exciting, fulfilling, passionate, or lovely. I was not going to allow fear to force me to accept a new story that was anything less than magnificent. I was not going to allow expectations of who or what I was at middle-age to play any significant or limiting role in who I would decide to become. Now, at the end of the yarn, I wanted to honor its importance to my past by harboring no anger, carrying no hurt, refusing to be damaged by its loss. I would only be strengthened by the knowledge that, yes, I had loved and been loved and the experience had made me the woman I was today.

Now it was time to make a new story for myself, time to refill my reservoir with new adventures and experiences. It was incumbent upon me to take the limited time I had left and celebrate by living my life to the hilt. I would not be someone whose life was always in the shadow of my divorce. I would not be damaged or cynical. I would not live a life that was staid or circumspect. I had not spent all this time painfully releasing the person I had been only to embrace caution and prudence and the status quo.

If losing my marriage and the love of my life meant redefining myself in the most fundamental way, then that definition was not going to be one in common usage, I would define myself anew, I would coin a new meaning for myself entirely. I now understood what Lagos had been offering when I first decided to stay after everything fell apart. Lagos was a wonderful absence of everything I had been, everything I thought mattered, everything I assumed I would need and want to survive. Because I had been given this amazing freedom from all those expectations, I had truly been set free to be myself.

As I lay naked, surrounded by friends, I had no idea who this new girl was. I had only a glimpse then of who she might turn out to be. But the fundamental obstacles to her becoming whomever she needed to be had been removed. I was truly naked. I was truly free.

And now it is midnight and my birthday. I leave my post on the cane chair and throw on a gold robe Shirene brought from Dubai. I raise the bright red glass Angel has filled with French champagne and greet my new year looking into the smiling eyes of my new friends. I'm saying goodbye to the old year: an ill-natured, unreliable, bad-tempered year. I'm toasting my new year — an uncertain future, but a better year for certain.

174

PART THREE

SAILING TO MOMBASA

I didn't really know I was traveling until I had packed.

It was another late night with Nora and Angel skinny-dipping in the apartment compound pool. The oil worker neighbors were all safely in bed and the three of us were floating under the watery Lagos moon. Six breasts bobbed to the surface, four of them considerably more substantial than mine. We floated silently for a time.

"I need to go somewhere," I blurted out.

"Where?" asked Angel, swimming to the edge of the pool to retrieve her glass of chardonnay.

"I have no idea. I just need to go. I got hiking boots for Christmas. I bought a new pack. I need to go... somewhere... soon."

Angel rested on her elbows at the edge of the pool and looked at me severely in the way she did when she was about to make a pronouncement. (Angel's pronouncements were always worth the wait.) She took a sip of chardonnay.

"I think you should go," she said.

Then Angel and Nora both dove under the water, resurfacing a few moments later.

"I'll watch Lucy," Nora said as she popped up.

But I had nowhere to go—and no real reason to go anywhere I could put my finger on. I had been living with Nora for more than a year and had passed the stage where I was telling friends, family, or even strangers that I was living in Lagos for any logical reason. The truth was I had been doing almost nothing. Doing nothing, it turned out, was what I had most needed to do. This time had been a precious gift; I was no longer the wounded and fearful woman who had first timidly peered under the bandages to assess the damages to her life, nor the woman who had tried (unsuccessfully) to imagine a new life in a wobbly pile of blocks. I felt whole again. And I was restless. The need for movement was becoming an almost constant pressure. It made no sense, but I knew I needed an adventure, a journey. Since deciding to stay in Lagos, I had increasingly felt the smartest decisions in my life were not made by careful adherence to a plan—or even as a response to rational thought. More and more I was convinced the best decisions often appeared freewheeling and irrational. Now I knew—for whatever reason—it was time to move.

Two days later, I was taking my usual run at sunset. The long, sunny days of the dry season had forced the bougainvillea to burst into bloom again. I watched as my feet landed on the piles of faded fuchsia petals. Ali, my leper friend, was sitting in his usual spot on his neatly folded mat of cardboard boxes. He smiled when he saw me, and I carefully placed a hundred-*naira* note between his fingerless upraised hands. I ran by the cobbler carrying his battered wooden box of shoe-repair tools. I said hello to the woman who sells oranges, the sweet citrus smell still in the air from the orange peels lying in a neat spiral on the cracked pavement. It was good to be in Lagos, I thought, good to be surrounded by the familiar and living in the comfort of Nora's home after so much upheaval. When I got home I took a warm bath and images of travel began to fade. I decided an early night would do no harm and went straight to bed.

Three hours later, I woke with a start.

"Get packing," She said.

"Pack for what? Pack for where?" This was nonsense, I knew. This was a dream. I fluffed my pillow and started to slip back to sleep.

"Get packing."

Wide awake now, I realized it would be pointless to resist. Maybe it was a hallucination. Maybe it was a peculiarly vivid dream. It didn't really matter. The same dead-certain voice had returned and She was telling me I needed to get packing—so I started packing.

I climbed out of bed and turned on a light. Lagos was dark, my window was cracked open, and I heard wind rattle in the palms. Where was I going? When was I leaving? It didn't matter; the important thing was to start deciding what I needed to take along—and to bear in mind I couldn't take much to… wherever I was going.

The more I packed, the more urgent it became. I tried on T-shirts, I tried on pants. Which ones were the lightest? I needed clothes that could be rinsed out at night and ready to wear the next day when I was… wherever I was going. I needed my clothes to match so everything could be worn with everything else. I laid all the candidates out on the bed together, shades of blue and green and brown mixed and blended. Those that clashed were tossed aside.

I packed my tent, my sleeping bag, my battery-powered toothbrush (a person needs at least one luxury) but decided I could get along with only three pair of underwear. I packed a water purifier, a fork, and a plate, but no pot or cookstove. I would have to find cooked food along the way—wherever that was. Did I want long underwear? It might be good to have them just in case there was a cold snap wherever I was going.

At last, I was through. I had packed all the clothes I needed for whatever journey it now appeared I was about to take. I decided I needed one more long skirt and headscarf in case there were Muslims wherever I was going. There are a lot of Muslims in a lot of places, so this seemed likely. I decided to have Nora's tailor sew a long skirt with a matching scarf if there was still time before I left—whenever that was.

Fully packed, I surveyed the small pile of matching clothes and camping gear tucked into my backpack. I poured myself a glass of wine and took it out to the pool. Floating under the moist Lagos sky, I noticed how much calmer I felt, now that I was packed.

The decision of where to go remained unresolved. In those rare moments when I looked at it objectively, I recognized the problem was that I really did not have much money to travel. Running dump trucks in Lagos had turned out to be a considerably less lucrative business once it was discovered the removal of fill from the sandbars was actually causing the island to erode. The state government had called an abrupt halt to the sand removal, and now Ismail and I watched our trucks sit idle most days. This made going to Europe unlikely.

178

Wherever it was I ended up going, it would have to be cheap. It seemed to me since I was already in Africa, I would likely be traveling in Africa.

I imagined going to Algeria, Tunisia, and Morocco. I would have loved to see them all, but somehow none of them resonated as the place I needed to go with my waiting backpack. As I ran my finger around a map of the gigantic continent, I realized I could spend a lifetime exploring Africa and never see more than a tiny fraction of what there was to see.

My finger rounded the northeastern coast and I saw the Kenyan city of Mombasa. I felt a jolt of recognition. More than fifteen years earlier I had performed in a play set during the Boer War. I didn't remember much about it (the plots of most plays had long since faded from memory), but I remembered the description of the East African coast and the vivid image of sailing a dhow to Mombasa in the moonlight. At the time, I had no idea what a dhow was or where Mombasa was located, but somehow that line — that description — had imprinted itself on my brain.

"Sailing a dhow to Mombasa in the moonlight," I said aloud, and I felt again that peculiar quiet certainty it was the thing I needed to do.

With a little research, I learned dhows are ancient single-sailed Swahili ships, virtually unchanged in a thousand years. When I also learned large seafaring dhows were becoming exceedingly rare, with only a few still leaving from Lamu, on the north coast of Kenya, the matter gained new urgency.

The next Saturday night, I was driving fast over the third mainland bridge with Angel, Azu, and her new friend, One-Eyed Mike, who was visiting from Uganda. (Mike had been given his Nigerian nickname because his eyes were not perfectly matched, much in the same way another friend of ours who was over six-foot-four was dubbed "Too-Short.") Angel's driver was at the wheel. We were passing back and forth a nice bottle of French wine and "You Can't Always Get What You Want" was playing as loudly as the stereo would permit. We were headed to The Shrine, the music venue created in the '70s by Fela Kuti whose son, Femi, was supposed to be playing at ten o'clock.

"But it will never start *that* early," Angel assured us as she passed the wine to the backseat.

When we arrived, the party was just getting started. Open to the night air with huge ceiling fans under a corrugated tin roof, the upper floor was adorned with long yellow-and-orange tie-dyed drapes covered with thirty years of dust, while on the spacious terrazzo ground floor tables and chairs had been set all around. Kitschy oil paintings of musical luminaries from the past hung behind the stage and Christmas lights had been strung up overhead.

A deadly earnest British film crew was there from Al Jazeera, and I got chatting with the director, who told me they were there to record for a six-part series called *Music of the Resistance*.

"Does it matter *what* they are resisting?" I asked the very serious director (as it did not appear to me that the young Kuti was resisting much of anything).

He looked at me sternly and answered, "*Of course it does.*"

Girl singers with their faces painted white and dressed in short skirts and Mardi Gras beads backed up a fifteen-piece band. The air was filled with pot smoke, the dance floor with men in dreadlocks. I bought a whole fish off the grill, which we shared with Jollof rice and Bailey's Irish Cream (which makes for a surprisingly tasty combination). Since One-Eyed Mike was from Uganda, I figured he might know if it was still possible to sail a dhow to Mombasa. So, over fish, I asked him.

"Absolutely!" One-Eyed Mike said. "But have you ever been to Zanzibar? It's close to Mombasa."

"No," I told him. Regrettably, I had not.

"You should go," he said.

And while I didn't know Mike well — and I didn't actually know where Zanzibar was — this seemed like it might be very good advice.

The following Thursday I attended my book group. It was a special meeting to celebrate the birthday of one of our senior members. I was at a buffet table filling my plate when I met a witty young Nigerian woman named Karen. Karen was talking to a Filipino woman who was observing it was a good time to visit the Philippines because airfares were low. The Filipino woman asked me if I was interested in traveling to the Philippines, and I said I planned to travel soon but had not yet decided exactly where.

"I would love that!" Karen said. "To have the time and money to travel and no idea where you will go."

"I'm not sure I actually *do* have the money," I told her, "but I know I can make more money. I'm pretty sure I can't make more time, and I have a feeling I need to go now."

I took my plate and sat next to Pauline, whom I knew casually from both the book group and the Yacht Club. Pauline was Welsh, a tall, elegant woman approaching retirement age. She wore beautiful jewelry and dressed well. Karen sat down beside us and said, "I'm going to remember what you said about not being able to make more time."

I told Pauline I was hoping to travel soon but had never actually traveled alone before. "Really?" said Pauline. "I spent a number of years trekking around the continent."

I was astonished. Pauline was about the last woman in Lagos I would have pegged as a solo backpack traveler, but it turned out that was exactly what she had been until quite recently. She and Karen started to discuss all the countries they had traveled through alone or, in Karen's case, as a young girl tramping across Africa with her European mother. They shared stories about crowded buses, last-minute accommodations, and the kinds of adventures that can only occur when traveling without an itinerary.

"I would never have met so many interesting people if I hadn't been traveling alone," observed Pauline, a quiet smile on her face.

Both women said I needed to trust my instincts, and they talked about how their instincts sharpened when they traveled. "I always have a heightened sense of when danger is near—and who I can trust," Karen said.

These two women, separated by thirty years, were kindred spirits, and yet they had never met before this lunch. It didn't feel like an accident, sitting there between them, but rather the gentle push I needed to pick up my already-packed backpack and leave.

I told them I had not yet decided where exactly I would go, but I wanted to sail a dhow to Mombasa, preferably in the moonlight.

"You know dhows sail only when the wind is favorable," Pauline warned, "and that is for only part of the year."

"When is that?" I inquired anxiously. She didn't remember. I needed to find out.

Back at Nora's, I did a little research and learned the winds for sailing dhows south to Mombasa would be favorable almost immediately. I also learned there was a music festival in Zanzibar in a month's time and I could catch a direct flight from Lagos to Nairobi, Kenya.

It was time.

I had no travel books and shipping anything into Nigeria was extremely slow, exorbitantly expensive, or downright impossible — depending on the item. Nora came to the rescue once again and let me ship a travel guidebook to Vienna and then have it brought into Nigeria by the Austrian consulate. (There are advantages to being the citizen of a small country.)

I had been warned about Nairobi: it was crime-ridden and dangerous, full of hustlers and con men. "But not like Lagos!" Pauline hastened to add. There would be corrupt border control officers, unscrupulous cabdrivers, pickpockets and touts at every bus stop. But everyone agreed that living in Lagos had inadvertently prepared me for the worst in international travel.

In just over a week, my flight from Lagos took off. I was alone — truly alone this time, as Lucy stayed with Nora and the Persians. There was no one waiting for me or expecting me. There was nowhere I had to be, nothing I needed to do. A deep peace settled over me. Flying across the dark continent (now literally very dark), I looked out the airplane window at the big night sky. I closed my eyes and fell asleep, feeling more at home than I had in a long time.

MISSOURI

I landed in Nairobi planning to find a hotel and then figure out how to get to the coast in the morning. But as the taxicab drove from the airport to the budget hotel district, we passed the bus station.

"Where are the buses going?" I asked.

"Everywhere — to the coast, mostly," the driver answered.

"Let me out."

Why spend a night in Nairobi if I could be on the road immediately? I paid the driver and hopped out of the cab. It was nearing midnight and a queue of buses were waiting on the curb. Nairobi was older, more compact, and much cleaner than Lagos. The streetlights were dim and it was raining lightly, so I ducked into one of the waiting buses and asked a driver how to get to Lamu. He told me I'd have to go to Mombasa first and then catch another bus north to Mokowe. So, I jumped aboard a bus headed to Mombasa, stashed my backpack overhead and, almost immediately, we were off. I dozed intermittently and, before I knew it, arrived in Mombasa early in the morning. There, I boarded another seemingly preordained vehicle and headed straight to Mokowe, the jump-off point to get to the island of Lamu — my last, best chance to sail a dhow.

The roads to Mokowe were impossibly bumpy and we were crammed in until every seat was full, side by side, elbow to elbow. But it was a beautiful day and the windows were open to let in the sounds and smells of the countryside. We drove by nomadic communities on the way, moveable houses made of long grass that looked like giant tea cozies, and we occasionally stopped to pick up more freight, drop off passengers, and buy things sold to us through the windows. I bought a bunch of small sweet bananas and some mysterious homemade candy called "Simpsons." No one seemed to know what they were; I later learned they were made from ground sesame seeds and sugar. They were delicious.

When we arrived in Mokowe, I hopped aboard an open-water taxi overloaded with about twenty other passengers and a variety of freight. I sat on a large roll of cowhide in front and thought I was clever, getting a seat on the bow where it was cool and not so crowded, until the boat got up to speed and I was soaked by the splashing waves. The other passengers glanced at me and then quickly away, trying not to smile.

Twenty minutes later, I was met on the dock of Lamu by the expected gang of touts and hawkers trying to lure me to various hotels. I told the hawkers I already had accommodations (which was a lie), then quickly settled into an open-air restaurant to get my bearings. While seated in the restaurant, I was approached by a very polite and nearly toothless gentleman with a bright yellow *kufi* perched on his head who politely introduced himself as Farouk. Farouk told me he could find me accommodations at a fair price. I liked his laid-back and self-assured demeanor, so after a dinner of curried vegetables and fish, I commenced a reconnaissance of Lamu with the assistance of my new guide. I had no idea what accommodations should cost or what to expect. Little and simple was the answer.

With Farouk's assistance, I found a lovely room for less than ten dollars a night, breakfast included. Then Farouk and I scouted out the liquor store (surprisingly easy to find in this Muslim town: it was located inside the police compound). On the way to the police station, I explained to Farouk my desire to take a seafaring dhow.

"Is it still possible?" I asked, knowing Farouk was the first person I had asked who might reasonably know the answer. I watched his wrinkled face and waited for an answer.

"Yes. Yes, I think so," Farouk said. I could tell he was searching his memory bank for dhow information and I didn't press him further. We agreed he would meet me the next afternoon.

On the way back from the police station/liquor store, I headed to my hotel through the labyrinth of close-walled alleyways. The entire city of Lamu is a World Heritage Site, an ancient place where Arab and Swahili traders met and mingled hundreds of years ago. The walls date from the 1600s and are made of coral covered in lime. The buildings are pressed closely together and entered through ornately carved wooden doors. Behind the doors are open courtyards and rooftop terraces at the top of several flights of winding stairs. Donkeys are protected on the island of Lamu and wander freely throughout the narrow streets. No private cars or trucks are allowed. There are only three vehicles on the whole island: a small tractor to pick up the trash in the mornings, a four-wheel-drive pickup used to transport injured donkeys to the veterinary clinic, and a three-wheeled ambulance used to transport injured people, though the ambulance often doubled as a taxicab (which seemed to me a reasonable concession).

Tacked to one ornate door was a hand-lettered sign pointing up a narrow stairway to an Internet café. There were no lights in the alley, but with the aid of my wind-up flashlight, I climbed the dark stairs to find a tiny, dim café with three computers. I decided I would let my family know I had arrived and sat down in front of one of the geriatric monitors. Preoccupied while waiting for my email to load, I didn't notice when I was joined by another customer and so I was startled when I looked up to see a Masai warrior dressed in traditional attire sitting beside me.

Head shaved with neat scars down his cheeks and elongated earlobes, he was tall and slim, wearing the traditional bright red tunic with lots of colorful beaded bracelets on his wrists and ankles and large ornate necklaces and earrings. Apparently nomadic life does not breed patience, as he was visibly annoyed with the slow Internet connection. I couldn't imagine what he was doing here on an island so far from cattle. I never thought of a Masai warrior on vacation (or on a business trip, for that matter), but there he was, muttering under his breath as his website failed to load. Eventually, we both got to our respective email inboxes. I wrote a short note to my family to assure them of my continued survival, and perhaps he did the same. Then I headed back through the twisting alleys to my hotel directly on the seashore.

My room was on the top floor of the three-story hotel and I threw open the carved wooden shutters to catch the breeze. I could see the outlines of small fishing dhows with their sails down, bobbing just offshore. I was tired; while sleeping is one of my few really notable skills, even I couldn't sleep properly on a bus that hit every pothole from Nairobi to Mokowe. The bed in my breezy room was firm, the sheets were clean, the waves were loud outside my open window. I knew I was exactly where I was supposed to be.

• • • • •

Here's my advice if you don't speak Swahili: when someone yells "Jambo!" at you, yell "Missouri!" right back at them and smile. Something that sounds very much like "Missouri" roughly translates to "Great! Fine! Terrific!" Say it with a big smile and you'll have it made. (Do not expect the same results if you get confused and yell "Wisconsin!")

Here's my advice if you want to meet a Masai warrior: don't bother with the expensive safari in the Range Rover and the fancy khaki ensemble. Go to the beach.

It turns out the Masai are an extremely adaptable bunch. It's getting harder and harder to make a living off cattle, with Kenya insisting some land is private and some cows belong to people other than the Masai. The Masai take a dim view of land ownership and scoff at the idea cows can belong to any one person. They take superb care of their cattle and rarely kill them, but they eat the curdled milk and drink their blood without doing the cow any lasting harm.

Nowadays, however, things are getting tight and the Masai prefer not to assimilate if they can help it. They've never cared much for European customs since they first encountered them and have never been shy about saying so, calling the trouser-wearing newcomers a name that translates to "those who confine their farts" (which isn't very nice in any language).

Now, instead of waiting around for the tourists to come and buy their beadwork, they were going to the beach. I had a nice conversation with a Masai named Joshua. He was walking down the beach in full red-robed regalia, jingling with beads like a human retail kiosk. I told him I was surprised to find him here, on an island beach far from cattle of any kind. He told me he was here on business (which was also the case with the Masai in the Internet café, I presume). He was visiting Lamu with his brother Solomon, whom I later met in town. This was good business for them, he explained. They travel to Lamu with a load of jewelry, sell some to the shops and some right off their bodies on the beach. When the jewelry runs out after about a month, they head back to their village and back to herding cows.

"We bought seven cows after our last trip to Lamu!" Joshua boasted.

Joshua was tall and slim. He had wonderful sandals made from motorcycle tires, extremely long earlobes, and a thoroughly disarming smile. The Kenya Airlines website said, of all Kenya's varied tribes, "the Maasai are the cutest." I thought this was a rather disparaging description of the Masai warrior I had featured in my imagination. But after meeting Joshua and his fellow cattlemen-turned-entrepreneurs, I had to admit this was probably accurate. I'd seen a lot of jewelry hawked on a lot of beaches, but never with the easy charm and elegant nonchalance of Joshua and Solomon. The Masai in Lamu were all young men: outgoing, well dressed, polite, personable, and traveling in pairs. They reminded me of Mormon missionaries, spreading the Masai brand—without all the proselytizing.

One final piece of advice: if you come to Lamu, under no circumstances accept a dinner invitation from a stout older gentleman with a scruffy white beard named "Ali Hippie."

My second day in Lamu, three other couples and I were seduced by Ali's offer of a home-cooked meal followed by live entertainment. He was recommended by *The Lonely Planet*, he assured us and had been doing this for thirty years. Ali Hippie had assembled a group of seven visitors to Lamu, and we all followed him into town and down a dark, narrow alleyway until we arrived at an ancient, elaborately carved wooden door. Inside was a completely bare lime-walled room with bright green linoleum covering half the floor. Shoes were removed at the demarcation of the linoleum. There was not a piece of furniture, not a pillow, not a picture on the peeling white walls. The room was airless and hot. The only thing in the room other than Ali and the seven of us was Ali's electronic keyboard sitting on the floor. I had a bottle of wine in my backpack that I had bought at the police station and, with Ali's blessing, I opened the wine and we split it seven ways as the food began to arrive. The first dish was purportedly crab samosas, but I had a bad feeling about that crab from the moment I tasted it.

We then had grilled red snapper we ate with our fingers while seated on the linoleum, followed by rice and beans and then for dessert a sweet that was not a Simpson, like I had on the bus, but a close cousin. Then Ali fired up his keyboard and sang traditional folk songs. His son drummed on some plastic jugs, his daughter sang harmony in English, and his eight-year-old granddaughter sang along in Swahili. Everyone had a fine time, and between songs, Ali told us about the good old days when Lamu was full of hippies.

"Oh, I liked those hippies," Ali reminisced. "They didn't have plans or tight schedules. Sometimes they stayed in Lamu for months—sometimes a whole year!"

The evening broke up, I got out my trusty flashlight (a woman with a bottle of wine and a wind-up flashlight is a highly-valued companion), and we all headed back to our respective hotels. Then two o'clock arrived and... I will spare you the details. The next afternoon, when I was finally ambulatory again, I made inquiries and discovered I was not Ali's first victim. The writer of *The Lonely Planet* either got lucky that night or had a cast-iron stomach because, apparently, Ali had been poisoning tourists from all over the globe for years.

Meanwhile, my guide Farouk had not been idle.

There was a rumored dhow arriving that night loaded with mangrove poles and headed to Mombasa in the morning. Farouk and I hustled down to the port authority, a cluttered, dusty office run by yet another cheerful and dentally challenged man. The boat appeared to be a well-substantiated rumor.

"Yes, I would be happy to take the American lady along," said the captain, another Ali, when, after a lengthy search, we located him on the pier. For sixteen dollars he said he would take me; fresh fruit and grilled fish were included in the price. I paid him 100 shillings (about $1.25) as a deposit for my trip.

On the walk back to my hotel, Farouk assured me, "The captain is a reliable man." (I wish I'd asked him about Ali Hippie.) Farouk promised to meet me at my hotel the following afternoon to firm up the deal.

Before retiring to my hotel, I chatted with the group of old men who sat on the pier all day drinking tea and watching the boats come and go. One of them, Mr. Abbas, generously offered to find me a husband in Lamu. I told him that was a very kind offer, but I was hoping to find a dhow and sail to Mombasa. Mr. Abbas frowned. He seemed to feel my chances of finding a husband were better than finding a large seagoing dhow. Even with all the potholes, he told me, hauling mangrove poles on the road to Mombasa was much faster than taking them by dhow, what with unpredictable weather and tricky winds.

"All the dhows have been replaced by trucks," he added wistfully.

But I was undeterred. Just as I had known, without forethought or examination, I should stay in Lagos, I knew my desire to sail a dhow to Mombasa was now more than a whim, but somehow important to the person I was becoming. In the absence of a plan, I had put my trust in the enterprising Farouk. It felt like the smartest decision I could make.

THE REAL FULL MOON

Farouk did not arrive at my hotel at his appointed hour. He had always been on time, even early. I asked Boniface for another cup of coffee and waited for fifteen minutes, then thirty. Boniface was a cheerful, round-faced young man who worked at the hotel. He made breakfast for me in the morning, did the laundry, made coffee for me in the afternoon, and was endlessly curious about why I was not married.

"Have you seen Farouk?" I asked Boniface when he brought the coffee. No Farouk.

I finished my coffee and walked to Farouk's house, a tiny cottage made of coral stone directly on the seafront. His wife shook her head. She spoke no English, but it was clear she didn't know where he was. I walked farther down the pier until I came to a Rasta couple named Countryman and Zawadi (which means "gift" in Swahili). Every day they set up a lopsided table on the sidewalk to sell the Rasta caps Zawadi made and an assortment of used books in English and German. They called it their "office." Whenever I came by they said, "Hey, step into the office!" and I usually did.

"Have you seen Farouk?" I asked Zawadi, who was crocheting a green, yellow, and red cap.

"No, Carrie, sorry. No Farouk."

I walked farther down to the pier, hoping I would see Farouk on the way. I made it all the way to the end of the waterfront. No Farouk. No Captain Ali. Mr. Abbas was in his usual spot, drinking sweet tea with his cronies on the pier.

"Mr. Abbas, have you seen Farouk?"

"No, ma'am, no Farouk."

"How about Captain Ali?"

"Ali who?"

I suddenly felt foolish. At least every other man in Lamu was named Ali. No one knew a Captain Ali taking mangrove poles to Mombasa. No one had seen Farouk. The underpinnings of my plan seemed more than a little frail.

As I walked back to my hotel, it was starting to get dark. I wondered if there had ever been a boat. I felt very alone. Then I saw a familiar yellow *kufi* on a briskly bobbing head walking toward me.

"Carrie!" It was Farouk. He told me he had been going back and forth to the pier waiting for word from Captain Ali.

"Let's go visit his wife," he suggested, and we walked quickly back to the end of the waterfront.

When I walked alone, all the Rastamen called out, "No hurry in Lamu!" — but I had to hustle to keep pace with the nimble Farouk. We rounded the corner and headed into a low warren of small stone houses at the far end of town, then knocked on an unadorned wooden door. A very pregnant woman answered. She opened the door and we took off our sandals and sat on a wood-frame cot. She and Farouk spoke in Swahili while I teased her young son, who pretended to be shy.

I heard "dhow" and "Ali" and "Mombasa" and not much else I understood. Apparently, the boat was not loaded and had not left the village for Lamu yet. We thanked Ali's wife and started back. Farouk explained if they came in too late, they would not leave the next morning. We would wait until ten o'clock that night. If they were not in by then, the trip would not happen until the following day.

I walked back to my hotel and met Ali Hippie, who smiled broadly and called out, "Hullo, mummy!" as he always did whenever he saw me. I ignored him. He knew I was annoyed with him for my night of food-borne illness. In the interest of public safety (and a bit out of spite) I had not remained quiet about it. I told Mr. Abbas and his tea-drinking colleagues the morning after I recovered that I had been poisoned by Ali Hippie.

"You are not the first," Mr. Abbas replied, shaking his head.

But some good did come of the evening with Ali Hippie because it was then I met Katie and Tom. They were young college graduates from Ottawa who had been traveling for three months and planned to travel another three before returning to Canada. Katie's dad (a lawyer-turned-organic farmer) told them, since there were no jobs in Canada, they might as well travel. They were on a very limited budget and Katie was watching every shilling while having a fine time. Tom was tall and quiet. Katie was pretty and outgoing; she had crazy curly hair and always looked a little surprised.

Katie and Tom had spent Christmas in Egypt. Katie told me breathlessly how they fell prey to a complicated and diabolical scam that began by giving a ride to a phony schoolteacher with broken eyeglasses and culminated in an exorbitantly priced camel ride to the pyramids. I was not able to catch all the details, but I believed her when she concluded breathlessly, "It was awful!" shaking her curls ruefully.

They then traveled throughout Ethiopia with a professional party clown named Steve from California, whom they met on the way. The clowning business was in a slump, apparently, and so Steve decided to visit Ethiopia. Now they were taking their time in Kenya with plans to go to Uganda, Tanzania, and possibly Malawi, which Katie said (with a surprised look) "is supposed to be really *nice!*"

I told Katie and Tom the latest on my search for a dhow.

"Oh, it would be too bad if you left before the dhow race!" Katie said, wrinkling up her forehead in sudden concern.

I knew about the dhow race, of course. All over town sailors had been repairing their sails, putting extensions on their masts, and adding long planks to the dhows to serve as counterbalances. The young men racing dhows stood far out over the water on wooden planks in an effort to keep the small boats upright and to travel faster, even as the dhow itself tilted farther and farther in the other direction from the force of the oversized sail.

A mysterious race sponsor, either British or French (reports differed), was offering a prize of 20,000 shillings (about $250) to the winner. There was going to be a big party with food and music on the nearby island of Manda. I began to wish for a day's delay to see the race. A few hours later, my wish was granted. The dhow had not arrived, Farouk reported dejectedly. We asked him if he could find us transportation to see the race and he arranged for a small dhow to take Katie, Tom, and me over to Manda the following day.

The next morning, we sailed across to the island of Manda. The dhow left us at the shore and it appeared we were early. There was no group assembled, so we headed to a low house built of raffia surrounded by balboa trees and found we had stumbled into the sponsor's house. The sponsor, David, was an older man with curiously bright, wild-looking blue eyes. He was seated in a cottage made entirely of woven raffia on a bamboo couch. The only other guests were an affluent-looking couple from France. Fortunately, Tom and Katie (being good Canadians) spoke French.

Katie immediately hit it off with the retired French couple who told her about the tragic death of their daughter, who had been Katie's age, and in the course of their short conversation, Katie was invited to come and stay with them in Nice to study French. (Katie told me the French were always delighted when they heard of Canadians seeking to improve their colloquial French.) The French couple spoke almost no English and David's speech was so deeply slurred I couldn't determine his nationality.

Soon we were joined by a seemingly endless queue of people coming to pay their respects. They dropped to their knees and spoke to David, inches from his face, and he seemed delighted to see everyone. The chiefs of both Lamu and nearby Shela arrived and we were introduced. They sat beside me on the couch and I complimented them both on the admirable job they were doing to promote tourism.

"I have a half acre of land in Shela you might like to see," the chief of Shela said, inching toward me on the rattan sofa. I was flattered that I was already being courted as a new resident.

Then it was time for lunch and it appeared we were David's guests. A head table had been set up behind the raffia house and we were seated with David, the chiefs, the French couple, and a few others we hadn't met. In front of the head table, a number of large raffia mats were spread on the sand under the balboa trees. Several of the largest cooking pots I had ever seen appeared (Katie and I could easily have both fit in one), and I was told they had killed three cows and two goats for this party. There were platters of fish fillets covered in tamarind, coriander, cardamom, and garlic. The raffia mats soon filled up with a mass of people seated closely together. We were served first at the head table and lunch was delicious.

After eating, the boat captains all assembled with David and the chiefs. When given the signal, they raced to the boats and sailed off en masse. It was a magnificent turnout: eighteen dhows set off together. Each boat was loaded with approximately ten sailors, some to pull the ropes and some ready to scurry on and off the cantilevered plank to keep the boat upright. Eighteen tall white sails aligned themselves in the wind; eighteen huge triangular sails spread taut under the sun.

The course was a clockwise circuit, twice around, with buoys on either end. Everyone sat under the trees drinking passionfruit juice and beer and cheering on their favorite dhow. When the winning boat came in, David congratulated the winner in Swahili. I've no idea if David's Swahili was any more intelligible than his English (or French), but when the winner was announced everyone cheered. Then Brazilian music was turned up to top volume and everyone boarded their boats to go home. Katie and Tom and I reluctantly boarded a dhow and headed back to Lamu in the late afternoon.

When I returned to my hotel, Farouk was waiting with more news: the mast had broken.

Farouk had walked all the way to the village several miles away where the dhow was being loaded to see it with his own eyes. When the dhow was half loaded, the tall mast had broken and now had to be replaced. Captain Ali was very sorry and had returned, by way of Farouk, the 100 shillings I had given him as a down payment for my ride.

"When will the mast be replaced?" I asked Farouk.

"Three days," he told me. Captain Ali said the dhow would leave on Wednesday. There was a fishing boat going to Malindi (about halfway to Mombasa) if I could not wait.

I received this news while standing with Countryman and Zawadi in their sidewalk office. This broken mast was not good news. In Africa,

Wednesday might just as well mean Friday. I had hoped to be in Zanzibar before the music festival was over. We were standing under a nearly full moon, discouraged by Farouk's news. I thought how nice it would be to sail a dhow under the full moon.

"When will the moon be full?" I asked Zawadi.

"Tomorrow," she said. "Tomorrow is the full moon party; do you want to come? There will be a celebration up in the hills," she added. "There is always a party with drumming and music when the moon is full."

"Yes," I said, "I would like to come." (Who could say no to a party under the full moon?)

I was waiting for my dhow, but now I began to wonder if perhaps my dhow wasn't waiting for me.

•   •   •   •   •

The next evening, Tom and Katie and I climbed high into the hills with Countryman, Zawadi, and Countryman's friend Popo. In the last couple of years, there had been a mad dash to buy up the land around Shela. As the land was purchased, the land's former occupants moved up into the hills.

We went to this new village high in the hills. We could see the ocean far below. The hills were made of the same soft white coral sand found on the beach. Under the moonlight they appeared bright white. There were palm trees and low brush but little else. The houses in the community were made entirely of palm. Under palm canopies, there were woven cane chairs and some low wooden tables. There was a party going on, but it was very subdued—perhaps because it was not really a full moon after all. Katie and I determined the ridiculously oversized moon, however lovely, had a slightly furry edge, indicating it was one day off from full.

Katie and Tom and I were the only foreigners at this quiet gathering. Everyone was drinking palm wine out of recycled glasses that had been spice bottles in a former life. Popo told a story about a ghost chicken with little ghost chicks, which he said gave him gooseflesh before they disappeared like smoke! Katie told us about her father taking her to the cleansing of a haunted house built on an Indian burial mound in Canada because he thought it would be an educational experience for his nine-year-old daughter. Then Countryman told a story about the small men the fishermen see walking on the waves when they fish overnight: tiny men carrying lanterns who trick the boats off their course to crash into unseen rocks.

From the edge of the gathering an older fisherman said quietly, "I've seen them. I've seen them with my eyes," and fell silent. We told no more ghost stories after that.

Then there was some drumming and some singing, mostly in Swahili except when Zawadi worried Tom and Katie and I might feel left out. Then we sang "Sunshine on my Shoulders" and "Country Roads," which everyone knew. (Say what you will about John Denver, he was making world music before the term was coined.)

We drank more palm wine and then Popo, lying on his back in the sand looking up at the giant moon, asked, "Why, if there is only one God, are there so many religions?"

"That's a good thing to discuss, but not when drunk," Zawadi answered.

"But I'm *not* drunk," Popo insisted, still staring at the moon.

"Fine, but I *am*," Zawadi said, and that was the end of that.

Then we walked through the soft sand, now cool on our feet, back to Lamu.

When I got to Farouk's house the next morning, his wife gave me the note that was waiting.

Dear Cary
Sorry for the Trip to Mombasa by Dhow To much Wind and also not finished repair boat so sorry.
So see around.
Ali Captain

This was not a "Wednesday might mean Friday" kind of note, this was an "it ain't gonna happen" note. I was defeated. I had hoped to catch at least part of the four-day music festival in Zanzibar and it would soon be underway. There had been no other word of a boat of any kind leaving the Lamu harbor since I had arrived other than the usual day trips hawked by the beach boys and a rumored fishing boat going to Malindi. But Malindi was only halfway to Mombasa, the fishing boat was small, and riding overnight with slowly decomposing fish didn't sound like the trip I had envisioned.

It was hard to believe the dhow I had been waiting for was still sitting in the mangroves, going nowhere. I showed the note to Zawadi as she sat crocheting yet another Rasta cap in her office. She read it silently as she crocheted and nodded sympathetically.

"Likely it's the strong winds that are keeping it from going," she said. The wind had been unusually strong for the last two days.

I bought a "Swahili pizza" from a street vendor, which was nothing like a pizza in either taste or appearance: a thin wheat flour crust wrapped around egg and onion, fried in a pan over the fire, and served with spicy tomato sauce. It was good, but it did not lift my spirits.

After dinner, I sat by the waterfront watching the anchored dhows bobbing in the low tide. The wind had died and the moon (the real full moon now) was shining brightly. I was joined by the always-cheerful Boniface from the hotel and I told him my sad news.

Boniface pointed to a large dhow called *Ashraf* anchored directly in front of us I had not noticed before. "This boat is going to Kilifi tomorrow morning," he said.

"Tomorrow? Where is Kilifi?" I asked.

"Just north of Mombasa," Boniface said, his round face breaking into a wide grin.

The owner wanted this boat taken to Kilifi, Boniface told me, and another dhow brought back to Lamu to use for tourist excursions. Boniface had already told Farouk, and Farouk was on his way to find the boat's captain, Captain Shallow.

"Oh, Boniface!" I said, and I almost hugged him. Boniface beamed.

Less than fifteen minutes later, Captain Shallow and Farouk were at my hotel. Farouk left me so I could discuss the details with Captain Shallow, who was dressed in a festive lacy pink robe and wearing a lot of pleasant, sweet cologne; he did not fit my preconceptions of a seafaring captain. But it turned out he would not be taking the boat out himself. His brother, Captain Sheffield, was to have left with the boat yesterday, but there was a death in the family. Sheffield was now returning from paying his respects in the village. The boat would leave at four o'clock in the morning.

The only question remaining was, what would he charge me? This boat was about to become a tourist excursion boat, and I knew the overnight tourist excursions from Shela cost hundreds of dollars. I told him I had planned to pay 1,500 shillings for the mangrove dhow and would pay him an extra 500 shillings, for a total of about $26, if he provided food. He accepted without hesitation and told me to be outside waiting at four o'clock in the morning. It was now after ten o'clock at night and I still needed to pack, buy water (the one thing I would not count on Captain Shallow to do), and say my goodbyes.

I hurried down the waterfront.

"No hurry in Lamu!" the Rastamen scolded as usual.

"I have to hurry, I have a dhow to catch!"

I saw my Masai friend, Joshua, and stopped to tell him the good news. He was happy for me but sorry to see me go. We exchanged email addresses and took a photo together. He promised to write. I continued down to the pier and met Mr. Abbas. I told him I had found my dhow.

"Come back to Lamu soon," he urged. "I will find you a good husband — one with no other wives!" I told him I appreciated that very much and continued down the waterfront.

I met Countryman and told him I was leaving. Zawadi had already gone for the day, but Countryman promised to tell her I had found a dhow and wished me safe travels. After a bit of hunting, I found Tom and Katie's hotel room, up several winding flights of dark stairs in the oldest part of town. Katie looked surprised I was leaving so quickly.

"Maybe we'll meet again in Tanzania?" she suggested as she hugged me.

At last, I returned to the hotel and Boniface offered to make me a couple of hard-boiled eggs for the journey. When Farouk returned, I told him it was all sorted out and I was leaving in the morning. He broke into a smile from ear to ear, revealing his almost complete lack of teeth, and then unexpectedly gave me a huge hug. I was utterly taken aback. He appeared to be every bit as delighted as I was. I gave him another 200 shillings, as I had done on the days when he had arranged something for me, but clearly that was not the point. He was genuinely delighted I had found my dhow.

I thought about my time in Lamu: Tom and Katie ready to keep rambling around East Africa, Zawadi and Countryman hard at work in their office on the sidewalk, Boniface and Mr. Abbas lining up matrimonial candidates, the gentle and charming Joshua and his brother Solomon saving up for more cows, the indispensable Mr. Farouk—and even Ali Hippie poisoning the next batch of tourists. I realized, with a sudden wave of sadness, that in this incredibly short time I had found a community, and now, with very little warning, I was leaving it.

Packing took me until midnight and there was only time for a short nap. I looked out over my balcony at the *Ashraf*. The tide was coming in. The real full moon was shining. It would still be shining when I set sail on my dhow.

SWAHILI DREAMS

A seagoing dhow rocks like a cradle and snores like an old man. It is low and broad and made of wood from the mango tree. It has only the one tall mast and a second pole, even longer, that holds the single large triangular sail aloft. When the sail is raised, these two long beams rub against each other, making a low moaning noise. The full moon was still shining brightly when we left Lamu and there was very little wind. The sail of the dhow rippled listlessly, and I lay on a raffia mat on the deck under an enormous moon. It is a wonderful thing when your imaginings are matched by reality: the dhow is a perfect vessel.

There were five of us on the dhow. I introduced myself at the dock, ready to make pleasantries and get to know my fellow crew members. I immediately realized this would be hard. Captain Sheffield had a smattering of English at his disposal as long as the question was fairly obvious and accompanied by a few hand gestures. The other three crew members spoke no English at all. We pulled away from the Lamu harbor a little past five o'clock in the morning. The early morning call to prayer was just beginning and I heard the lonely sound rising in the dark from mosques at either end of Lamu. In the center of town, a donkey brayed. Then I heard nothing but the waves and the boat.

Captain Sheffield had none of the flamboyance of his brother Captain Shallow. He was thoughtful, rarely smiled, never laughed. He spoke little in Swahili and less in English, but he was clearly concerned about my comfort and obviously the man in charge.

Muhammad was the first mate, if such a title exists on a dhow. He was tall, strong, and handsome and seemed to be as much a part of the boat as the rudder or the sail. He could walk on the railing of the dhow without holding onto any line and he fixed the mast overhead, climbing to the top of the pole in seconds. When Captain Sheffield was not at the rudder, it was usually Muhammad taking his shift. Muhammad was a natural storyteller. Almost as soon as we set sail, he began one of his long, animated stories, building up to a riotous climax. He laughed loudly and waited for his listeners' laughter to subside before continuing.

During this dramatic pause, I asked Captain Sheffield, "What is Muhammad saying?"

Captain Sheffield thought for a moment and then answered, "He is telling about when he was fishing on another boat." Not for the first time, I chastised myself for not learning some Swahili before I left.

Muhammad manned the charcoal grill on the bow of the dhow and in the morning was kind enough to boil water with Kenyan coffee in it, then pour the boiled mixture into a thermos. (The grounds would settle out and make great coffee.) I was putting the coffee in the pot on the first morning when he suddenly took my hand and expended his entire supply of English.

He pointed to himself: "No English." Then he pointed to me. "No Swahili?"

"No," I had to answer. I watched his face fall as he stood holding my hand. So many stories to tell, a captive female audience, and I could not understand a single word. He shook his head. It was a great disappointment.

Bacari was next in the chain of command. He was also very strong, which was important for raising the giant sail or tacking. He pumped the manual bilge pump whenever it was needed (which seemed to be much of the time) and cleaned the fish we caught. He was soft-spoken and liked to sleep whenever he could.

Jaro was the youngest and seemed diminutive for this kind of work. He had a lively sense of humor and was the only one with a cell phone, which he kept in a plastic bag. There was rarely a signal, but he seemed to know when there was one and would quickly turn his phone on and start making calls and receiving messages for the few minutes the signal lasted, then turn it off again to save the battery. Jaro was the acknowledged fishing expert on board, and he took the line in his hand and played with it, singing a crazy fish-calling song and laughing. I teased him about his fish-calling, mimicking his fish song, until twenty minutes later when he pulled a large tuna on board just in time for dinner.

During the second night, Muhammad was at the rudder and all around us was dark and foggy. Everyone else was asleep. There was no compass on board, no charts, no GPS. Sailors navigate the open sea by watching for the tiny lights from shore and on the sprinkling of islands along the way. We were a long way from the shore, headed toward some islands, I presumed, but I could see nothing through the fog. I was thinking of the fishermen's stories about the small men with lanterns walking across the waves and I saw how easily one's eyes could be fooled. I shivered. Every year dhows are lost when they hit rocks below the surface.

Suddenly Muhammad called for Jaro to wake up. Jaro sprang up from his mattress between the ribs of the dhow, Muhammad asked him something in an urgent tone, and Jaro silently scanned the shoreline for several seconds before he excitedly answered in the affirmative. Somehow, they knew where we were; Jaro could see lights on the distant shore when I could see nothing at all. Now Jaro's small stature made more sense: it was good to have a crew member with better than 20/20 vision, even if he was not the strongest man in the harbor.

During the day the sun was hot, but there was a little sunshade made of raffia over a portion of the deck where Captain Sheffield manned the rudder and where I could escape the worst of the sun. I would lose myself in the sun and the waves, the creaking mast, the gently rocking boat. Sunset came quickly, and the setting sun played tricks on my eyes, making the waves look like distant boats at first and then faces looking out at me from within the waves. Then it was dark and the stars were out immediately. There was no trace of ambient light in the sky, just the stars reflected in the waves and the splash of the rudder.

I never slept through the night but drifted in and out of sleep the nights we traveled. There on the dhow, I found my tranquil sea. In the deep of the ocean, I lost track of time and felt a profound peace. The hull of the dhow held me like a womb, rocked me like a cradle, loosened my grip on notions I didn't even know I was still holding. I don't know why a boat carved of mango wood on the East African coast was the transport I needed, but on the dhow I was able to let go of the last bonds to the person I had been, the life I had lived, the expectations I had harbored so faithfully for so long. Riding the dhow, in this utter void of ocean and boat, I thought of all the things that had been so important to me, and without any careful consideration, I knew those things wouldn't matter anymore. I would never return to business. I would no longer pine for my lost marriage. I would never again be as strong as I had appeared to be, as hopeful, or as sure. Riding the dhow, I felt an unaccustomed vulnerability as the past evaporated like fog and the future remained as remote and inscrutable as the distant shore.

A strange white woman on a seafaring dhow, my only companions the Swahili crew of this ship, I had no agenda. I needed nothing. I fell asleep at sunset watching the faces in the waves watching me. When I awoke, I saw the moon waiting overhead and either Sheffield or Muhammad at the rudder, and I would listen to Muhammad sharing another long story filled with laughter. Just as I fell asleep, I understood Swahili perfectly and the story became part of my dreams.

•   •   •   •   •

We arrived in Kilifi at eight o'clock in the morning after a beautiful sunrise on the dhow. Sadly, there was no coffee, as we had used up the last of the charcoal frying fish the previous evening. But this day had a few more disappointments in store.

I was sitting on deck eating a mango as we pulled into a leafy harbor that seemed to be used exclusively by the dhows fishing out of Kilifi. The fishermen having breakfast were surprised to see this large seafaring dhow arrive, more surprised yet to see a white woman jump out.

"*Jambo!*"

"*Mzuri!*" (a better spelling for "Missouri").

I briefly conferred with the fishermen. My plan was to cross into Tanzania by bus and try to get a cargo boat from Tanga to Zanzibar. The fishermen thought this could be done, but my travel guidebook was not entirely encouraging. I decided I would try; Dar es Salaam was the next point from which I could catch a ferry to Zanzibar and it was considerably farther south. The music festival was now underway, and I had an appointment to be dancing in Stone Town.

I started to climb the steep hill away from the harbor with Captain Sheffield. At the top of the hill, I turned to look back at the dhow and saw Muhammad had climbed to the top of the mast to wave goodbye. High above the palms, he waved to me. I waved back, then headed to the road.

A minivan stopped almost immediately to let me in. I said goodbye to Captain Sheffield, my pack was thrown into the van, and I was off. The ride was fast and friendly, and I soon arrived in Mombasa to another waiting minivan, this one going to Tanga.

The minivan to Tanga was crowded. They took one look at me and determined the price was eight hundred shillings. For that amount, I said, I wanted a window seat. They said, "Of course!" — and of course there was no window seat. I was squeezed into the middle, a mother and baby in the seat to my right and a man to my left. It started to get very hot in the van.

Just out of Mombasa we had to put the minivan on a ferry, which required all the passengers get out and walk in the midday heat onto the ferry, then reboard the minivan once we were across. This process took an hour. Shortly after we got moving again we arrived at the Kenyan border, where we had to file out of the minivan again, walk a few hundred meters, fill out forms, and get back in. We then drove for about fifteen minutes, came to the Tanzanian border, and did it all over again. (I have no idea what country we were in after the Kenyan forms and before the Tanzanian forms.)

As I entered Tanzania, it dawned on me that if I were to find a boat in Tanga, I would have no Tanzanian currency to pay for it. There were signs everywhere at the border telling me not to deal with touts, but I didn't know where else I would get cash. I jumped out of the minivan and was swarmed by money-changers when I realized I had neglected to find out what the exchange rate was. I really hadn't the slightest idea what I should be getting for either the euros or the Kenyan shillings in my wallet. I went into my default Nigerian bartering mode.

"How much do you want to change?" several touts shouted in unison.

"It depends, what rate will you give me?" I said, trying to sound defiant.

"Fourteen!" one shouted. (Fourteen what? Fourteen hundred? Fourteen thousand? I literally had no clue.)

"*Fourteen?!*" I shouted back. "Are you crazy? I may as well just go to the bank!" I acted as if I might hop back into the minivan out of sheer indignation.

"Okay, okay! I'll give you fifteen!" one of the touts shouted back.

The sum was calculated at a rate of 1,500 Tanzanian shillings per euro and I knew there was an excellent chance I was handing over 100 euros for ten percent of their worth, but at that point I was committed. The heat was terrible; I had a headache and I was almost incapable of doing even simple math. The money was exchanged and I was hustled back into the minivan.

Immediately upon entering Tanzania, we were confronted by major road repair. The highway was now a rough gravel road; clouds of red dust were thrown up by every passing car, and keeping the windows closed in this minivan was not an option. We stopped yet again, this time to pick up more passengers. The driver decided there was room for two more men in the seat to my left—in addition to the man already there. When I protested there really was not room for six people on one bench seat of the minivan (there were three in front and three plus a baby in back), I was told, first of all, the baby didn't count and, second, these men would be out "soon." They rode all the way to Tanga.

I was soaked with sweat and covered in red dust. The baby in back threw up and we stopped to throw some sort of blue powder on it (the vomit—not the baby), then continued on our way.

Arriving in Tanga, the minivan was surrounded by touts, hustlers, and cabbies. I had no idea how to get to the harbor and it was already three o'clock. I picked out one of the less aggressive would-be "guides" and told him I would pay him something if he could help me find a boat to Zanzibar.

"No problem, I will find you a boat," said a guide who claimed the improbable name of "Steve."

He took my backpack and we hoofed it down to the shore, but we had not actually set foot in the harbor when we were stopped by the port authorities.

"Can I help you?" asked an official in a brown uniform who did not look as if he had any interest whatsoever in helping me.

"I'm looking for a boat to Zanzibar."

"There is a boat leaving on Tuesday." It was Friday.

"I would be happy to take a cargo boat."

"That is forbidden to foreigners." This sounded highly suspect. The official continued, "I suggest you spend the weekend in Tanga."

I looked at the customs official. He did not show any sign of easing up on the "no foreigners allowed" stance. If it were morning, I figured I could come back and try to sweet talk the next official on duty or find a boat captain in town and get on board somewhere other than directly in front of the port authority office. But the last bus to Dar es Salaam was scheduled to leave in an hour and I realized I didn't have time to fight this battle. Steve was clearly of no help. Steve knew no one in the harbor. Steve knew very little about anything, as it turned out. I felt a bad case of crabbiness coming on.

I sulked back up the hill to where the buses were gathered, and Steve insisted I should get on an "Air Bus" rather than into another minivan, as he told me this was a more "luxurious" ride.

"How much is this luxury going to cost me?"

Thirteen thousand shillings was the answer.

I had no idea what that meant, still unsure of the exchange rate. It sounded like a lot. But I was running out of time and it appeared the bus was filling with working-class Tanzanians, so I had to assume this was the going rate and I parted with 13,000 shillings in mystery currency. I also realized I had eaten nothing since that mango outside Kilifi. I tried to buy something from a street vendor near the bus, but everything was fly-covered and greasy. I remembered Ali Hippie and thought better of it. Instead, I bought a bottle of water and a package of biscuits. I told Steve I was giving him 1,500 in mystery money and I didn't need any more help.

Steve was outraged. "I deserve 5,000 shillings!" he insisted.

"You were supposed to find me a boat to Zanzibar, remember?"

"I found you a boat!"

"You did not!"

"I found you a boat—you just have to wait until Tuesday."

I gave him 2,000 shillings and took my biscuits, water, and a seriously bad attitude aboard the luxury Air Bus. Steve was still hollering when I took a window seat on the bus.

"Give me a biscuit at least!" he said. "I'm a young man—I need to eat!" I handed him two biscuits through the window of the bus and he went away.

I have a high tolerance for ramshackle buses, but that luxury bus was the most uncomfortable ride of my life. The seats were apparently plywood covered with the thinnest possible layer of foam and some newish fabric. The angle of the seats was such that I couldn't sit straight and I couldn't slouch over. Every part of my anatomy began to hurt almost immediately. I had red Tanzanian road grit under my eyelids and inside my ears and a sleepy soldier sitting to my right, slowly elbowing his way into my limited space.

The road was worse than before and the ride took more than six hours. When I finally arrived in Dar es Salaam, the biggest, busiest city in Tanzania, it was after ten o'clock at night. With no idea where I would stay, I had pulled out my travel guidebook and tried to find a hotel as close to the dock as possible as I wanted to catch the ferry to Zanzibar in the morning. Because the currency fluctuates so frequently, no prices were listed, only a cautionary note that hotels were expensive in Dar es Salaam. So, I picked a hotel that had the price listed as a "3" out of a possible "10," figuring that was probably as much as I wanted to spend. As soon as the bus stopped, I was swarmed with cabbies and touts once again. Once again, I was seriously wishing I had learned at least the rudiments of Swahili. I had no remaining reserve of politeness and desperately wanted to get to the hotel I had selected without either the benefit of Swahili or a lot of runaround.

"Can you understand me?" I almost shouted into the face of the first cab driver I saw. He looked shell-shocked.

"No? Okay, fine! CAN YOU UNDERSTAND ME?" I inquired of the next.

I continued this utterly baffling behavior until an older cab driver stepped up to the plate (to use an expression that would also be incomprehensible to a Tanzanian cab driver).

"YES!" he shouted. "I UNDERSTAND YOU!"

"GOOD!" I bellowed. "LET'S GO!"

The decrepit hotel room he brought me to was easily, without dispute, the most nightmarish I have ever stayed in. I did not protest. (When I did figure out the money, it turned out to be a $7.50 room in this expensive city, so I will let you imagine for yourself.) I turned off the lights and turned on my wind-up flashlight, so I couldn't see it quite so well. I showered in the I-don't-want-to-think-about-it bathroom until I had removed a good portion of the collected dust. I set my alarm for six o'clock and fell instantly to sleep. I dreamt I was swaying in the cradle of the dhow, back and forth, back and forth, back and forth...

DANCING LESSONS

The large, comfortable ferry going to Zanzibar had none of the romance of the dhow or the discomfort of the bus. It moved so smoothly away from the port in Dar es Salaam I didn't even notice we had departed until I looked out the window and saw a dhow filled with fishermen. The passengers were a more conservatively dressed group of Muslims than most I had seen in Kenya. The women were bringing along baskets of mysterious things wrapped in newspaper. One woman shared a piece of cake with me as a movie starring Sylvester Stallone (in English, subtitled in English) played on the TV overhead. I found some consolation in learning Sylvester Stallone and Brian Dennehy were no more understandable to the residents of Dar es Salaam than I was without subtitles.

Zanzibar still had a somewhat reluctant alliance with Tanzania. Zanzibar didn't become part of Tanzania until the 1960s, and I had read of tourists being required to purchase a second "visa" or pay an immigration tax upon entering Zanzibar. When we landed in Stone Town, I tried to sidestep immigration (as it appeared all the Tanzanians were doing), but as the only white face, I was called out of the exiting crowd by immigration officials and asked to produce my passport.

"Where are you staying?" the officer inquired. I confessed I did not know.

"How long are you staying?" Again, I claimed ignorance.

"Do you have friends here?" he asked, starting to look me suspiciously as he flipped through the pages of my well-worn passport.

"Not yet, but I will," I assured him. "If you are my friend, I have a friend in Zanzibar already!" I attempted my most winning smile.

He looked up at me and snorted as he inspected my Tanzanian visa (which had already been stamped at the border). He stamped it a second time as a reluctant smile spread across his face.

"Welcome to Zanzibar."

"*Asante*." (I was grateful I could at least say "thank you.") I had officially entered Tanzania for the second time in two days without leaving.

Although the rainy season had not yet arrived, Zanzibar seemed prone to short rainy bursts, usually under a shining sun. There was one such outburst as I stepped off the dock. I ducked under an awning with a group of unperturbed Zanzibaris. As soon as it let up, I headed to the nearest budget hotels and discovered (not surprisingly) with the music festival in full swing, many of the family-run hotels and guesthouses were full. At my third stop, I found a room on the second floor with a shared (but very clean) bathroom and a balcony overlooking a busy street.

Stone Town was much like Lamu on a grander scale. The winding, curving streets were too small for cars, although cars drove around the perimeter of the island. The narrow streets were filled with hundreds of tiny shops selling antiques and curios, paintings and fabrics, spices, and ornately carved wooden furniture. Everywhere there was the smell of jasmine, incense, and curry. There were fewer donkeys but more bicycles careening around the blind corners of the winding stone streets, ringing their bells to warn the unsuspecting tourists who were constantly standing in harm's way.

Wonderful food was sold on the street. There were pastries and spicy vegetable dumplings, spongy sweet rice cakes, and fruits I had never seen and could not pronounce but loved to eat. Every night at sunset, two dozen tables were erected in a public park right on the water and an amazing variety of fish, seafood, beef, chicken, and falafel was grilled to order on portable charcoal grills. The vendors all wore chef caps and white coats (which looked peculiar but impressive) in order to comply with some obscure government requirement, and they cooked by the light of kerosene lanterns. Fresh sugar cane juice was squeezed on the spot and served with grilled flatbread, samosas, and more Swahili pizzas (except here they were called Zanzibari pizzas). Potato mango soup was dished into steel bowls and garnished with cassava chips and chili peppers. But there was no time to linger over cassava chips; the music festival had begun.

I bought a ticket and headed to Omani Fort, a 300-year-old structure near the sea with thick stone walls enclosing it and age-blackened towers at the corners. In its long history, the fort repelled the Portuguese, served as a jail, housed the Zanzibar Ladies Tennis Club, and held public executions—not necessarily in that order.

Now, it hosted Zanzibar's annual music festival. Within its walls a stage had been erected, and people sat under the stars on the grassy lawn to hear music from all over eastern and southern Africa. On the first night, I sat near two young Zanzibari men with limited English and a young Canadian man they had befriended who was holding forth on the universal appeal of beer. (He seemed to have considerable firsthand experience.) The second night I sat between two Muslim families: one comprised of three women fully covered in black and accompanied by their male chaperone, the other a young couple with two young children, the husband in dreadlocks and the wife and smallest girl in sequin-covered blouses and lots of jewelry. The little girl clapped her hands in time, her eyes wide. The ancient walls of the fort reflected the stage lights. Banners hanging off the stone parapets flapped in the breeze. The announcements were sometimes given in Swahili, sometimes in English, but everyone got the general idea.

In addition to large ensembles playing traditional music, small combos from many regions of Africa performed pop music, hip-hop, jazz, and blues, their music flavored with Indian, Arabic, and Western influences. One night, the legendary Bi Kidude took the stage. Her age was unknown, but the earliest recordings of her were made more than eighty years ago, so she could not have been much under 100 years old. She stood on the edge of the stage and the wind picked up her flowing robes. The crowd fell silent. I worried the wind might knock over this frail wisp of a woman eclipsed in billowing robes, but then she opened her mouth to sing. Bi Kidude's voice rolled off the stage and echoed against the ancient stone walls. Her voice was larger than her entire body. It filled the ancient stones of the fort; it burst into the night sky. Her voice was bigger than us all.

I sat on my little batik cloth from Nigeria watching the crowd and listening to the music, surrounded by people from all over the globe. The audience was mostly Tanzanians, but a lot of Kenyans from Nairobi had come for the show. There were backpackers from all over Europe, a handful of Brits, a group of Chinese, and a surprising number of Canadians, but few Americans.

The last performance on Sunday night was a large ensemble of veteran Tanzanian musicians who had played throughout the festival in various groups. There were huge drums and a massive wooden xylophone in the orchestra and a chorus of brightly costumed singers. The ensemble played classic songs that all the Zanzibaris knew by heart. As the festival was coming to a close, they played a traditional song with new words for the occasion.

The chorus was now, "Obama! *Ubarikiwe*. Obama! *Ubarikiwe*."

I watched in amazement as every person in the ancient fort rose to their feet. People from all over the planet swayed together. Our hands in the air, we all sang in Swahili: "Obama! Blessings to you. Obama! Blessings to you."

I looked all around me; there was not another American in sight.

·   ·   ·   ·   ·

The music festival was over, but the festivities continued at a beach resort a few kilometers out of Stone Town. Since I figured it would be easier to attend the party if I was already staying at the resort, I had made my only reservation of the trip at the site of the party. The shuttle bus that picked me up at the hotel was filled with Europeans and, surprisingly, one American: a Californian named Michael who had gotten out of the real estate business in the nick of time, right before the market crashed. He now lived half the year in Florianopolis, Brazil, and half in Santa Cruz. We struck up a conversation as the bus rattled and lurched its way over the gravel roads to the north end of the island. Michael had not made reservations; the whole music festival was a wonderful surprise for him. Actually, all of East Africa was.

He told me how he had met a Ugandan batik artist in Brazil who had invited him to come and stay with her family should he ever find his way to Kampala. He said he could not have found Uganda on a map at the time, but he immediately recognized this as a good suggestion and booked his ticket to Kampala direct from Brazil. He had a wonderful time in Uganda, then found his way to Tanzania and on to Zanzibar, where his arrival serendipitously coincided with the start of the music festival.

"I did the same thing in Shanghai," he told me. "A stranger said I should see it and I just had a feeling I should listen."

We fell silent, looking out the windows at the Zanzibari coast; glimpses of brilliant white sand appeared behind the trees.

"Shanghai was great," he said.

I told him how I was also here on the advice of a Ugandan, One-Eyed Mike, and Michael and I agreed these chance meetings were the best source of travel inspiration. We arrived at the resort and it was, not surprisingly, fully booked. I wished Michael happy travels and we promised to stay in touch.

After three weeks on the very Muslim east coast, the resort, frequented almost exclusively by Europeans, was a startling change. Situated on an embarrassingly beautiful beach, the soft white sand was sprinkled with pale orange and green coral, the waves were gentle, and the water was a perfect blue-green. From my vantage point under a raffia umbrella, I had an opportunity to watch unprotected pale flesh turn a variety of deep and painful hues over the course of the day and to observe the comparative rate at which tourists from various parts of Europe changed color under the unforgiving tropical sun. The British burned first and most severely, but they were also more reserved and left a little less real estate exposed to harm. Scandinavians of all types burned less severely than the Brits, but they left more delicate territory unprotected, the women donning string bikinis regardless of age or body type. Italians (especially the men) wore the least, but they had a Mediterranean advantage, so they browned like small, plump birds slowly turning in a street-side rotisserie.

The party began once the sun had set and I met an eclectic assortment of travelers, nomads, and semi-permanent residents of Zanzibar. The Masai on Zanzibar were a far more worldly bunch than those in Lamu (some clearly faux Masai, cashing in on the latest hot trend). They were obviously enjoying their status as the new chick magnets on the beach, dancing in their red robes and many ankle bracelets in the sand under a disco ball, a European college girl on either side. As the party progressed, I watched the Rastamen (some of them faux Rastamen) look on forlornly. There was a time not long ago when dreadlocks, a Bob Marley T-shirt, and a couple of joints in your pocket were all that was required to snag a northern girl on winter holiday. Times change.

I chatted with an intense-looking Italian, bronzed by the sun, who told me he had been a philosophy major until he dove beneath the ocean waves many years ago.

"There I discovered a better world," he informed me.

Now he travels the world as a dive instructor. He told me he would give me free lessons. But as I looked into his dark and somewhat feral-looking eyes, I was not sure I was ready for a better world just yet and I politely declined.

A frustrated Finnish photographer was there updating the resort's website. He had spent the better part of the afternoon trying to get one decent photo of a nervous blonde in a bikini perched on a rattan couch in one of the more luxurious rooms. I shared a thermos of coffee with him and we talked about his travels and mine. He told me he had friends here and was going to look at a piece of property tomorrow to see if he might like to buy a place.

"It is important," he said, "to do it before you are too old."

"Do what?" I asked.

He searched for words for several moments before he finally said, "Find your harbor."

The party went on till late, but I suddenly discovered I was not in the mood for existential musings under a disco ball. I went to bed in my little rattan hut close to the beach with a mosquito net around me and listened to the music outside. I did not sleep for some time.

I had no harbor.

The burst of ambition that had motivated me to secure a dhow, to make it to Zanzibar and the festival, was now spent.

Where is my harbor? I wondered.

Where did I belong? I had no idea. The idea of a harbor sounded inviting and necessary, but I had no image to attach to it. I understood leaving everything behind entailed finding a new place and discovering the new person who would live in it. I had a deep yearning to better know the creative girl who had been released in Lagos, the vulnerable woman who left the last of her old life on the dhow. I now knew the irresistible impulse I had felt to travel — to leave Lagos and the comfort of Nora's home — was a desire to find out who this woman was.

All I knew about her was, at forty-six, she was a lot older than the college girls dancing under the disco ball outside — and yet she did not feel (in any of the ways that seemed significant) particularly old just yet. She was newly single, no longer in business, and not nearly as sensible as she used to be. Before I found the all-important harbor my Finnish friend spoke of, perhaps I would need to become better acquainted with the woman who now needed it.

In the morning, I headed back by minibus to Stone Town. The bus made regular stops along the way to pay modest bribes to Zanzibari policemen who seemed very relaxed and not very ambitious by Nigerian standards. With the concert over there was no shortage of lodging, and I checked into a sweet little guesthouse with an elaborate four-poster bed and a lovely rooftop sitting area from which I could see the ocean in two directions. It seemed like a good place to spend a day or two. I decided to stay.

Sitting on the rooftop drinking a cup of dark Tanzanian coffee, I was again surprised to meet some Americans, three this time, all Peace Corp volunteers from Zambia. They had taken the Tanzar train, a 42-hour ride from the border of Zambia to Dar es Salaam.

"It was awesome!" they assured me.

This was the second time I had heard someone say the train ride was well worth the trip. I took a few notes on Zambia and their travel suggestions, which included a purportedly spectacular waterfall that one could camp very near.

"Just watch out for the baboons!" they added.

"Thanks for the ideas," I said, looking into their excited, sunburnt faces.

"No problem," a young volunteer from Ohio replied, then added: "Vonnegut said peculiar travel suggestions are dancing lessons from God."

I wish I had said that.

ALONE

I was alone in the water when I saw a flash of blue on the shore.

The blue was my wrap—I recognized the color immediately. A moment earlier, two young boys had been walking down the beach. I saw them just as they grabbed my wrap. The wrap covered my bag, which contained everything I had brought with me to the beach. They saw me in the water and they ran—fast—into the jungle with my bag.

"No!" I yelled from the water. "No! No! NO!"

But my yelling inspired them to run faster and they were now totally out of sight. I started to run into the jungle and attracted the attention of several men nearby (a woman in a rainbow-striped bikini yelling "No! No! NO!" at the top of her lungs will attract attention) and they came running. A lack of Swahili hampered things for a moment. But a professional training in theater had sharpened my pantomime skills in preparation for just such a moment, and they got the idea quickly enough. We all stormed off together into the jungle in a furious line.

I remembered later where I had seen those two boys and why I was so certain they were boys, not young men. I had seen them on the beach earlier, playing like puppies, challenging each other and trying to do push-ups sitting on each other's back. Even from a distance, I could see they were egging one another on to greater deeds of daring.

It was a quiet day at the beach. I was staying on Pemba Island, the lesser-known island of Zanzibar, a place that sees perhaps a dozen tourists at a time, and most of those taking organized diving tours. There were no tourists today on this long, lovely stretch of beach. There were no prowling professional vandals because there were no tourists to steal from. There were only a handful of fishermen standing waist-deep in the low tide with nets stretched between them, slowly working their way down the shoreline, and because it was a Saturday there were a couple of families with cold boxes sitting in the shade, drinking beer, and eating the food they had prepared out of large plastic bowls.

Which was why I remembered those two boys. I saw the flash of blue and my indispensable daypack disappear with my camera, nearly full journal, sunglasses, sunscreen, telephone with Tanzanian SIM card, earphones and MP3 player, seventeen-year-old hat that had traversed the world on my head, and a little notebook with the names and addresses of people I had met along the way, a few phrases in Swahili, and a list of ladies from Lagos who might like to take pole dancing lessons. (While the last item's importance could be argued, it certainly was not replaceable.)

The race into the jungle was fruitless, as you might have imagined it would be.

It is only in the movies the perpetrators are caught by the woman in the rainbow-striped bikini leading a posse of outraged vigilantes. In real life, the men in hot pursuit lose interest almost immediately and the woman in the striped bikini gets her legs scratched and realizes there are countless little rabbit trails heading off in every direction and she cannot possibly guess which one the boys took. And she returns empty-handed.

As soon as it was obvious what had happened, the required self-recriminations began along with the inventory of damages. First and most importantly: no money was lost, and also no passport, tickets, credit cards, or other items of great worth. One of the many useful things about traveling in general, and traveling alone in particular, is it requires the exercise of deciding what I could afford to lose and what I was willing to carry. This is a valuable exercise, whether one is traveling or not.

Before I left Lagos, I had a long and interesting argument with Nora about the ethics of cutting apart a travel book in order to carry only that part of the country I planned to visit. This seemed eminently sensible to me but on the order of a felony offense to Nora, so I acknowledge there are differing points of view. But, however you come down on the subject of book mutilation, extended travel is an exercise in weighing — literally weighing — one's priorities.

I followed my father's advice and purchased a camera that, in his words, "would not ruin your vacation if it fell off a mountainside" (or, presumably, disappeared into a jungle). I briefly chastised myself for taking the camera to a place as risky as the beach, but I stopped before getting too deeply into self-flagellation. I wouldn't take any pictures if I didn't bring the camera. If I brought the camera, I risked losing it. These two facts of travel were inextricably linked: hence my father's off-the-side-of-a-mountain school of camera-shopping advice. I was not thinking about the monetary cost. I was thinking of all the pictures I would not be taking.

I guessed these two boys were not professional thugs. They were not desperate or hungry; they were not driven to criminal acts out of a sense of outrage or entitlement. Snitching a lady tourist's bag could have no real repercussions because there was no real victim. The victim was an abstraction: a ridiculous foreign white lady with a beach bag, nothing to do with anything real.

More than likely someone knew them, I thought. So, I made myself a bit more decent (my beach wrap was not taken — another blessing) and, accompanied by the would-be vigilante men as interpreters, I approached the nearest picnicking family and inquired if they had seen anyone meeting my rather vague description. I received a few sad head shakes, a bit of sympathetic tut-tutting, but nothing to indicate these boys had anything to do with the family on the beach.

And so I was startled when the patriarch of this family, a fat older man with no shirt sitting on a cold box, asked me in English and in a loud voice: *"Why are you alone?"*

I felt my eyes begin to sting as I tried to form an answer in my head. *Why am I alone?*

Surely, I am a fool to be alone. And I realize I must seem (and probably am) ridiculous: a middle-aged woman with no partner, no plan, no excuse — a foolish white lady in a black country who has lost her bag. This is not worth upsetting your picnic, disturbing your peace and I do—I really do—understand that.

Why am I alone? I have spent nearly every day for the past three years wondering that very thing. I didn't exactly expect to be alone at this point in my life, if you really have to know, Mr. Cold Box. Given my druthers, I would have had a travel companion and a beach-bag guardian, I wouldn't be quite as vulnerable and ridiculous as I surely seem to you. But things didn't turn out quite as I hoped.

Still, I don't think that means I deserve to have my bag stolen. I just lost the camera I was going to use to take pictures of your island to show my family. I lost my journal with things in it I really didn't want anyone else to read. I lost my notebook with the names and addresses of all the friends I've made since I started traveling. I've already lost quite a bit in the past couple of years, Mr. Cold Box, and I really didn't feel like losing anything else today.

All this was circling through my head as I felt dangerously close to crying, and he again demanded: "*Why are you alone?*"

"Because I am!" I yelled back. And I stomped off in my rainbow-striped bikini, a ridiculous figure.

Early the next morning I got on the ferry leaving Pemba. It was a beautiful day and the water crossing over to the mainland was a color I could never have captured on the camera that was no longer mine. It was neither the turquoise blue of Zanzibar nor the slate blue of the open sea. This blue was a sapphire blue, a true, clear blue that seemed too intense for my eyes to take in. The crew of the ferry was playing a live recording of the Egyptian singer Om Kolthoum. I could not remember ever hearing a more haunting voice. Leaning on the rail of the ferry, I stared out at that blue, blue water and listened to her voice for hours.

I got a sunburn (my sunscreen was now somewhere in the jungle), and when I landed, I hopped onto a bus that broke down after about an hour. Everyone from the expired bus climbed into the next bus that came along, which was already full before it took us aboard. I have no idea how many of us there were altogether, but as we headed up into the mountains everyone was fine. We were standing too close together for anyone to fall.

The conductor helped me from this new bus onto yet another bus, which took a lot of sharp switchbacks and eventually brought me high up into the mountains after dark. I landed in a tiny town called Soni and a little hotel called the Old Soni Hotel, where the hotel manager woke up when I arrived ("You must be hungry!" "Yes, actually I am!") and was kind enough to make an omelet for me at a very late hour.

When I woke up in the morning, I opened my curtains and was astonished to see a gorgeous sheer cliff and a waterfall, vines loaded with big trumpet-shaped blossoms, and pine trees absolutely filled with monkeys—a troop of monkeys staring right back in my window at me! The monkeys bobbed their heads up and down and looked at one another knowingly, and I knew what they were thinking.

"Ridiculous!"

·　　·　　·　　·　　·

The monkeys left sometime during the day.

It might have been when I took a motorbike from Soni to visit the Sakharani Monastery, where the Benedictine fathers raise dairy cows that wear large brass bells, making gentle music on the steep green pastures. The fathers grow delicious hazelnuts. (I bought some with the notion of bringing them home to my father, but they didn't make it through the night.) The fathers also make a lovely Chenin Blanc wine with just a touch of effervescence from the grapes in their vineyard. The monkeys were gone when I returned from a hike to the waterfall across from the hotel, but by then it had started to rain, so I thought perhaps they were simply hunkering down somewhere under their monkey umbrellas.

The next morning there were no monkeys looking in my window. At breakfast, I asked the hotel manager where the monkeys were.

"They have moved on," he said simply. I decided I should probably do the same.

I left Soni in another small bus which climbed higher into the mountains and delivered me to the beautiful town of Lushoto, high in the Usambara Mountains of Tanzania. The first thing I noticed was the light. I thought perhaps it was because it was partially overcast, which it often is. At about 5,000 feet above the coast, the clouds do not settle in and get comfortable; they skitter in and out, obscuring the sun for a few minutes, dropping a bit of rain perhaps and then moving on. But even when the sun was shining full, it was not the brilliant, flat equatorial sun I had grown accustomed to. The colors appeared unnaturally vivid to my eyes; my depth of field was sharper than I was used to. It was as if someone had doctored my color palette and everything was several shades more intense. Finding my way around in this surreal environment, I headed immediately to the wonderfully well-informed cultural tourism center, where they told me I could hire a guide and take a several-day hike into the mountains. For lodging, they advised me to go to St. Benedict's Hostel. Having had such a pleasant experience with Benedictine Chenin Blanc and hazelnuts, I was an easy mark.

I walked down the tidy main street of Lushoto, a red dirt road lined with bougainvillea on either side, to the Catholic church, a lovely old sanctuary surrounded by a cluster of white stucco buildings trimmed in blue with clay tile roofs and surrounded by overflowing flower gardens. Coming up the drive was a group of impossibly neat schoolchildren in uniforms that seemed to be a purple too intense to be real (again, I credit the strange quality of the light). They were surprised to see me and eager to try out their classroom English. "How are you? I am fine!" (hysterical laughter).

A timid young man named Leonard, who was employed by the church, showed me to a spartan little room in one of the stucco buildings: a narrow bed, a red-painted floor, a spotlessly clean bright blue bathroom, a wooden chair, and a table covered with a crisp white cloth looking out over a flower garden.

I had already decided I was not going to rush out of Lushoto. The tourism center had told me about several wonderful hikes in the area and, if nothing else, I wanted to enjoy the amazing light. Father Sabuni, the priest of Lushoto's only Catholic church who also served as the manager of the hostel, introduced himself as I sat in the screen porch. I told him I might be staying for a while. He asked what I did for a living and I mentioned something vague about projects involving engineers.

Father Sabuni immediately began to tell me about a water project he had been trying to get off the ground in a mountainous region outside Lushoto that did not have potable water. He had submitted a grant request to an international agency that had indicated some interest, but he had not heard back from them and he wondered if I might be willing to take a look at his proposal to see if I had any suggestions for how it could be improved or who might be interested in seeing it. He said he would be happy to take me to the villages that were without water to see for myself.

My luggage had not yet made it to my neat-as-a-pin room when I was presented with Father Sabuni's carefully written (if somewhat disjointed) grant request for the water project. Later that evening, I was taking notes on the proposal when the power went out. Moments later, there was a quiet knock at my door. I opened it to find Leonard presenting me with a two-and-a-half-foot-tall brass candlestick and a burning taper to put on the floor of my neat-as-a-pin room so I could continue working.

I had been warned about the many risks of travel in Africa: disease, robbery, high altitude, bad water. I recommend you watch out for the Benedictines. They are a sneaky bunch.

The following morning Father Sabuni and I were rattling along in a Jeep he borrowed from the diocese. I was somewhat surprised to see it was pimped out with gold braid and exhortations to Jesus for safety in several languages, but I saw the prudence in this as we climbed up the increasingly narrow and partially washed-out roads higher and farther into the Usambara Mountains.

Father Sabuni explained as he drove, "There is water in the mountains but it cannot get to the people. The hotels have stolen it. The women in the villages must walk two kilometers every day for water, the school children must haul it even farther to the elementary school — here — where there is water everywhere!"

We stopped to look at a spring that came out of the mountainside. A pipe had been installed by a luxury hotel (without anyone's knowledge or permission, Father Sabuni noted) and now all the water flowed directly to the hotel. We drove on until we came to one of the remote mountain settlements, a cluster of neat clay buildings with potatoes planted on the cliff's edge. The drinking water was kept in five-gallon buckets taken from a surface source and did not look clean.

When I was staying in Zanzibar, I thought I might find something useful to do, but my attempts to be of use were unsuccessful. I tried to volunteer at the public school but was told I needed a permit from the Ministry of Education. I went to the women's vocational training center, thinking I could tutor in English, and was told no one was interested in language classes. I finally went to the orphanage figuring I could at least read stories in the evening and was told my help was not needed because the orphans tended to "scatter" when school let out. I walked in the evenings right under the orphanage, located above a tunnel in the center of town. There was a forlorn-looking group of children sitting above the tunnel every evening, swinging their bare feet over the street; they didn't seem to be scattering far. But an unwanted volunteer is a nuisance and a source of more work if one is not expecting or looking for one and I eventually gave up my efforts to be useful in Zanzibar.

I waved goodbye to the folks in the mountain village as Father Sabuni started up the diocese jeep and headed down the deeply rutted road, gold braid swinging. Wanting to be useful is not enough, I thought, as we bounced down the treacherous road home. You have to be willing to offer help when and where it is wanted. Their water was nearly undrinkable, but the people of the village were optimistic. They knew they had a champion in Father Sabuni, who did not require any permits or persuasion to lend a helping hand and did not wait for volunteers to offer their services—but poached them directly from his hotel before they had time to unpack.

BRIGHT BLOOMS

The next day I hitched a motorbike ride from Lushoto and the driver dropped me off at a waterfall high in the mountains. After hiking up the many layers of the cascading waterfall I headed back, taking a path that broke off the main road. I could have taken the same road back to Lushoto, but this path (according to the motorbike driver) was shorter. Perhaps more importantly, I had not taken it before. The clouds blew in and out through giant eucalyptus trees, everything was in bloom at the end of the dry season, and the mountain air was crisp.

At first it seemed to be nothing more than a drainage ditch heading steeply downhill through banana plantations and pear orchards, but then I saw traces of foot traffic. A moment later, two women came up from behind.

"*Jambo!*"

"*Mzuri!*"

"Lushoto?" I asked, pointing down the barely visible trail.

They nodded and I followed them, watching their feet on the path. The older one had lightweight canvas shoes, the younger one was barefoot. They were both wrapped in colorful *kangas* and walking briskly. We crossed a steep green valley surrounded by mountain peaks on either side, past tidy farms and gardens. The sun was bright, but it was cool and pleasant.

"Lushoto," the younger one said to me and pointed to the left while they veered off to the larger path headed right. I was now on a real footpath—barely wider than my foot. The path had been there some time, I could tell, for it was raised on either side above the grassy hill, which had eroded away. I came to another split in the path and this time there was no one to direct me. I decided to go the way the water was flowing.

A few minutes later I met a group of people walking. I pointed: "Lushoto?" They nodded and smiled and I continued on and soon entered the forest. Should I worry about entering the forest alone on a narrow footpath? I didn't think so. The eucalyptus trees towered overhead, draped in vines as thick as my forearm. It was noisy with birds and I saw a monkey jump from one branch to another. I was taking a new path in Lushoto; I was just following my feet—not anticipating, not planning, not worrying.

That night I went to dinner at a small hotel and met David, a middle-aged New Yorker and self-described atheist. David explained to me in a pronounced New York accent that he had been coming to Lushoto and staying for several weeks at a time for the past six years. He loved going to church, he told me, which surprised his New York friends. David spent most of every Sunday attending church. He knew the starting times for all the denominations and went from one service to the next, sometimes arriving late for one and leaving early from another so he could catch as many services as possible.

"I also volunteer to teach English," he told me, "and occasionally teach Samba dance!"

The next day was Sunday and I decided I would attend the Lutheran church. The Lutheran church in Lushoto was the main church in the diocese (the "cathedral," locals called it, which sounded rather un-Lutheran to me). I figured I had given the Benedictines enough of my business and, raised in the Lutheran church, I knew they supported a lot of humanitarian projects in Tanzania. I wondered if there wasn't a way I might rope the Lutherans into Father Sabuni's water scheme.

Unlike the Catholic church, the Lutheran church was new, located on a wooded hill. It was a contemporary design with a green metal roof and pews facing the altar from three directions. There were lots of windows on all sides and a beautiful view of the surrounding forest. It was a nice service, entirely in Swahili, with good music, and the sermon was only twenty minutes long (short by African standards), during which I listened for words I knew and watched the minister struggle to deliver jokes. Whatever the topic was, he was clearly more in his element during the earnest bits than when he was trying to get a laugh. I was sympathetic; comedy is hard.

Unfortunately, immediately after the service, there was the annual financial report. This was only marginally more interesting in Swahili than it would have been in English. A good percentage of the congregation slipped out the door before the minister saw and gently chastised them. He then presumably assured the remaining congregants this would not take long—which was a bald-faced lie.

The church treasurer started his report and I could see he intended to make the most of this rare opportunity in the spotlight. The report droned on. I recognized only the words for which Swahili does not have the vocabulary, including "Sunday School," "Financial Report," and "November." (I had to admire a language that has no word for "Financial Report.")

I was sandwiched between two groups of women who were either more devout or less agile than the others, as they stayed put. Pinning down my end of the pew (and closest escape route) was an elderly woman who looked determined to go the distance. This excruciating monologue continued for more than twenty-five minutes until the minister could sense he was losing his audience. He thanked the treasurer and put out a call for questions, and of course a pompous-looking man in a Western-style suit took the opportunity to hear himself speak, which seemed to delight the treasurer, as he then gave a lengthy response. By then everyone was squirming in their seats.

Three women to my right snuck past the determined elderly woman and I was sorely tempted to do the same. But just as I was about to attempt my escape, I noticed through the thinning crowd I was not the only *mzungu* (white person) in the church. David the atheist was there sitting with an extremely pale man. I figured if church-hopping David could sit through this, I certainly could.

Finally, after the third question, the minister resolutely picked up his Bible and hymnal (a not very subtle sign this discussion had come to an end), thanked the treasurer, and said the benediction. We all proceeded out of the church to "Rock of Ages" sung in Swahili.

I stepped into the bright sunshine and said hello to the minister, who was standing with David and the very blond young man. The minister asked if we had been introduced (it wouldn't do for three *mzungus* not to know each other) and I said I had met David but was then introduced to Oscar, who turned out to be from northern Sweden. He said he had seen me around town and I told him I had been trailing around with Father Sabuni looking at a rural water project, but I hastened to add I was not a water engineer, I was just looking at Father Sabuni's proposal.

"Oh!" said Oscar, "I actually am."

Oscar was a water engineer trained by the Swedish Air Force. Until recently, he had been installing water distribution systems in Uppsala. I asked him if he was working on a project here and he said no, he was here doing a residency with the Lutheran church.

Our friend David the atheist had to leave — he had several more churches to visit that morning.

"The next service is the Apostolics!" he said, sounding very excited.

We waved goodbye to David as he scampered off.

"Let's have breakfast," Oscar suggested. After an almost three-hour church service, this sounded like an excellent idea.

Over breakfast, Oscar told me how he had been a highly-compensated water engineer when he started to sense God didn't want him to be an engineer in Uppsala. Unfortunately, God was not immediately forthcoming about what he should be doing instead. So, while waiting for further instructions, Oscar enrolled in theology classes in Sweden and eventually ended up in Tanzania, where he thought his residency might be more useful than in Sweden. We talked about the water plan. I told him about the springs that had been diverted and the five-gallon pails filled with dirty surface water.

"Do you think the Lutherans might be interested in helping?" I asked.

"I don't know. I don't think they cooperate much with the Catholics. The Christian churches here are very competitive. You can be excommunicated from the Lutheran church in Tanzania for drinking. They are trying to outdo one another with their devotion because they are all competing for souls with the Muslims."

"I can't imagine the church of Martin Luther excommunicating its members for drinking!" I said, thinking of the former monk's well-documented fondness for beer.

"Ya, well, that's how it is here. But I think we might try to talk to them. They are saying they want to become more ecumenical. This might be a good chance."

We sat for a moment in silence, drinking dark coffee from Kilimanjaro.

"God has been quiet, but I am fairly certain I am supposed to be in Lushoto," Oscar said, looking out over the lush forest. "I'm just not sure why."

"Maybe, while you're figuring it out, you might see if you could help Father Sabuni," I suggested.

Oscar smiled. "Ya," he said, "I can do that."

Walking back from breakfast, I stopped at the outdoor market. It was full of an amazing variety of fruits and vegetables that thrived in this temperate mountain climate. Earlier in the week I had walked to the Benedictine convent and discovered the nuns there made a simply wonderful Gouda cheese. I had a small wheel of it back at the hostel.

"I'll bet I can get Leonard to make a proper salad out of nun's cheese and these avocados!" I thought as I headed home with my bag full of vegetables.

I returned to the quiet Benedictine hostel and poured myself a glass of the monk's slightly effervescent Chenin Blanc. I was happy to be alone in my monastic little room. I imagined church-hopping David, coming back year after year to teach Samba dance, and Oscar, leaving his well-trod path in Uppsala, waiting to hear from God in the Tanzanian mountains. I looked out the window at the garden in the twilight and wondered what would happen next in this peculiar and uncharted life I now found myself.

"Perhaps the monkeys were right," I said to myself, "Perhaps I *am* ridiculous."

I sipped my Chenin Blanc and smiled.

•   •   •   •   •

I knew it was time to leave: the signs were everywhere.

First, I started decorating my room at St. Benedict's Hostel. I hung colorful scarves from Zanzibar on the mosquito-netting framework over my bed. The mosquito netting was blue and so were my scarves, in varying shades, so it was quite a nice effect, I thought. Then I brought in some bouquets of bougainvillea and put them on my little wooden table.

But soon I was no longer content to inhabit my room. As Oscar, Father Sabuni, and I sat working together on the water plan in the open-air dining room, the artificial flowers started to bother me. I was waiting for Oscar to arrive one morning when I filched a fistful of fresh flowers from the abundant gardens surrounding the church and put them in an empty Chenin Blanc bottle from the Benedictine monastery. When Father Sabuni arrived, he admired the flowers and said they were just what was needed at the hostel. That was all the license I required. Soon all the tables had fresh flower arrangements. The soft-spoken Leonard demonstrated a hitherto-undiscovered talent for floral arrangement. He padded out to the church's flowerbeds, kitchen knife in hand, and returned with bouquets of bright blooms. He culled the faded blossoms and replaced them with new flowers in the afternoon.

Yes, I had stayed too long.

I instructed Leonard in how to make coffee and he did an exemplary job. He also prepared the salad I liked with fresh avocado, tomato, cucumber, bell peppers, and Gouda cheese. Now Leonard could barely be restrained from new displays of domestic accomplishment. He served avocado salad whenever Oscar came over to discuss the latest developments.

Oscar was very thin and always hungry. He was leaving soon for Tanga and then on to Sweden to continue his theological studies. He had delayed his departure two days so he could scoot around by motorbike to most of the affected areas in Father Sabuni's water distribution plan. He discovered the survey was badly out of date and the first order of business was to get a new survey done.

Oscar set up an appointment at the Lutheran diocese headquarters and the three of us met with the assistant bishop. The meeting was friendly; the Lutherans seemed pleased to suddenly find themselves with the ambitious Father Sabuni in their corner and a project already in progress that would benefit a large number of their parishioners. Father Sabuni was clearly delighted to find an audience for his lonely crusade. We discussed how the existing survey was out of date and it soon came to light the Lutherans had an in-house engineer and Father Sabuni had a bit of pull with the Ministry of Water. Between the two, we concluded, they should be able to update the survey rather easily.

Both parishes had been called upon to increase their ecumenical activities without much to show for it. But by the end of the meeting, it was agreed an ecumenical partnership would be formed to implement the water project. The Lutheran and Catholic Bishops would both have to sign on, but neither side seemed to think there would be any difficulty in getting their respective bishop's approval.

Father Sabuni was delighted.

"I believe this is all part of God's plan for Lushoto," he told Oscar and me on the way back to the hostel. Then he and Oscar ate an entire bag of the tiny, tasty sugar cookies I had brought back from the market and served with Leonard's coffee.

I felt a bit guilty about delaying Oscar's departure. "You were supposed to leave days ago!" I reminded him over coffee and cookies.

"No, no, I don't mind," Oscar insisted, helping himself to another cookie. "This project is the first thing I've done during my residency that has had tangible results. I'm glad I got to do something concrete before returning to my books in Sweden."

I thanked him again and gave him a bag of cookies for the bus ride to Tanga.

The next day I planned to head out into the mountains for my much-delayed camping trip. A guide named Mouhdi from the Usambara Tourism Center had been checking in with me less often, apparently unconcerned I would disappear without hiring him, as I seemed to have taken up permanent residence in the Benedictine hostel.

I was hoping there might be another hiking group I could join, but things were slowing down for the season and there were fewer hikers and no campers heading into the mountains in the next few days. I finally decided I would head out alone with Mouhdi. I told Mouhdi I wanted to camp for three nights and would like to spend at least one night "in the middle of nowhere." He promised to oblige. There was a lot of nowhere in the Usambara Mountains.

Before I went to my little room overlooking the flowerbeds for the night, Father Sabuni stopped by to wish me a safe safari and invited me to dinner when I returned.

"You will always have a home here at the hostel," he told me, and he suggested I should forget about my bill (eleven dollars a night with breakfast included). I declined his offer of free accommodation and accepted his invitation to dinner upon my return.

The sun had set in Lushoto; my pack was ready for the morning. Before I went to bed I admired Leonard's handiwork, and he promised to keep the bouquets fresh while I was away. I went to sleep happy — happy about the flowers, happy about the water project, happy about my time in Lushoto and getting the opportunity to do something useful. It's nice to admire flowers from a distance, I thought, but there comes a time when you need to bring some of those bright blooms inside.

THE DRUMS

Early in the morning, Mouhdi and I headed straight up into the mountains. I managed to keep a lively conversation going with Mouhdi for all of it except the steepest bits, and Mouhdi said he liked having someone who talked while walking. (He might as well like it since he didn't get much choice in the matter.) I asked questions about the crops and the trees and what people were saying and what sort of fruit we passed. We popped in for a cup of really good tea in one tiny village, which amused everyone, as they had never had a tourist visit before.

We had a great dinner at a friendly guesthouse perched in the hills and then pitched our tents out back. No one at this hotel high in the mountains spoke a word of English, so Mouhdi was conversing for both of us in Swahili rather than relying on my marginally effective (albeit professional) pantomime skills. It was easier to let Mouhdi do the talking, and he seemed to consider it part of his guide services. Our second night would be our "nowhere" night, so the hotel was packing us dinner to take along. Mouhdi also asked them to pack us something for lunch so we would be well provisioned. We were going to stay at the top of a mountain, he said, but he confessed he had never actually been there before.

I crawled out of my tent the next day and had a cup of coffee from the guesthouse with the pleasant morning sun on my back. It was cool but the mountain sun was brutal. (I noticed I had reburned my nose during yesterday's hike.) I asked Mouhdi to get the bill, and while he was getting it, I tallied up an estimate in my head of what I expected it would be. We had agreed on a lower rate than Mouhdi would normally charge as a guide for a larger group, but I had said I would pay for food along the way.

When Mouhdi brought the bill, it was nearly three times what I anticipated. The simple dinner of rice and vegetables the night before and food for the next day was more than I had paid for a hotel since coming to Tanzania. I had not, as I normally do, asked what the food was going to cost before it was served, wrapped, and ready to go.

"What is this?" I asked Mouhdi. "How can a simple picnic cost eight thousand shillings?!"

"That's just what it costs..."

"Mouhdi! Eight *thousand* shillings? I trusted you to keep track of these things. I didn't know I had to watch every little expense, but apparently I do!"

"It's for both dinner and lunch... it's just what people normally pay!" Mouhdi tried to explain.

"Fine!" I said. "I guess I'll just have to pay more attention in the future." I handed him some money and he quickly got up and left.

Only then did I realize what a total ass I was.

Eight thousand Tanzanian shillings was less than six dollars. The hotel had packed four large boxes of specially prepared food for $1.50 each. The boxes alone likely cost half of that. Mouhdi had asked for lunch and dinner and the kind people at the guesthouse were not about to send us into the mountains hungry. I had just pitched a fit over a home-cooked meal costing less than a dollar and fifty cents.

I am not that person. I don't know who that person is, but I'm sure I don't want to know her.

I got up from my sunny spot, no longer pleasant, and went to find Mouhdi. He was on the other side of the hotel and obviously angry.

"I'm sorry, Mouhdi. I was wrong. I don't know why I acted that way. The food is fine—it's great. Please forgive me for being such a bitch."

Mouhdi sat with his back to me. "Nothing surprises me anymore," he said, which was not exactly the same as saying he forgave me, but he had a right to be angry.

We started hiking again, but this day there was no lively chitchat.

We walked in silence, Mouhdi playing the professional guide and me wondering what on earth would make me behave so badly. I had panicked, I realized. The blissful feeling of letting the path take me had vanished and I had panicked over my lack of control, my vulnerability, my dependence on strangers. I was deeply disappointed in myself, discouraged by this slow two-steps-forward-and-one-step-back method of becoming whoever it was I was becoming. I may not yet know who I was, but I was *not* that woman screaming at the hotel over her bill. I also noted both my feet now had giant blisters forming and were demanding my attention.

"Take a number!" I told them grumpily.

We stopped for a picnic lunch high in the mountains in a place that sees few hikers. As soon as we sat down, a group of children gathered and stared at me unabashedly. I tried to be as entertaining as possible while eating an avocado, as it seemed the white lady eating lunch was the best — and only — show in town.

After lunch, we left all villages behind and climbed nearly straight up the side of a mountain. In the thinning air, I felt my heart beating hard in my chest. My pack seemed impossibly heavy, my spirits were sunk, and my badly blistered feet were no longer even on my shortlist of concerns. We moved slowly toward the peak, and then, unexpectedly, we were there. There was only one tree on the mountaintop and a few low bushes. Mouhdi and I sat for a few minutes under the shade of the single tree and looked at the amazing landscape far below. Then we found level spots for our tents and went to take a nap. He told me to wake him later.

As the sun was about to set, I got up and started to gather wood. The sky was turning pink and I could see the lights in the villages far below. I woke Mouhdi as sunset was coming and we silently worked together to start a low fire. Just as the fire caught, the clouds rolled in and the villages disappeared entirely. We were on an island of land completely surrounded by dense fog on all sides. Then the sun set and it was dark. We tended our fire and I heard sounds coming from below, somewhere in the fog.

"Local drumming," Mouhdi said, speaking for the first time that evening. They were drumming in one of the villages below. The distant drumming continued, very faint.

We shared our packed dinner of potatoes fried in egg batter with peppers and cucumbers the hotel had prepared. It was delicious and I told Mouhdi so. I asked Mouhdi how he became a guide.

"My father was in the Tanzanian military—he's from Zanzibar. He first came to the Usambara Mountains to recruit for the army. He went to every household to make the young men enlist. Some of them didn't want to go and he had to... he used some tough tactics," Mouhdi said, looking into the fire. "After his recruiting days were over, he decided to stay in Lushoto. He met my mom and they had a family. He never went back to Zanzibar."

Mouhdi was the oldest son and his father wanted him to go into the military, but Mouhdi wanted to go into tourism and got a chance to study in South Africa.

"I fell in love with my ecology professor and we had a baby together, but we couldn't get along," he told me. "She's married now and still in South Africa. My parents are helping me raise my girl. When she's grown up, my daughter and I are going to have a business of our own here in the Usambara Mountains. This is my home," he said, still looking into the fire.

I felt raindrops and we figured it was time to take refuge in our tents. I kicked apart the small pile of burning sticks and Mouhdi gallantly offered to pee on the remaining embers.

As soon as I zipped up the door to my tent the rain started in earnest. The wind gusts billowed the sides of my tent in and out in abrupt, violent bursts. The lightning flashed bright in the sky, but the thunder was quiet and in the distance. What was suddenly loud was the drumming.

The strong wind of the storm carried the sound of the drumming to the top of the mountain as if it were close at hand. I could hear every hand beat, every stroke. I could hear the sound of flesh on flesh, the pause, the rhythm as it grew. The sound was no longer distant and alien. It was intimate and comforting.

"Yes, you will be scared sometimes," the drums said. "You will do things you regret. But be kind to yourself." Because everything will be fine, the drums assured me. Everything will be better than fine. Everything will be *mzuri, mzuri sana*.

•   •   •   •   •

Father Sabuni had me to dinner for a final farewell.

He had found another engineer who was willing to assist and was confident he would soon have the information assembled to rewrite the proposal for the water project. After dinner he told me again how meeting Oscar and me was part of God's plan and when I returned to Lushoto (I noticed it was "when" rather than "if") I would not be coming as a tourist, but coming home.

"May I pray for you, Carrie?" he asked.

"Yes, certainly."

"May I pray in Swahili?"

"Of course."

Father Sabuni sounded a bit reticent when he spoke in English. He was self-effacing by nature and every sentence sounded as if it might begin with an apology. But in Swahili, the reticence vanished. When he spoke to God in Swahili, he sounded as if he was continuing a conversation with an old friend that had begun long ago. I heard my name and "safari," and he mentioned Lushoto and Oscar and water. He prayed for several minutes and seemed to forget I was there. Then he said "amen" and he gave me a hug. I looked into his kind eyes and promised him I would send an email at the next opportunity.

In the morning, Leonard made a breakfast that looked as if he expected I would be traveling for a week without further nourishment. I knew it was time to leave, but as I took a final look around the cheery, flower-filled hostel, I also knew I was leaving another home and I would miss it. I had a last cup of Leonard's good coffee and headed out to where the buses collected in the morning.

The gathered buses all had names, but the meanings were often cryptic. Next to a bus called "No Discussion" there was a bus called "Hunting Knife" inexplicably illustrated with a pink-cheeked white girl feeding a bunny with a bottle. I got on a mini *matatu* that looked as though it was threatening to leave soon (departure was dependent upon having at least one passenger in every seat). My pack was thrown onto the roof and we were off.

For the first couple of hours we negotiated the spectacular curves of the Usambara Mountains, slowly winding our way down past Soni, past the sheer cliffs and waterfalls I had not seen when I arrived in the dark. Soon the traffic picked up and we made more stops and picked up more passengers till we were full to overflowing. I watched the peculiar politics of what was allowed in the bus and what was sent to the roof. Sometimes it was obvious, other times less so. The noisy, orange-billed geese went on the roof, but the bananas were allowed in. Why? Perhaps the narrow necks of the geese were more vulnerable to the shifting, shuffling feet in the aisle? Maybe the bananas complained less? I do not know.

All the way from Lushoto we had the same "conductors," young men who collected the fares, assisted with luggage, and let prospective passengers in each village know we were on our way to Tanga. A man with a "Chick-fil-A" T-shirt rode most of the way standing in the stairwell immediately in front of me until the bus became too full for him to stand even on the bottom step; then he had to sit in my window. With his butt blocking my view, his legs, head, and arms all hanging outside the bus, we careened down the steep, rocky road.

On the bus, I felt back in the flow. I was at ease surrounded by strangers, strange landscapes, strange languages. I rode neither completely awake nor quite asleep; the sights and smells and sounds formed an ever-shifting collage. I was part of the collective ride, joined with others in a way that was rarely possible for me at any other time in Africa. As we bumped and jostled down the road, for a few hours I ceased to be the white outsider and I relaxed utterly into the shoulders and hips of the passengers who entered the group, rode for a time, shifted position, and departed. No one on the bus forced their way or defended their space. The bus of people ebbed and flowed like water, human bodies filling the available space, making a single, living entity.

After Chick-Fil-A again found foothold inside the bus, I realized he had been providing useful protection from the sun. Since the sad loss of my daypack on the beach in Zanzibar, I had been struggling to find replacement sun protection. Sunglasses had turned out to be a surprisingly difficult thing to find in this part of Tanzania—although not as difficult as sunscreen. When I finally found it, the sunscreen had no effect whatsoever. The pharmacist had not sold a bottle in memory and was not entirely sure what it was used for. In Soni, I found an enormous pair of reflective sunglasses that gave me the appearance of a startled insect. My beloved and ancient hat had also been taken so, in Lushoto, I added a bright orange visor to my ensemble. The visor worked well and shaded my defenseless Scandinavian nose which had burned and peeled twice since the loss of my hat. I caught a reflection of myself in the bus window and saw I closely resembled one of the geese recently banished to the roof. When my insect-like sunglasses were added to the ensemble, nearly my entire face was obscured, and I looked as if I might be entering a witness protection program. I was thinking of making it my new signature look.

I had been debating where to go next. Originally, I thought I would head off to more mountains, leave the cool and friendly Usambaras and see the mighty snow-capped Kilimanjaro. But after my time in Lushoto, the idea of heading into Arusha (the gateway to Kilimanjaro)—with its big crowds, prearranged safaris, and legendary touts—no longer sounded appealing. Away from the coast for some time now, I found the ocean was calling. I had read one short paragraph about a mysterious place called "Mwazaro" along the south Kenyan coast. It was a bit tricky to get to, apparently, but it was supposed to be beautiful and a holy place to the Swahili. Like the enigmatic mention of "sailing a dhow to Mombasa," it sounded right.

The three-hour bus ride lasted only five hours and then I was back in Tanga. This time, trying to avoid the aggressive touts, I was searching for a motorbike to take me from the ATM to the next bus when I fell into a hole in the sidewalk, with my pack on my back, and badly skinned both knees.

Bloody and dirty, I finally made it to the bus stop and shared another bag of tasty sugar cookies with a primary school teacher from

Dar es Salaam while I waited for potatoes to be loaded on the roof of my little *matatu*. The schoolteacher was interested in my travels and impressed by the cookies. We promised to stay in touch. My plan was to jump out of the *matatu* and try to make it to Mwazaro Beach, just a few kilometers off the main road. With the slow-moving potatoes, however, I was afraid I might arrive after dark, and I didn't know what type of transportation—if any—would be available at the crossroads.

After a lot of unpaved road and an uneventful border crossing, I was deposited at what was not even a wide spot in the road and told it was that way to Mwazaro Beach. The light was growing dim. A motorbike was loitering at the side of the road.

"How much to Mwazaro Beach?" I asked the driver.

"One hundred shillings," he replied. A motorbike at that hour was a good deal at ten times the price.

"Terrific!" I said. "Let's go!"

Just then a second motorbike pulled up and asked me where I was going.

"Mwazaro Beach," I told him.

"I'll take you for 150 shillings!" he announced.

"I already have a driver—and he's going to take me for 100 shillings."

"He's crazy!" the second driver said.

"I know," I replied, "he's my friend. All my friends are crazy!"

Motorbike driver number two was still laughing as my new friend and I drove away with my pack on my back, my skinned knees and snappy orange visor headed toward the sunset. I didn't know where I was going, but I was almost sure I was headed in the right direction.

BAD BUFFALO

At first glance, the place seemed deserted.

A complex of small coral stone cottages facing the sea, the resort sat on the water's edge in a quiet cove. The electricity was all solar and wind-generated. The water flowed straight from the Usambara Mountains and was clean enough to drink right from the tap. (After Nigeria, this took a bit of getting used to.) The roofs that were not covered with solar panels were thick, well-constructed thatch, very high to allow the heat to escape and the ocean breeze to enter. There were washbasins outside made of three-foot-wide seashells. The water overflowed the giant shells and fell into shallow basins on the ground before draining so I could wash my hands and feet at the same time with the same water.

I found the owner before I found a receptionist. Hans was holding court in the open-air restaurant, a capacious, slate-floored structure with a towering bamboo roof, comfortable furniture made of mangrove poles, and a long communal table where everyone took their meals together. That was what they were preparing to do, as it happens, just as I showed up. Two Masai showed me to the camping area, as the coral-walled cottages were well beyond my budget. The camping area was lovely, with shade awnings built in a circle on the sand and a solar-powered bathroom just a few meters away. I quickly removed the road dust, rinsed my raw knees, threw a clean Zanzibar shawl over my shoulders, and joined the dinner party for a feast of curried *dorado*, salad, and a chocolate layer cake for dessert. The restaurant was full of large friendly dogs, two African grey parrots, and good conversation in English and German. There was a group of German television journalists, a Dutch designer and builder of fantastic Swahili-inspired beachside castles, and a couple of feisty ladies from Nairobi.

Hans was a retired German research doctor, I later learned, a man who had spent his professional career spreading misinformation about the safety of smoking on behalf of the tobacco industry throughout Africa. His life was abruptly changed on a flight from Frankfurt to Seattle when he suffered a heart attack.

Thanks to a quick-thinking young software engineer named Bill Gates, who also happened to be flying first-class that day, Hans survived. But he was told his liver was too compromised to withstand heart bypass surgery and he was given six months to live. Hans quit the tobacco business. He told everyone he was headed in search of "sandy beaches, hula girls, whiskey bars, and rocking chairs." He sold everything in Germany and headed to the coast of Kenya. That was twenty years ago.

The story continues: threats made against his life when his former tobacco industry associates became concerned he might start to talk about the tactics used to introduce tobacco in developing countries, the Kenyan partner who tried to assassinate him and the witch doctor's daughter who saved his life, his love affair with the beautiful karate expert who sadly met her demise doing a dangerous stunt in a Mercedes, and his second near-death experience when he was hit by a petrol truck as he was about to board the ferry to Mombasa. Fourteen were killed and Hans was dragged into the water, run over, and headed to the morgue when rescue workers realized he was still alive.

I have no idea if any of this is true.

The run-in with the petrol truck affected Hans' memory, so he told some of the same stories several times. He informed me at least two dozen times (each time with equal pleasure) his dog, Sammy, was a cross between an Australian dingo and an African ridgeback— "the first mixed breed of its kind!"

But Hans also told me about *mwazaro*.

"*Mwazaro,*" Hans said, means "a balance between the spirit worlds." I also read it meant "a place of prayer." I would imagine trying to balance the spirit worlds would require a lot of prayer, so I see no real contradiction. On the right hand, there were the forces of creativity, individuality, and invention. On the left were the forces of civilization, technology, and community.

"Mwazaro," Hans explained in strongly German-accented English, "is about bringing these two worlds into balance."

The word *mwazaro*, he said, was used in languages throughout much of Africa. Someone lacks *mwazaro* when they are out of sync, no longer in balance.

"This place was called *Mwazaro* long before I arrived," he continued. "It's a holy place. I made peace with the spirits on both sides before I started building."

I would hesitate to call Hans a spiritual guide: he used raunchy language, and his habit of punctuating every conversation with the announcement that his dog Sammy was "a cross between an Australian dingo and an African ridgeback—the first mixed breed of its kind!" somewhat undermined his more philosophical musings. But Mwazaro *was* a special place.

Low tide came in at about eight-thirty that morning and the white sand flats stretched far out into the distance. Every day for the next several days I watched, mesmerized by the tide's long creep in. First the mangrove trees were up to their toes and then over their knees in water. I walked out into the water on the soft white coral sand; the warm saltwater felt good on my skinned knees and the sand was soft under my feet. I walked until the resort was barely visible in the distance. The warm water slowly climbed up my body but, no matter how far I walked, I never reached a place where the water was over my head.

Long after I was out of the ocean, I could still feel the warm waves climbing up my body. I could still feel myself relinquishing control and relaxing into the slowly rising tide. By evening the tide had retreated. The mangroves stood on solid ground again.

I decided I would stay in Mwazaro a little while longer. As I felt the tug of my journey ending, I wanted to watch the tide advance and recede another time. I wanted to spend at least one more day in *mwazaro*.

• • • • •

I had not anticipated I would spend my last weekend in East Africa with 700 Jehovah's Witnesses.

While I knew I would not always feel the peace I'd felt in Mwazaro, as I left to catch the overnight bus to Nairobi I felt full to overflowing. As an additional incentive to move on, I had succeeded (after days of no apparent progress) in teaching Hans's two young African grey parrots to say, "Obama! Obama! Yes, we can!" The parrots were now saying it—loudly—for hours at a time. Hans was not happy about this. The African grey parrot has an expected lifespan of approximately eighty years. It was time to leave. Also, I had to meet my relative Kathy in Nairobi.

My former mother-in-law (a wonderful woman who had assured me after the divorce that we would always remain close) had written shortly after I arrived in Kenya to say she had family in Nairobi and they would love to meet me. Two days after leaving Mwazaro, I found myself in Nairobi seated in the Jehovah's Witness Assembly Hall for a two-day symposium titled "Stand Firm Against the Devil's Crafty Acts." This was the first event of its kind for me. I was there with Kathy, her delightful husband, their two teenage daughters, and their daughters' friend Tabu, who had come for this once-a-year meeting.

I knew Kathy was somehow related to my former in-laws, but upon meeting her face-to-face for the first time at her office in downtown Nairobi, it was soon revealed neither she nor I had any idea exactly how they were related.

"I was hoping you might know," she said.

I fired off an email to my former mother-in-law, who cheerily replied that Kathy was my former father-in-law's fourth cousin. This would make me the *ex-wife of Kathy's fourth cousin once removed*—which was far more information than Kathy's Jehovah's Witness brethren required.

So, when Kathy introduced me to her dear friends in the Assembly Hall as her "relative from America," she shot me a sly glance, we both smiled, and I quickly extended my hand and greeted them warmly to fend off further inquiries about the precise nature of our familial ties.

In spite of having no recognizable claim to even shirttail relations, Kathy and her family opened their home to me in a remarkably generous fashion, providing me with a bed on a busy weekend, meals with their family, and a welcome taste of home at the end of a long journey.

Kathy had lived in Kenya since she first came from Canada as a missionary in 1968. She met and married her witty and charming Kenyan Jehovah's Witness husband and had clearly found a loving home in Nairobi. The Assembly Hall was built (as I learned they often are) in two days, like a giant barn-raising. Everyone contributed their labor: laying block, painting walls, cooking meals, or minding children. This hall in Nairobi was simple but attractive, with giant baobab trees painted on either side of a stage in front and large louvered windows along the walls to allow plenty of fresh breeze to flow through. It seated seven hundred comfortably.

Kathy had Witness friends she'd met when she first came to Nairobi more than forty years earlier. The members of the congregation were a diverse mix of Kenyans, Indians, and British. The atmosphere was jovial and affectionate. The symposium consisted of a series of talks, each given by a male member of the Assembly or a missionary. Women shared their experiences by having a male monitor ask them questions, which they answered while holding microphones. (This avoided the appearance of the women preaching, which the opinionated Apostle Paul cautioned against.)

At the lunch break, we had a picnic in the shade outside by the car and I found myself alone with the girls' friend Tabu. Tabu told me she was a seamstress. I asked her about her work and she told me the sorts of things she sewed. Then, with no one else within earshot, she impulsively blurted out, "But my passion is environmental conservation. I want to protect Kenya's natural resources—that is my dream!"

I told her I thought it was a wonderful ambition and suggested she look into European programs offering college scholarships to African students in the field of environmental studies. She thanked me for the advice, then we packed up the pasta salad and returned to learn more about the devil's crafty acts.

We learned Satan's crafty acts are found in the fields of technology, entertainment, and education. We were told how Satan urges us first to waste money on useless computer gadgets and then to waste time figuring out how to make them work. We ran the risk of encountering Satan at all-inclusive resorts (which I had no trouble believing), and it was Satan who encouraged us to run into debt buying useless electronics and visiting Disney World. I found these admonishments to avoid the pitfalls of consumerism and debt refreshing. In fact, I was wholeheartedly behind this exposé of Satan's craftiness until we got to the field of education.

It was then explained how Satan was luring young people into "higher education," which was primarily a tool to achieve "prominence," earn more money, and spend time studying things with no practical value to one's spiritual life. Higher education, it was explained, was a shaky ladder. Parents who stood by while their children foolishly climbed it, did so at their peril.

We watched a short skit in which a Jehovah's Witness elder counseled a young woman who had won a university scholarship and was planning to accept it until she was warned about the dangers of higher education. A little education was a good thing, it was explained, but higher education just puts you into Satan's hands. Two young people (including one of Kathy's daughters) came onstage and testified how their lives had been blessed by their decision not to go to college.

We then sang a song about the joys of serving Jehovah in the face of ridicule and abuse (a common refrain), followed by a short talk on the importance of staying spiritually awake, which was timely at this point in the afternoon when it appeared a number of us were struggling to maintain wakefulness of any kind.

The last talk was given by a British missionary on the theme: "Beware of Overconfidence." His metaphor for the topic was the story of a buffalo. The missionary told us he had seen this foolish buffalo with his own eyes while on safari in Masai lands. The buffalo in question strayed from the herd, attracting the attention of hungry lions, then returned to the herd. When he strayed a second time, the lions drew near, but his fellow buffalo surrounded him and got him safely back into the herd.

But then our friend the buffalo strayed a third time, and this time his fellow buffalo apparently felt he had strayed once too often and he was eaten by the lions. The lesson for the Assembly was not to stray from the herd. The lesson for me was that I would make a really bad buffalo.

The next day I slipped away from the herd and went to Nairobi National Park. I anticipated problems, as my travel guidebook said I would need a vehicle to enter the game preserve (so as not to be eaten by lions) and I obviously had none. But the Park was only a kilometer from the Assembly Hall, and Kathy and her family gamely dropped me off at the gate.

Upon entering the park, I saw a bus about to enter the game preserve. It was a school bus filled with excited schoolgirls in maroon uniforms. I approached the ranger leading the tour as well as the girls' teacher and asked if I could ride along. The ranger was reluctant, but the friendly young biology teacher, Emily, had no problem sharing her seat with me on the fully loaded bus. I boarded, the lone foreigner with a busload of lively Kenyan schoolgirls from out of town on a field trip.

The schoolgirls and I had a great time. We saw giraffes, zebras, three types of antelope, wildebeests, impalas, ostriches, warthogs, baboons, egrets, secretary birds, bushbucks, and, of course, buffalo. The girls, I learned, were all members of a high school wildlife club. I took a group picture of them with Emily and asked them what they wanted to do when they grew up. They all wanted to be rangers and biologists. They were ecstatic about the weekend-long trip with the enthusiastic Emily and eager to see and preserve Kenya's wildlife.

Later, I sat on the outdoor deck of the National Park restaurant watching the warthogs and antelope at the watering hole just a few meters away. Two families of baboons were quarreling over who would get a table at the most popular acacia tree. I was drinking my coffee and thinking about my trip and those excited schoolgirls, just a few years younger than Tabu, who also loved wildlife. I remembered the warning about climbing that treacherous ladder. I realized it was my last day in East Africa and I suddenly wished I could see Tabu again.

I wanted to tell her that not every ladder topples and that not everyone who wanders alone is eaten by lions. I wanted to tell her that sometimes you have to do some climbing to get to where you want to go and sometimes you have to go alone if you're going to go at all. But most of all, I wanted to tell her that it was worth it—worth going alone, worth the risk of lions, even worth the occasional fall.

WHAT HAPPENS NEXT

Flying out of Nairobi I saw the cookfires on the outskirts of the city and thought of the conversation I had with Karen and Pauline at book club that had propelled me to East Africa. Eating our plates of spicy Jollof rice, Karen had told us how she was traveling with her own young daughter, now only four, and how she wanted to travel more as her daughter grew older.

"She can already carry a pack and hike for four hours!" Karen said delightedly of her small girl covered in braids and beads, now sleeping soundly in her lap.

"Do you still travel alone?" Karen asked Pauline.

Pauline shook her head. "No," she said, "I stopped several years ago."

"Why?" Karen asked.

Pauline looked down at her polished nails and was silent.

"Why did you stop traveling, Pauline?" Karen persisted.

I imagined the elegant Pauline would laugh and say she had done enough traveling out of a backpack and she now preferred more comfort. But when Pauline answered, her voice was wistful. She looked up, remembering.

"It was the wood smoke in the evening," she finally said quietly. "I would be traveling alone on a bus as the sun was setting, and everywhere I went I would smell wood smoke. I knew I was passing someone's home and they were making dinner and I would become homesick for a home of my own."

Now I could smell wood smoke and I knew it was—finally—time to go home.

After more than three years in Africa—and with very little warning—I knew I was ready to go back to the house under the maple trees and face an uncertain new life. After months of not being able to contemplate a return to any kind of familiar life, then months of doing nothing but healing, then a few months of discovering who this new person was—this middle-aged woman without a marriage, a job, or a harbor—I now knew it was time to go back to where it had all started and try to begin anew.

I landed in the Lagos airport on a sunny afternoon. On this particular day, the baggage carousel was not operational. Nigerian passengers were sitting patiently, congregated around the motionless conveyor belt, ready to wait out the latest Nigerian delay. The American oil workers from Texas were red-faced and annoyed, pacing to and fro and complaining into cell phones. Meanwhile (perhaps a harbinger of things to come), a determined group of Chinese passengers were working their way into the bowels of the baggage handling system, seeing if they couldn't fix it themselves. Since I only had my backpack, now slightly worse for wear, I headed to the door and the waiting crowd of shouting faces.

Emeka had come out of retirement to pick me up at the Lagos airport. He tried to look businesslike, but he immediately broke into a huge smile once he caught sight of me outside the airport door. On the drive back to Nora's he told me about his new business making concrete blocks. Rachel, the woman he hoped to marry, was pregnant. Their house was nearly finished.

"Rachel's going to have a baby? When are you going to marry her?"

"Soon! Weddings are expensive!"

I wished him luck and told him we would be in touch.

Nora was happy to see me, greeting me with a giant hug. Lucy gave me a startled look when I walked in the house, then turned her back and feigned indifference. In my absence, she had commandeered Nora's bed away from the two Persians, each more than twice her size, and forced them to sleep on the floor. Now that I was back, Lucy moved back to my bedroom and the Persians sheepishly reclaimed their former place on Nora's bed.

While I was away, Ismail and Shirene had moved to the neighboring country of Benin. Ismail had temporarily abandoned his ambitions to start his own construction company and was putting his skills to work as the project manager of a large building contract in Cotonou. I visited them in their new home in a cool and shady neighborhood. The house had a wall around the yard filled with mature trees but with no barbed wire at the top of the wall. There was electricity all the time; no one had generators running. The streets were remarkably clean. The former French colonials had left behind a tradition of good bread, sold from wicker baskets on the street corners by cheerful Beninois. Cotonou was a calm, quiet paradise compared to Lagos. Ismail and Shirene's children were doing well, moving effortlessly to this French-speaking country from their French school in Lagos. Their oldest son, a shy teenager in Lagos, was shocked to unexpectedly find himself on the receiving end of female attention in Cotonou. Ismail had hired a Beninois cook and Shirene was delighted to be able to drive herself around town without the bother of a driver, long lacquered nails tapping in time to music.

After dinner, Ismail, Shirene, and I sipped tiny cups of strong Lebanese coffee on their balcony looking over the treetops in the low evening light. I told Ismail I was no longer interested in business. He was sorry we wouldn't be working together anymore, but he understood, as he always seemed to.

"I just can't do business anymore, Ismail. I'm not sure what happens next. I think I might want to write — which I know is crazy — but it seems to be the only thing that makes any sense."

"You do what you need to do, Carrie. I'll always believe in you."

I looked from Ismail to Shirene and back to Ismail and felt tears come to my eyes. As long as I lived I would remember these friends who I could quite literally trust with my life.

I returned to Lagos and went to see Azu. He now had a gallery space, although it was still under construction. I walked past piles of sculpture outside and paintings stacked in the halls and threw myself into an overstuffed chair in his dim, cluttered office.

"I've missed you!" he said, the familiar scent of coconut greeting me as he gave me a hug.

"I'm going back," I told him.

"For how long?"

"For good, I think."

"Really?"

"Yes. And I wanted to thank you."

Azu listened in the peculiarly intent way he had, as if there were not another person on earth he wanted to talk to at that moment.

"I want to thank you for being my inspiration and for starting... whatever it is that has started in me. I want you to know I will always think of you as my muse."

Azu smiled his Cheshire cat smile. "No problem, my dear. I'll always be there for you." And, as wildly untrue as I knew that was, I also knew it was true.

•   •   •   •   •

"Where will we all be in five years, I wonder?" Nora asked as she slowly swam circles around the pool. "What will we be doing in twenty years?"

It was the last time we three—Nora, Angel, and I—would be skinny-dipping in the compound pool. Angel snorted. Angel was not one for idle speculation. I didn't answer—but I speculated. I imagined Nora's life in five years: in another position somewhere in the oil-producing world, or perhaps hunting precious gems in some exotic location. I imagined Angel starting up a new venture somewhere in Africa, or perhaps chucking journalism and putting her considerable entrepreneurial skills to use back in France. But when I tried to imagine my life in five years—or in twenty—I saw nothing.

I couldn't imagine a future flying down a sunny desert street on a moped, skirts whipping in the breeze, racing off to a new love with a very different kind of man. I couldn't imagine the girl I had been, the girl with all the ideas and dreams for a life filled with fun, finally freed. I couldn't imagine a future for Nora, no longer in the oil business or business of any kind, not drilling or digging anything but herbs in the garden and nursing a baby. And I couldn't imagine Angel. I couldn't imagine any of what awaited Angel. Maybe that was just as well.

•   •   •   •   •

And now, once again and finally, I began to pack. Lucy watched as I packed the same two boxes that had tumbled in the snow on that cold day in January more than three years ago. I packed some art, some souvenirs for my family, and my journals. Books, furniture, and household goods were left behind. Clothes, including all my black suits, were given away to the fabulous Ghanaian cook, Celina, who looked much sexier in them than I ever had. She modeled them as she told me about the import business she was starting in Accra. I wished her success and hoped the suits would help. I did not think I would be wearing black suits again. My upstairs room at Nora's was empty. Lucy jumped into her carrier and looked at me expectantly.

"Yes, Lucy. It's time."

And now it is evening and I am flying over Lagos, dressed in sandals and white linen trousers, a pale blue scarf from Zanzibar wound around my neck. I look out the plane window into the growing darkness and see the tiny lights of the homes below and the small cookfires burning far off into the distance. I wonder if there will be a home for me when I finally return home.

"Listen," She says.

I am startled to hear this voice again after so long. I had begun to believe She was no more than a much-needed hallucination brought on by stress and grief. But this time I am not stressed, and my grieving has abated. This time, when I hear her again, I do not argue or wonder. This time—for the first time—I simply listen for what happens next.

"Everything matters," She says. I smile—then discover I am crying.

Flying over Lagos, I look at my old life, the life I left kicking and screaming, and I see that even if it were possible to go back, I would no longer fit inside that life. The pain—which I never sought and always dreaded—has transformed me. Everything matters. Nothing was wasted. It is all fare for the next journey. It is a huge and unexpected gift.

I claim this gift by remembering the blue yarn, remembering how it began and how it ended, remembering and accepting all the magic and all the pain between the two. While it may not be a happily-ever-after story, it is a story with a lot of happiness in it—and because it is not a fairytale, a lot of sadness too. Everything matters, even now. Everything matters, especially now.

The next big thing is here and it is me. Flying home in the rising sun, I look out the window with wet eyes and smile into the bright, blank page ahead.

•   •   •   •   •

After nearly three and a half years living in Lagos, Nigeria, I returned to my little farmhouse in Wisconsin and began the long and fruitless hunt for my kitchen knives. Returning to the house under the maple trees was emotionally exhausting, and chief among the unpleasantness was the ordeal of sorting through dust-laden boxes in the basement containing household goods that had been there since the dissolution of my marriage and subsequent move to Africa, a lifetime ago. Amidst the boxes of pots and pans and plates were long-forgotten items that used to have meaning and purpose—photo albums and Christmas decorations, souvenirs and scrapbooks—and these boxes now seemed like tiny coffins I had to exhume one by one.

In the midst of this disinterment, I am called off to testify in court.

My ex-husband's second marriage has come to a sudden and terrible end, with a custody battle over his infant son and criminal charges of domestic violence leveled against him. It appears the charges have been made so Azi, who is Iranian, might remain in the U.S. He asks if I will serve as a witness on his behalf.

And so, without any real contemplation, I do.

This is only my second time in a courthouse and it is only marginally better than the first. I am in another new blond wood building, testifying again under oath.

"No, he was never violent with me. No, I never saw him violent with another person."

"No, he was never unfaithful to me," I tell them, because this is what I believe.

I give my testimony to a room of attorneys and a video camera and my ex-husband is quickly cleared of all charges; there was no actual evidence of violence. After the trial, I make lasagna for his large extended family, who have all gathered in his new bachelor apartment, with its packing-crate end tables, to show their support.

"You can't be our sister-in-law anymore, Carrie," his oldest sister says over a dinner on mismatched plates, "so you'll have to be our sister." I feel tears start and give her a hug.

On the night before I fly home he says he wants to talk to me. We have dinner together in a quiet Italian restaurant and then go back to his semi-furnished apartment. It is then, sitting on the floor together more than three years after the end of our marriage, it is only then I finally learn of his affair, of the beautiful girl and her son in Brazil.

"I kept saying I would end it, but then I would go back and I wouldn't," he tells me in a voice choked with pain. I see how hard this is for him to say. I feel no anger as he speaks, only a terrible sadness.

"When it was over, I still could not tell you," he continued. "I just couldn't."

There are tears in his eyes. I know this is the conversation we should have had under the maple trees before any of the rest of what happened began. I know this is the piece of my story that was missing—the piece I always felt was missing—from the very first. But now that I finally know my story, I feel no relief. What I feel is an unbearable sadness for all the suffering: my suffering in not knowing why I lost my marriage and everything that mattered most; his suffering in not being able to tell me, in returning again and again to Brazil and continuing with a relationship he knew was not right; the suffering we both experienced that drove him to a dark-haired Brazilian girl to begin with.

I look in his eyes, now red and filled with tears and see the gray that has grown around his temples and spread into his hair in the last three years. I see the suffering etched in new lines on his face and all I feel is an overwhelming sorrow for everything we have both been through. There is a silence between us as I look at him.

"I would have forgiven you," I say.

"I know that," he answers. "But I could never forgive myself."

I know we have spoken the truth to one another. I know he never wanted to hurt me. I know it is late, but now that the truth has been told, our story finally has its conclusion.

• • • • •

I returned to the house under the maple trees and to the ultimately futile search for my kitchen knives. But before my search was completed, I was whisked off on an Alaskan cruise to celebrate my parents' fiftieth wedding anniversary. This was no ordinary cruise: my parents being staunch Scandinavians, they had selected a small cruise ship that held only a few dozen passengers committed to energetically educating themselves on the many natural wonders to be found sailing up the narrow arms of the Inside Passage.

The occasional bout of gluttony was permitted so long as sloth and other deadly sins were rigorously fended off by means of frequent frantic rushes on deck dressed in insufficient clothing to observe the disappearing fin of a large sea mammal. We remained outside in the frigid air just long enough to confirm the animal's permanent departure and court hypothermia. My sister's two young children, Isabelle and Beau, were the only children aboard, and I was the only single adult with the exception of some crew members and an 82-year-old widower. The ship was filled with a perpetually rotating cast of biological experts, and it was strongly implied I might be required to pass an exam on marine life in order to retrieve my passport.

Beau was nineteen months old and his vocabulary grew by leaps and bounds over the twelve-day cruise. He learned to identify orcas and acquired a taste for kelp plucked from the cold water on our excursions in an inflatable raft. When one of the Filipino wait staff cheerily hailed him with "Hi, baby!" our first night onboard, Beau inferred this was the correct form of address to every new person he met. He startled and surprised the passengers, most in their sixties and seventies, with an exuberant "Hi, baby!" at every opportunity. Beau spent copious amounts of uninterrupted time with my father, his adored grandpa, and if for some reason Grandpa was not in attendance, there was a ready supply of surrogate grandpas to take up the slack.

My niece, Isabelle, was now six and delighted to discover there was not just one, but two magicians aboard. This was sheer coincidence, not programmed entertainment. (Magicians, as it turns out, vacation just like Masai warriors and party clowns.) Isabelle was entertained with card tricks, mysteriously knotted ropes, coins materialized out of ears, magical wands, and even a disappearing banana. When she had exhausted the seemingly endless patience of one magician, the auxiliary magician appeared—as if by magic—just in time for the next act. After a couple of days, it was routine to find Isabelle, long separated from her family, sitting at the bar with a magician in the club lounge, learning sharp card tricks and consuming quantities of meatball hors d'oeuvres. It was an idyllic holiday for a six-year-old.

It was also ideal for me. Removed from Africa, not quite back in the U.S., not quite back on land, for two weeks I lived on the tranquil sea in a never-never land where it was perfectly permissible to eat two desserts a day (and cookies in the club lounge at two o'clock) so long as I made it on deck just in time to miss the next exhibition of marine life. The rules were simple; the routine quickly established. I watched the land advance and recede. There would be time enough for uncertainty. Now it was cookie time.

I shared a cabin with Isabelle. Like all six-year-olds, Isabelle was wise beyond her years. She was also strong-willed and opinionated. As soon as she learned she would be sharing a cabin with me, her first question was, "Will we have a disco ball?" Of course we did. (Imagine, before the Internet, a person might not know where to purchase a travel-sized, battery-operated rotating disco ball.) Isabelle was also unfailingly polite. When we hit some rough water and had to retire to our cabins, she quietly said, "Please excuse me," before making a dash to the bathroom and losing her dinner.

Still, even with Isabelle—even with the mirrored ball, the two o'clock cookies served promptly in the club lounge, the spectacular scenery, and the opportunity to spend quality time with my family— even in the midst of a rare sunny day on the Inside Passage with whales spouting off the side of our ship and seabirds trailing behind—even then, I sometimes found myself feeling a little sad.

Sometimes I remembered, when this long-awaited trip was planned, I had never imagined I would be a single woman traveling with a disco ball. I had a husband beside me not so very long ago, I remembered. I would have been another couple on this ark of two-by-two passengers.

I remembered I was returning to live under the maple trees alone after spending more than half my life married. I was returning with no clear idea of what the future would hold or what would happen next. Sometimes, especially right before going to sleep, sometimes for a moment or two I was overcome with sadness.

It was a night like that. I was already in bed and Isabelle was in the nearby twin bed. Even though it was late, the room was still light, so far north on nearly the longest day of the year. Isabelle was quiet, but she was still awake.

"I am sad, Isabelle," I said into the quiet room.

For a moment I thought perhaps she was asleep after all. Then, out of the silence, I heard Isabelle's small voice.

"My mommy and daddy say when I am crabby it's because I'm hungry or tired but it's not true," she said. "I'm crabby because I don't get my way."

I thought about all the things I had wanted and all the times I had wanted my way. Now I was learning to let life be—even the parts that made me crabby. Now I was living a life I no longer pretended to control. I thought for several moments before asking, "So what's the answer, Isabelle?"

Without missing a beat, Isabelle said:

"Deal with what you get.

"Like what you've got.

"Play with what you have.

"Don't ask for things."

There was a brief pause as she thought for a moment.

"And be polite."

A few moments later, I could hear her breathing slow and deepen and I knew she had fallen asleep. I lay in the soft summer twilight and felt my half-empty glass fill to overflowing again.

"Yes," I said, to whoever might be listening. "This is what happens next."

THE END

ABOUT THE AUTHOR

Carrie Classon is a playwright, newspaper columnist, and memoirist. Her first career was as an Equity actor, working in theaters on both coasts before founding a professional theatre. Carrie later received an MBA and worked in Central Asia and West Africa. She returned to school yet again for an MFA in creative writing from the University of New Mexico. She resides in the somewhat surreal city of Los Alamos, New Mexico, with her husband, Peter.

Thank you so much for reading one of our **Biography / Memoirs**.
If you enjoyed our book, please check out our recommended title for your next great read!

Z.O.S. by Kay Merkel Boruff

"...dazzling in its specificity and intensity."

–C.W. Smith, author of *Understanding Women*

CPSIA information can be obtained
at www.ICGtesting.com
Printed in the USA
FSHW010829070819
60755FS

9 781684 332267